T H O M A S

F A T H E R O F

O H I O S T A T E H O O D

Thomas Worthington

Father of Ohio Statehood

BY
ALFRED BYRON SEARS

Ohio State University Press
Columbus

Illustration on p. ii courtesy of the Ohio Historical Society.

Library of Congress Cataloging-in-Publication Data

Sears, Alfred Byron, 1900–
    Thomas Worthington : father of Ohio statehood / by Alfred Byron Sears.
        p. cm.
    Originally published : Columbus ; Ohio State University Press for the Ohio
Historical Society, [1958]
    Includes bibliographical references and index.
    ISBN 0–8142–0745–6 (pb : alk. paper)
    1. Politicians—Ohio—Biography.   2. Ohio—Politics and government—
1787–1865.   I. Worthington, Thomas, 1773–1827.
    II. Title.
    F495.W73 1998
    977.1'03'092—dc21
    [B]   97–51221
                                                                      CIP

Cover design by Gore Studio, Inc.
Printed by Cushing-Malloy, Inc., Ann Arbor, Michigan.

The paper used in this publication meets the minimum requirements of
the American National Standard for Information Sciences—Permanence
of Paper for Printed Library Materials. ANSI Z39.48–1992.

9 8 7 6 5 4 3 2 1

DEDICATED TO
JAMES T. WORTHINGTON
1873-1949

VIRTUTE DIGNUS AVORUM

PREFACE

IN THE movement to secure Ohio's admission to the Union and in the framing of an enlightened and democratic constitution, which excluded slavery, banished executive tyranny, and safeguarded private and public liberties in a comprehensive bill of rights, no one displayed greater leadership than Thomas Worthington. In a very real sense, Ohio is a monument to his memory. Yet his political services have never been adequately recognized, and no biography of him has hitherto appeared.

Worthington was a dominant figure in early Ohio politics. Following his arrival in the Northwest Territory, he was appointed justice of the peace, lieutenant colonel of militia, and judge of the court of common pleas. He served in the territorial legislature, 1799-1803, and twice helped defeat the plans of the Ohio Federalists to set the western boundary of the state at the Scioto River. A member of Ohio's first legislature, he was elected to the U. S. Senate in 1803, and served a second term from 1810 to 1814, resigning on his election as governor. As senator, he was considered an authority on western lands and Indian affairs. As chairman of the Committee on Public Lands, he introduced many legislative measures to improve the distribution of the public domain and to safeguard purchases made by settlers. In 1812 he sponsored the bill which led to the establishment of the General Land Office.

Throughout his public career Worthington was a staunch advocate of internal improvements. In the Senate he was a leading figure in the movement for the construction of the Cumberland Road. During his governorship he promoted plans for building the Ohio canals, and at the close of his last term of office he served on the commission which made the surveys and started construction.

Although Worthington was a strong Jeffersonian Republican, he was critical of President Madison's foreign policy, and in 1812 voted against the declaration of war; he prophesied it could end only in military and financial disaster. Having made his position clear, however, he took part in the war effort with all the impetuous energy of his nature.

For thirty years Worthington kept a diary in small paperbound books filled from cover to cover, chiefly with business details but also with travel notes and private observations concerning life in general. Moreover, he carefully preserved his correspondence and drafts of his business letters. His diary and most of his papers were passed on by his widow to his eldest son, General James Taylor Worthington; by him to a grandson, Richard T. Worthington; and in due course to a great-grandson, James T. Worthington, to whom this biography is dedicated. Now and then, some portions of Worthington's papers and parts of his diary were lost to the family, but fortunately these were collected by the Library of Congress, the Ohio Historical Society, the Ohio State Library, and the Ross County (Ohio) Historical Society. In 1949, on the death of James T. Worthington, the papers remaining in the family were acquired by the Ohio Historical Society.

In this study I have endeavored to be objective. Realizing, however, that complete objectivity is impossible, I am bound to apprise the reader that I have come to admire Worthington for his sturdy manhood, his unflinching moral courage, his faith in democracy; for his refusal to compromise with weakness, incompetence, or evil; for his religious convictions and the high intellectual and spiritual level at which he sought to spend at least a portion of his days; and for his devotion to his wife, family, friends, and servants. He had a deep respect for his fellow men—for their rights as citizens and as free moral agents. He was a true patriot, completely dedicated to what he believed were the best interests of his country. In his private and public life he adhered strictly to the principles of industry, integrity, and sobriety which, he believed, were the cornerstones of individual achievement and service.

It is impossible to mention all of those who have helped with this book during the extended period of research and writing. The advice and encouragement of Carl F. Wittke, Eugene H. Roseboom, and Harlow Lindley were indispensable. Chief among those to whom gratitude is due are James T. Worthington and his sisters, Mrs. Elizabeth Worthington Costello and Mrs. Anne Worthington Newton, great-grandchildren of Thomas Worthington. Others are Thomas P. Martin and John de Porry of the Library of Congress; Mary A. Hicks of Friends House, London; James H. Rodabaugh and Henry Caren of the Ohio Historical Society, Columbus; Eugene D. Rigney and Martha Bennett of the Ross County Historical Society, Chillicothe; and Eleanor S. Wilby and Marie Dickoré of the Historical and Philosophical Society of Ohio, Cincinnati.

I recommend that the reader visit Adena, the federal home designed by Benjamin H. Latrobe which Worthington built in 1807 a mile northwest of Chillicothe, and which has recently been restored to its original status by the Ohio Historical Society. With its gardens and grounds, it constitutes a notable exhibit for all who are interested in beauty, history, and early American architecture.

Norman, Oklahoma   ALFRED B. SEARS
September, 1958

Contents

SPECIAL ABBREVIATIONS
USED IN THE FOOTNOTES

HPSO	Historical and Philosophical Society of Ohio (Cincinnati)
LC	Library of Congress
OHS	Ohio Historical Society (Columbus)
OSL	Ohio State Library (Columbus)
RCHS	Ross County Historical Society (Chillicothe)
WM	Worthington Manuscripts, Ohio Historical Society (Columbus)
WMOSL	Worthington Manuscripts, Ohio State Library (Columbus)
WRHS	Western Reserve Historical Society (Cleveland)

THOMAS WORTHINGTON

FATHER OF
OHIO STATEHOOD

i

A Virginian Transplanted

I⊤ IS probably just as well that the facts concerning the early antecedents of most of America's illustrious sons are shrouded, at least to
some degree, in romance, anecdote, and tradition. Preëminence in
colonial days was a matter of achievement rather than of family,
and if the first immigrants had put their trust in noble lineage rather
than in energy, sobriety, and economy, they and their progeny would
have had little occasion to assume heraldic trappings. Until financial
success had crowned the labors of the migrant and made him visibly and acceptably superior to his fellows, noble ancestry was no
social asset. The wilderness was no place to boast of gentle blood;
God, not the king, was here the arbiter of the destinies of men; let
them who could, follow in His train.

Yet among many of the colonists there was a constant appreciation
of the importance of heredity, the desirability of family pride, and the
challenge which the achievements of their ancestors presented to
each succeeding generation. The Quaker records of England, Ireland,
and America show the forebears of Thomas Worthington to have
been upright, civic-minded citizens of the communities in which they
lived. In conformity with the practice of members of the Society of
Friends, they let their daily actions reflect that moral rectitude and
excellence of breeding to which they laid modest claim. From these
Quaker records are derived the authentic data relating to the immediate progenitors of Thomas Worthington.

2

The motto of the Worthington family of Cheshire, England, was
Virtute dignus avorum ("In virtue worthy of one's ancestors"). Each
branch of the thirteenth-century Lancashire family of William de
Worthington inherited not only this motto but a coat of arms: "Argent
—three shakeforks, sable, two and one; crest a goat passant, argent,
holding in his mouth an oak branch proper (or vert), fructed, or";
which, translated, means a silver shield with three black, triple-tined
stable forks, one below and two above; the crest, a side view of a

silver goat, holding in its mouth a green-leafed oak branch with golden acorns. This motto and coat of arms may be seen in Chorley Church, Wilmslow Parish, Cheshire, where lived the particular branch of the family in which we are interested.

From Norman times on, the family had been a fertile one; in the sixteenth and seventeenth centuries the Worthingtons were numerous in Cheshire and adjoining Lancashire. Many were devout Anglicans and eminent scholars; for instance, John Worthington (1618-71) was master of Jesus College and Vice-Chancellor of Cambridge. Others were nonconformist ministers: John of Dean Row, and Robert of Mottram-in-Longdendale, who in the 1640's fought the power of the established church. Others remained true to the Catholic faith, notably Thomas (1549-1622), president of Douay College, and his son Thomas (1671-1754), Dominican Prior of Barnhem, Flanders, and Prior Provincial of England. Many joined the Pietist Society of Friends and fostered in their communities the industry, sobriety, and integrity associated with the will of the righteous God they tried to serve. Their faith in the spiritual value of each individual and the equality of all men fostered social democracy; liberty of conscience and the inner light established tolerance and sympathy; emphasis on education and service furthered social reform and the advancement of the social gospel; devotion to the cause of the enslaved, the oppressed, and the underprivileged promoted a policy of world-wide reconciliation. Relatively few in number, they were extremely influential in their own day, and continued to be so in the new world in the person of leaders like William Penn and, in our own time, scholars like Rufus Jones.

3

Thomas Worthington's great-great-grandfather was John Worthington (1606-91) of Morley, Wilmslow Parish, northeastern Cheshire, England; he called his farm Quarrel Bank (stone quarry). He and Mrs. Worthington (Mabel Owen) were Friends, two of the earliest followers of George Fox, the founder of the society. Worthington's son Jonathan (or John) of "the Quarrel Bank in Pownall fee" died December 18, 1717, aged eighty-eight, leaving his widow Mary (1639-1723) with a large family. One of their children was Robert, sometimes called Robert the Quaker, born in 1667. Aided in part by a collection made up for him by the Morley Monthly Meeting, in 1695 Robert left Quarrel Bank and moved with his wife (Alice Taylor) and his three boys (Samuel, Robert, and John) to Ballignihee, King's

County, Leinster Province, some seventy miles west of Dublin, Ireland. The next year they moved a short distance to Ballinakill, a small village in County Westmeath, where they were members of the Moate Monthly Meeting. There, seven more children were born to them (Jacob, Ephraim, Esther, Martha, Eliza, Philip, who died thirty-one days later, and Rachel). In 1712, Robert's eldest son, Samuel, migrated to Salem, New Jersey, and the parents and the other children followed him there in 1714. They joined the Salem Monthly Meeting of Friends and became active participants in its work. In 1722, Robert Worthington was dismissed by the Salem Meeting to the Philadelphia Meeting, and moved his family to the vicinity of Philadelphia, where he established himself as a merchant, farmer, stock raiser, and dealer in lands. Unhappily, a few years later Mrs. Worthington was taken sick and died. After the proper interval, her husband, old in years only, married Mary Burtis of the Friends Meeting at Burlington, New Jersey, on July 30, 1729.[1]

Deciding to leave Philadelphia and move westward, Worthington divided his estate into nine equal portions, retaining one for himself and distributing the others among his eight children, who, with the exception of Samuel and Jacob, were not interested in moving into the wilderness.[2] In 1730, having completed the purchase of three thousand acres of northern Shenandoah Valley land from Joist Hite for fifteen pounds, he moved his wife and infant son Robert to the area west of the Blue Ridge Mountains just south of the Potomac.

As early as 1726, Morgan Morgan had established a home in this wilderness near Bunker Hill on Mill Creek, and shortly afterward a few families founded a hamlet called Mecklenburg (Shepherdstown) on the south bank of the Potomac near Pack Horse Ford. When Robert Worthington settled there in 1730, a group of families followed him, including, before the year was out, the Shepherds, Harpers, Foresters, Lemons, Mercers, Van Meters, and Van Swearingens. Worthington was probably the first Friend to settle there, but the next year he was joined by a considerable number of Quaker families from Philadelphia.[3]

His purchase lay on Evitts Run and the north fork of Bullskin Creek,

---

[1] The marriage certificate and deposition of Mary Burtis Worthington are in the Orange County Courthouse, Orange, Virginia. Quaker records in England, Ireland, New Jersey, Pennsylvania, and Virginia were investigated by James T. Worthington of Washington, D.C., and by the author for much of this early data. Most vital statistics for the United Kingdom are in Somerset House, London.

[2] Thomas Worthington's "Account of His Ancestors and of His Own Early Life," a twelve-page manuscript written for his children in 1821 (in WM), has been used in this chapter.

[3] Charles H. Ambler, *A History of West Virginia* (New York, 1933), 51.

tributaries of the Shenandoah, in the southwest angle formed by that river and the Potomac. The Quakers seem to have thought they were still within the William Penn Grant[4]—just why it is not easy to understand. In 1732 Joist Hite and fifteen families moved in from Pennsylvania and settled farther up the valley about five miles south of what is now Winchester, where several Pennsylvania-German families had lived since 1728. In fact, every year brought large groups of Germans, Hollanders, Scotch Irish, and English from the North to this beautiful and fertile valley. Knowing the value of land in England and having seen it appreciate near Salem and Philadelphia, Worthington was ambitious to rebuild his fortune by land speculation in the Great Valley.

When he found that he was within newly organized (1734) Orange County, Virginia, he applied for and received a patent for his three thousand acres from the king's lieutenant governor, William Gooch. He agreed to pay a quitrent of five pounds in Virginia currency for his land, thereafter locally referred to as Worthington's Patent.[5] There, near the present site of Charles Town, West Virginia (laid out on a mill site by George Washington's brother Charles in 1786), he labored diligently as farmer, stock raiser, and dealer in lands. There he built the first stone home west of the Blue Ridge and called it Quarry Bank (later Piedmont), "new stile for Quarrel Bank."[6] The house is still in use today as a part of the lovely home of John Briscoe.

In mid-October, 1735, while at Snowden's ironworks near Patuxent (now Warderville), Maryland, Robert Worthington was taken ill and died at an inn close by. On October 2, he had had an attorney draw a will which divided his estate of three thousand acres among his widow, his children—Robert, Jacob, Mary, and Martha—and a grandson, Bobby Dunblaen, first son of Samuel, who was Worthington's eldest son by his first wife. However, since the lawyer failed to specify that the land was to be held in fee simple by each devisee and his heirs and assignees forever, the Virginia law operated to give the heirs only a lifetime estate, with reversion to Bobby Dunblaen on their deaths.

Soon after her husband's death, Mrs. Worthington married a farmer of the locality, Samuel Brittain, and the children were made his wards. He treated Robert harshly and in 1740 bound him out to a severe master. As a result, the boy ran away to Philadelphia, where he worked until

---

[4] Letter of Thomas Chaukley to the Friends of the Monthly Meeting at Opequon, May 21, 1738, in Samuel Kercheval, *History of the Valley* (3rd ed., Woodstock, Va., 1902), 42. See also John W. Wayland, *Hopewell Friends History, 1734-1934, Frederick County, Virginia* (Strasburg, Va., 1936), 126, 183.

[5] For a description of the grant, see Virginia Patent Records, XV, 339.

[6] Frederick County Court House, Winchester, Virginia, Deed Book, I, 286.

he was eighteen. Returning to the Valley in 1748 to receive his patrimony, he took up farming, surveying, and land-dealing in his own right. A tireless worker, he was soon able to buy the reversionary claims to most of his six hundred acres from his nephew Bobby, who, after a period of prosperity as a speculator in Valley lands, seems to have dissipated his holdings rapidly. In 1752, Bobby sold 700 acres to Lawrence Washington, and in 1754, he sold Piedmont (Quarry Bank) and 1,279 acres of land, which was perhaps all he owned by that time, to Charles Dick.[7] Years later, Mrs. Brittain told her grandson Thomas that Bobby had drifted West penniless, but since he had received £2,200 from Dick for the Piedmont estate, she was either in error or he owed many debts.

Having had little schooling, Robert secured a tutor for himself and soon became proficient in his studies, especially in mathematics, which he needed for surveying. He sometimes worked with George Washington as a chain carrier in the lower Valley, where the latter was employed as surveyor by Lord Thomas Fairfax.[8] They often stayed at Fairfax' splendid mansion, Greenway Courts, thirteen miles southeast of Winchester. The bachelor lord's five and a half million acres between the Rappahannock and the Potomac and an approximately equal area in and beyond the Shenandoah Valley itself gave them plenty to do.

Washington was Robert's junior by two years; both served Virginia in Braddock's campaign, and were lucky to get back home alive. George Washington himself had a farm on Bullskin Creek. Harewood, Samuel Washington's home, lay next to Worthington's, between Bullskin Creek and Evitts Run.

In 1759, Robert married Margaret Matthews, an Irish lass from Fredericktown, Maryland. For marrying outside the Quaker communion he was "disowned" by the Hopewell Friends Meeting. By diligent effort he and his wife built up an impressive estate near the present Charles Town. They called their home, a stone house halfway between Quarry Bank and the Washington estate at Altona, the Manor House, and finished out their lives there; they also owned a town house in the village of Martinsburg, which they called the Mansion House. Robert invested in several tracts of Ohio country land and at his death owned at least a score of slaves.

---

[7] *Ibid.*, 414. In 1770 Charles Dick sold Piedmont to James Nourse. Nourse sold it to Dr. John Briscoe in 1780. The Briscoe family still owns it. See the Charles Town, West Virginia, newspaper, *Spirit of Jefferson*, September 6, 1933.

[8] Worthington's signature appears on a survey made by George Washington, November 19, 1750, reproduced in the United States George Washington Bicentennial Commission, *History of the George Washington Bicentennial Celebration* (5 vols., Washington, D. C., 1932), I, 152.

During the latter part of his life, Robert was a justice of the peace, the first coroner of Berkeley County (established in 1772 from Frederick, which had been separated from Orange in 1743), a collector of tithables, captain of the first of nineteen companies of Frederick County militia (1773), and in general an influential citizen of the community. Deeply religious, he was instrumental in erecting St. George's Chapel, the first church in Norborne Parish (separated from Frederick in 1769), on land which he and Thomas Shepherd of Shepherdstown had donated. The land was set aside in 1769, the church was erected the next year, and a good endowment was secured from Thomas Shepherd's son Abraham, from other members of the Shepherd family, and from James Nourse.[9]

For his services in the French and Indian War as lieutenant of Virginia militia, Robert was awarded a grant of two thousand Virginia acres by "the Right Honorable John, Earl of Dunmore, Governor of Virginia, dated the 9th day of April 1774 and directed to the surveyor of Augusta County . . . which land he is entitled to by his Majesty's proclamation issued in the month, October, 1763."[10]

The year 1774 was a critical one in the history of the British Empire in North America. By such belated awards as that made to Worthington, Dunmore doubtless hoped to placate the rising fires of discontent in the back country. His efforts were vain, however, for the resentment over British policy toward the colonies had grown in the two decades since Braddock's defeat on the Monongahela. Colonial casualties, interruptions to trade and commerce, large debts, and high taxes created bitter resentment, even though the Frenchmen had been driven from the continent. Moreover, the Proclamation of 1763 and the gradual emergence of a plan to exploit the West from London with British capital was a shock to colonial financiers, who hoped to carve fortunes from land speculation in the Ohio country. The Grenville and Townshend tax schemes had aggravated the ills of the colonial businessmen, and, with the First Continental Congress but five months away, Dunmore perhaps hoped to enlist Robert Worthington's aid against the Indians and hold him loyal to the crown; at least he could hope not to find him in the opposition.

After 1749, many Virginians, including George Washington, Patrick Henry, Hugh Mercer, William Preston, William Christian, and John

---

[9] *Spirit of Jefferson* (Charles Town, W. Va.), September 6, 1933; Roy B. Cook, "The Story of St. George's Chapel, Norborne Parish," *West Virginia Review*, X (1932-33), 194-197, 214. See also William Meade, *Old Churches, Ministers and Families of Virginia* (Philadelphia, 1857), II, 290.

[10] Deed in WM.

Connolly, had secured or were seeking lands on the Ohio River. Most Virginians, including Dunmore himself, if we can judge by his actions, echoed Washington's sentiment that "notwithstanding the Proclamation [of 1763] that restrains it [settlement] at present . . . I can never look upon that Proclamation in any other light (but this I say between ourselves), than as a temporary expedient to quiet the minds of the Indians."[11] By 1774, both in England and the colonies, it had been decided that the Indians were to be sacrificed for the speculators, as Charles Lee put it, in a war "carried on by the governor of Virginia, at the instigation of two murderers on the frontier [Michael Cresap and John Connolly], and in spite of the declamations of the whole continent against the injustice of it . . . an impious, black piece of work."[12] That Dunmore was playing a double game is fairly obvious, for he had to operate as an agent of the king while he himself wished to speculate in land in the Ohio country. It was doubtless with reluctance, therefore, that he announced to the Virginia Assembly in May that, for the time being, no further grants would be made. His announcement was relayed to Robert Worthington in a letter[13] from George Washington:

> *Williamsburg, June 1774*
>
> Sir:
>
> *Your purchase of the within claim has been attended with several unlucky Circumstances, and must, I apprehend, turn out a loosing bargain—I did not get down to the very first of the session, & as it turned out, was not here whilst the Council were sitting. Whilst I was waiting therefore for this Event, the Governor received orders to Grant no more Lands upon the Western Waters til further orders, so that no more warrants can now Issue & a total stop is put to all future proceedings in Landed Claims till his Majesty's further pleasure is known— Under the circumstances I return your assignment from James Smith and am*
>
> Sir Yr most H'ble Sev't
> G. Washington
>
> *To Mr. Robert Worthington*
> *In*
>   *Berkeley Cty.*

This action was in conformity with the royal circular of February 3, 1774, which forbade further allocation of western lands, except

---

[11] Washington to William Crawford, September 21, 1767, in John C. Fitzpatrick, ed., *The Writings of George Washington from the Original Manuscript Sources, 1745-1799*, prepared under the direction of the United States George Washington Bicentennial Commission and published by authority of Congress (37 vols., Washington, D.C., 1931-41), II, 468.

[12] Charles Lee to Edmund Burke, December 16, 1774, in the "Lee Papers," in the New York Historical Society, *Collections, Publication Fund Series*, IV (1871), 149.

[13] Original, RCHS.

as compensation to veterans, until after they had been surveyed into lots of one hundred and one thousand acres, after which they might be sold at not less than sixpence per acre (the price to be set by the governor) with a quitrent of a halfpenny sterling.[14] Worthington's application was for issuance to him of the warrants due Smith for his war service, but the governor's action indefinitely postponed their issue and did not permit Worthington to qualify for them under the veterans' compensation provision in the proclamation or the February circular.

Worthington took no part in Lord Dunmore's War, and that in spite of the fact that he owned at least 2,170 acres of frontier land (the "Potato Garden") on Raccoon Creek in western Pennsylvania. He had purchased this tract from William Crawford in 1772 for one hundred sixty pounds in Virginia currency, and it was very advantageously located on the Mingo Path in the area west of Pittsburgh, only seven miles from the Ohio River. He also owned a tract of perhaps sixteen hundred acres west of the Ohio on Yellow Creek (Columbiana County, Ohio). It is likely that his Quaker training made him fundamentally a man of peace, especially when it came to despoiling the Indians, with whose plight, it is reasonable to believe, he was sympathetic. On the other hand, with the coming of the Revolution, Captain Worthington was not slow to espouse the patriot cause. He and Captain William Darke hurried east to offer their services to Washington upon his appointment as commander of the Continental Army. Of his services we have no record. However, we do know that four years later Worthington was back home endeavoring to raise a troop of cavalry, chiefly at his own expense, when death overtook him in 1779 at the age of forty-nine. His wife died the next year, leaving six children: Ephraim, Martha, Mary, William, Robert, and Thomas—the last a boy of six (born July 16, 1773).

According to the father's will, drawn up July 30, 1779, by the local Episcopal minister, the Reverend Daniel Sturges, each child inherited an equal share of the $200,000 estate (about 1,466 acres each or the equivalent), and Ephraim was made sole executor. All the children had had the best of private tutors, since the father had been eager to give them a good education—a privilege of which he had been deprived. Thomas Worthington recalled years later that "tho [he was]

[14] L. W. Labaree, *Royal Instructions to the British Colonial Governors, 1670-1776* (2 vols., American Historical Association, Beveridge Memorial Fund Publication, New York, 1935), II, No. 765. Dartmouth's letter of July 6 to Dunmore repeated this injunction, but in the same month Washington and others were made a grant of lands near Pittsburgh which had been applied for before the circular of February had been issued. Thomas P. Abernethy, *Western Lands and the American Revolution* (New York, 1937), 110.

not five years old," his father had expressed anxiety to hear him read and had promised his tutor additional rewards for teaching him. Ephraim had been sent to William and Mary College at Williamsburg, but withdrew to serve with the Virginia troops under General McIntosh in the Ohio country. Toward the end of the war he came home, was married, and after the death of his parents moved Effie, "his pretty and very illiterate wife who made his life miserable," into the Manor House. Mary, William, Robert, and Thomas lived for a time in the stone Mansion House in Martinsburg, but the pinch of war conditions, among other things, shortly led Ephraim to insist that Mary seek another home. He bound out William to a Winchester merchant and took Robert and Tom to live with him at the Manor House. The Mansion House was then rented.

The boys were indifferently schooled by Ephraim. Robert soon established a hack-and-hauling service to Alexandria and Baltimore, married, and moved out of the Manor House. Young Tom for some time was used by Effie as nursemaid for her children, a role he naturally resented. He was a sensitive boy, who particularly missed Mary and his two brothers and never felt any great affection for Ephraim or Ephraim's wife, whom he remembered as abusive. "Night after night," he wrote years later, "did I wet my pillow with tears. It was then for the first time, tho my parents had been dead but 2 years that I was sensible of being an orphan, and mourned the loss of my more than kind sister Mary, than whom a better woman never lived."

When Tom was about fourteen (1787), his brother William came of legal age, married Elizabeth Machie, and took the boy for a year as his ward to the Mansion House in Martinsburg. Tom went joyfully, expecting to better his surroundings, but William was an indifferent guardian. When he decided to remove to Kentucky,[15] Thomas replaced him with an old friend and associate of his father, Colonel William Darke of Shepherdstown. He proved to be the type of friend and counselor the young Worthington needed. Tom was sent to school and given a real home by Colonel and Mrs. Darke: "This gentleman was to me a father, and his good lady a mother. On my part I repaid all in my power their kindness—I lived happily and progressed in my studies."

During his schooling under the guardianship of Colonel Darke, young Worthington studied navigation, for he "had long indulged the

---

[15] William died in 1801 at or near Maysville, Kentucky. Thomas Worthington was his executor. Worthington's diary, August 26, 1811. All references to the diary refer to the Worthington notebooks in the Library of Congress and the Ohio Historical Society. See also letters of Eliza Worthington to Thomas Worthington, February 1 and March 7, 1801, in WM.

inclination to go to sea." So, despite the fact that he was almost of age and about to enter on his inheritance, he asked consent to try his luck on the ocean.[16] "My guardian . . . reluctantly assented and on the 7th day of May 1791 I bid this kind family farewell except the youngest son who would accompany me to Georgetown, District of Columbia, where I shipped as a common sailor on board the Brittania of port Glasgow, Scottland, requiring no other pay than my food."[17] This voyage took him to Cuba, Jamaica, Glasgow, and the Baltic. In Jamaica, endeavoring to double his small capital by venture, he invested it in molasses. When the ship arrived at Glasgow the young merchant opened his casks and to his disgust found that he had purchased and transported a consignment of salt water. For the rest of the voyage he was a common seaman by necessity as well as by choice. In June, 1792, he shipped from Glasgow with Alexander Blair, master of the brigantine "Home," for Barbados. In November of the same year he served aboard the "Mary of Glasgow," the master of which was James Taylor, who had long been engaged in the Greenland, Nova Scotia, and New England trade. Off the coast of Scotland they were boarded by an English press gang, who paraded all hands on deck. The ruddy, tall American, who looked every inch a healthy Britisher, was among those seized, and it was only after violent expostulation by him and his captain, accompanied by a complete examination of the ship's papers, that Tom escaped participation in the Napoleonic wars. He showed his gratitude years later when he named his first son James Taylor Worthington. After a voyage to America, he was paid off, honorably discharged, and landed by Taylor at Alexandria, Virginia, on January 18, 1793.[18]

In Captain Taylor young Worthington had found a most admirable and amiable friend and enjoyed, as he put it, "a degree of happiness in being with him that I had never before experienced from any other gentleman of his profession. . . . Expression fails when I would wish to paint his Character in a Proper light." A correspondence was attempted between them, but it was thirty-one years before the captain learned that he had a namesake in Ohio. He regarded it as the highest compliment he had ever received.[19]

After almost two years at sea Worthington was happy to return to the

[16] For a more elaborate account, see Sarah Worthington Peter, *Private Memoir of Thomas Worthington* (Cincinnati, 1882), 10.
[17] This is the end of the account by Worthington. Mrs. Peter's *Private Memoir* will be followed in the remainder of this chapter except as otherwise noted.
[18] "Seamans Journal" (manuscript log kept by Worthington), June 4, 1792, to January 18, 1793. Photostatic copy, RCHS.
[19] Taylor to Worthington, July 20, 1824, RCHS.

hills of his childhood, to his friends and his work. Colonel Darke took an even more fatherly interest in him now, for his youngest and favorite son Joseph had been killed, and he himself wounded, while serving with the incompetent and gout-ridden St. Clair against the Indians of the Northwest in 1791.

Worthington, now twenty, established bachelor's hall in the modest home which he had inherited and which he called Prospect Hill. He had a few colored servants to wait on him, among them his devoted housekeeper, Aunt Hannah. He kept busy working his estate, surveying, acting as deputy for Sheriff Cato Moore, and speculating in western lands. He had at least 1,873 acres on Raccoon Creek, Pennsylvania, a third of which he had inherited; presumably he had bought the shares of William and Robert.[20] He was also engaged in courting at least one of the belles of the countryside and listening to tales of the rich lands in the territory northwest of the Ohio River and of emigration in that direction. He prepared himself to serve against the Indians, for the defeats of St. Clair and Harmar had shown the necessity of a well-regulated militia; he secured a lieutenancy in the 55th Regiment, Militia of the Commonwealth, in September, 1794, and in March, 1795, was commissioned first lieutenant in a company of artillery attached to the 16th Militia Brigade. A fortunate turn of events in Indian relations perhaps kept him from suffering the fate which had befallen half of St. Clair's command, for on August 11, 1794, Anthony Wayne at Fallen Timbers dispersed the conquerors of St. Clair and Harmar. By the spring of 1795 the Indian opposition had faded since it was evident that England and the United States were not going to war. When the British came to terms with John Jay, the Indians were forced to sue for peace at Greeneville.

4

After the papers opening two-thirds of Ohio to settlement had been signed, migration increased to a flood, and Worthington, now captain of an artillery company (Third Regiment of the Third Division), caught the "Ohio fever." Having purchased a considerable number of Virginia military warrants, including some from General Darke, he proposed to go and locate them himself. On this trip he decided to keep a diary, and to it we are indebted for most of the detail related here.

[20] Alex White, 3rd, to Worthington at Travelers Rest, Berkeley, June 2, 1796, in WM; Tiffin to Worthington, March 10, 1798, in WMOSL. Numerous documents (in WM) show Worthington to have been a deputy sheriff and collector of tithes in 1795-96. See Joseph Swearingen to Worthington, February 3, 1794, regarding his west Pennsylvania land, in WM.

He set out on horseback for the Ohio River on June 20, 1796. Several days later, he arrived at Wheeling village on the Ohio, where he left his horses and took the mail canoe to the mouth of the Muskingum, noting along the way the splendid farming possibilities at Buckhill Bottom, thirty miles below Wheeling—an area well watered and full of sugar maple, beech, elm, and walnut trees. At Marietta he secured a place in a sailing packet boat, and was much intrigued with a girl and her brother who were passengers as far as Belpre, the home of their father, Colonel Israel Putnam. Sailing day and night, they passed George Washington's Kanawha bottoms on the twenty-eighth of June, and the French settlement at Gallipolis on the twenty-ninth. On the thirtieth the packet dropped him at the mouth of the Scioto, where, by agreeing to handle a paddle, he got a place in the mail canoe going up that river. For the first twenty miles he was disappointed with the country; not more than one-eighth of the land they passed was the rich bottom land he had been led to expect, and the river was "the most meandrous" he had ever seen. On July 1, after pushing the canoe all day, he went ashore in the evening and got lost in a swamp, where he saw many deer and turkeys. Not finding the canoe, he walked five miles north. Overtaken by darkness, he napped for a few hours, and was half-devoured by the myriad mosquitoes. At daybreak he walked north another five miles and caught the canoe when it came along. They pushed on eighteen miles that day, "passing several fine prairies."

The next day, July 3, he went ashore at Indian Creek and picked up a guide in the person of one Charles Fournash, who had been a prisoner of the Indians for four years and knew their language. They walked north to Nathaniel Massie's farm (Station Prairie) at the mouth of Paint Creek, where Massie's men with thirty plows had put three hundred acres of virgin soil in cultivation the first week in April which now showed a splendid stand of corn. Three miles farther north they came to Massie's Town (Chillicothe), established in 1795 by Nathaniel Massie and his father, Henry Massie, who had migrated from Virginia to Kentucky in 1783 to survey and purchase lands there and across the Ohio River. In 1791 they had established a post on the Ohio near the mouth of Ohio Brush Creek and named it Massie's Station (now Manchester).[21]

Worthington and Fournash found Massie's Town in the first stages of settlement. It was made up of the scattered cabins of the settlers who had purchased hundred-acre outlots from Massie at £25, each of

[21] See John McDonald, *Biographical Sketches of General Nathaniel Massie, General Duncan McArthur, Captain William Wells, and General Simon Kenton* (Cincinnati, 1838).

which carried a bonus of one inlot and one four-acre outlot to the first hundred settlers.[22] Some twenty clapboard-roof cabins were already built or in the process of being built. They found very little to eat there—no reflection on the hospitality of the settlers but an indication of the situation in the new settlement: few garden plots yet, no mill, no store or tavern deserving the name, everyone living off the game and wild fruit in the woods and sharing or selling imported flour and bacon with the greatest reluctance.

The next day they made a canoe and continued to prospect the river country. By evening, Worthington had decided that the finest piece of land he had seen was the high-bank prairie in the Congress Lands opposite the mouth of Paint Creek, an area "9 miles long & 2 miles wide." They stayed at Fournash's house, "fifty [sic] miles down the river," that night. Starting for the Ohio on the sixth of July, they met with difficulty when their canoe was upset by logs in the high water and Worthington almost lost his saddlebags, papers, and clothes. From the seventh to the thirteenth they inspected the land on both sides of the Ohio near Graham's Station, Massie's Station, and Limestone. With fresh horses and a new companion, Daniel Bollinghouse (perhaps he furnished the horses), they prospected the shady bottoms on the west side of the Scioto on their way back to Chillicothe, which they reached on the fifteenth. They had had little to eat on the trip, and very little was available in the hamlet. The same day, Worthington got Duncan McArthur, Massie's brawny, twenty-four-year-old surveyor, to take two men and start surveys for him on a fine piece of land to the northwest of the settlement. He watched the beginning of this process with great satisfaction; that night they "supped on flour and water." The next day McArthur decided to go in search of food. He and Michael Thomas started after a deer while Worthington celebrated his twenty-third birthday alone in camp "on baked flour & almost starved." The following morning, leaving McArthur to continue his survey of this wonderful area, which included both fertile valley and pleasant wooded upland, Worthington scouted his way through his land, exhilarated by the clear air and alternate sun and shade of the hills and the damp, aromatically scented valleys. He lay in the woods all night, and the next day followed an Indian trail back to the village. That day he purchased several lots.

He spent the next day thrashing his way through the Scioto bottoms, and after another night in the open, he started for Limestone on July 20. For two days it had rained, and the streams were swollen.

---

[22] Williams Brothers, *History of Ross and Highland Counties, Ohio* (Cleveland, 1880), 46-47.

In fording Ohio Brush Creek near its fork, Worthington's horses were swept down the flooded stream for sixty yards before he could get them ashore. On the twenty-first, he crossed the Ohio into Mason County, Kentucky, at Limestone, and going by way of Washington, the county seat, reached his brother William's in the evening.

After visiting a few days with his brother, during which time they attended Monthly Court at Washington, where he met several acquaintances from Berkeley County, Worthington left for home. At Graham's Station he caught a sailing packet up to Wheeling. There he picked up his horses on the eighth, and that evening was in Washington, Pennsylvania, where, tired as he was—but not too tired to drive a bargain—he bought six hundred acres of Scioto Brush Creek land from Henry Smith at four shillings an acre. He reached home after two more days of hard riding via Bardstown, Beesontown (Uniontown), Laurel Hill, Faucets, Potters, Lumpkins, Tumbleton, Steckers, Cumberland, and Oldtown.

This first trip to the Scioto country completely won his farmer's heart and alienated no little part of his affection for that equally fertile but definitely limited Shenandoah Valley land on which he had been reared. He returned home firmly determined to remove to the promising Ohio region at no distant time. His friends, however, strongly urged him not to go to that far-off wilderness; John Blackford wrote on September 5, 1796, "I hope you . . . have concluded to take to your arms that sweet little woman that propitious heaven has ordained for you . . . and set down at your ease and become a good member of society."[23] Worthington took only part of this advice; on December 13 he married the beautiful Eleanor Swearingen of Shepherdstown, who was to prove a devoted and tireless companion throughout his life. She was a niece of Mrs. Abraham Shepherd (née Strode) of Shepherdstown,[24] in whose home the wedding took place. Eleanor, familiarly known as Nellie, had been left an orphan, her mother having died in 1786 and her father in 1795; but since she had inherited a good deal of property, some stock, and several colored servants, the young couple was extremely well-to-do for the times. In fact, Sam Washington, George's nephew and the proprietor of Harewood estate near Charles Town, wrote in a letter to Worthington in October, 1796, "Knowing that you are the only man in our neighbor-

[23] Letter in WM.
[24] The *Private Memoir* contains some personal history and a picture of Mrs. Worthington. The Swearingen family Bible gives the place and date of the wedding. See also Virginia Lucas, "Thomas Worthington of Virginia, 1773-1827," *West Virginia Review*, VI (1929), 140-42.

hood that has money [by which, of course, he meant the only man who saved his money], am induced once more to impose on your good nature in lending me a Hundred Dollars for Three Weeks. . . ."[25]

It seems probable that Worthington and his wife spent their honeymoon in Philadelphia, where Worthington visited Congress, informed his friends of his decision to move west, and solicited a position as surveyor in the Northwest Territory.[26]

In May of 1797, Worthington's brother Ephraim died, and his widow, Effie, prevailed on him to settle the estate. That summer, Worthington, accompanied by Edward Tiffin—a thirty-one-year-old doctor from Charles Town, a close friend who had married his favorite sister Mary in 1789—made his second trip to the new country, bearing more warrants which he wished to locate. He was amazed to find that the cluster of cabins at Chillicothe had grown to almost a hundred, that another hundred families lived within a radius of ten miles, and that new settlers were arriving daily. As to their nature, "So far as I have seen," he wrote his wife, "they are exceedingly well disposed and remarkably industrious. As yet there is no magistrate, nor, though I have inquired, do I hear of any quarrels. There are four or five little stores from which you can buy anything necessary. . . . The Indians are quite peaceable, and from what I learn among those of them who speak English, there is not the most distant prospect of war."[27]

On August 2, he entered into an agreement at Chillicothe with Duncan McArthur for the location of 7,600 acres in the Virginia Military District,[28] the great area located between the Scioto and the Little Miami rivers which had been reserved by Virginia for her soldiers when the cession of western lands was made to Congress. The warrants that Virginians were locating there were, therefore, those that had been issued to them as Virginia soldiers or that had been purchased by them from the original holders. For his services for Worthington, McArthur received one-fifth of the quantity of land specified in the warrants he located, which was the ordinary percentage; in addition, Worthington had to pay all expenses connected with surveying and entering the lands. This would seem to have been a rather large price for the mere locating of lands, but actually the locater was a most important person, for in the Virginia Military District the camelback (sometimes called the "zigzag cut and carve") survey was used, which permitted the surveyor to parallel the water courses and elimi-

---

[25] Letter in WM.

[26] Richard Z. Blackburn to Worthington, January 1, 1797, in WM.

[27] Peter, *Private Memoir*, 22-24.

[28] Signed memorandum in the McArthur Papers, LC.

nate all shallow, rocky, or otherwise undesirable land.[29] McArthur, having supervised the first survey, congratulated Worthington on the fine quality of the land (apparently 2,866⅔ acres) which he had located for him.[30] These two continued to work together in land deals for many years; although such deals were a minor issue with Worthington, they were McArthur's chief business.

On this trip Worthington again met his old friend and fellow Virginian, Nathaniel Massie, with whom he carried on much business afterward. They discussed with avidity the opportunities in the West, the necessity for post roads, and the desirability of petitioning Congress for a grant of land for the support of a university to be established in the not too distant future. Already, these young men of Jefferson's generation and persuasion were anticipating educational advantages for the many.[31]

This second trip to the West confirmed Worthington's faith in the new country and strengthened his determination to move there. The rapid increase in population stimulated his visions of profitable investment. The Greene Ville Treaty seemed to have ensured safety for the inhabitants, and the beauty of the rolling verdure-clad hills and of the fertile Scioto and Paint Creek valleys delighted him. The location appeared to be healthful, and since the three lots he owned in Chillicothe were so inviting, Worthington thought it wise to build a house before some squatter usurped the best site in his absence. Consequently, he and Dr. Tiffin agreed to build log-cabin homes immediately. About one hundred fifty yards south of the easterly bend of the river, near the present corner of Paint and Second streets, Worthington erected a modest log cabin on a lot which included an Indian mound some thirty-five feet in height on which he planned to have a summer house.[32] He lost no time, for the prospect of an heir made him anxious to return to Virginia. On July 9, 1797, Abraham Shepherd of Shepherdstown wrote him as follows: "Mrs. Worthington . . . Mrs. Shepherds nease [sic] has thirty young ducks I see her paying great attention to every day and she begins to show she is a married woman. I suppose you will feel strange when Papa is called."[33] Back

[29] See William T. Hutchinson, "The Bounty Lands of the American Revolution in Ohio" (unpublished Ph.D. dissertation, University of Chicago, 1927), Chap. 3, for a study of surveys in the Virignia Military District.
[30] McArthur to Worthington, October 30 and November 17, 1797, in WMOSL.
[31] See letters in David Meade Massie, Nathaniel Massie, A Pioneer of Ohio (Cincinnati, 1896).
[32] Worthington to Mrs. Worthington, May 17, 1797, in Peter, Private Memoir, 23. See also Alice Worthington Winthrop, "Thomas Worthington, A Memoir" (typed copy, n. d., annotated by the author), RCHS.
[33] Letter in WM.

in Virginia by September, the Worthingtons and Tiffins began to prepare for their exodus in the spring. Worthington's slaves were all manumitted and either placed with friends or included in the plans for the West. The Worthingtons' first child was born November 19, 1797, and named Mary Tiffin.

Worthington endeavored to dispose of most of his Virginia property, making a particular effort to secure Ohio lands in trade. Prospect Hill and most of his Berkeley County lands were traded to his neighbor, General Stevens Thomson Mason of Raspberry Plain, for land warrants in the Virginia Military District.[34] Nathaniel Massie, originally from Berkeley County, was invited to make a visit to his old home county and give advice on land locations and general prospects in the Ohio country. Since Massie was unmarried, Worthington tried to ensure his visit by telling him of the fair and well-endowed maidens that could be had for the asking. He proposed, moreover, that they go to Philadelphia and petition Congress for a post road from Wheeling to Limestone and for a land grant to establish a college at Chillicothe. He mentioned in passing that he was watching the French Revolution carefully; he hoped the Directory might have "pure principles and bring harmony to the country."[35] Already this twenty-four-year-old Virginian was evidencing the political philosophy and the practical statesmanship which were to make him one of the Ohio country's leaders.

The Wheeling-Limestone road became an actuality that same year (1797), when Ebenezer Zane established it over the horseback trail known as Zane's Trace which he had opened in 1795. Travel and commerce over it from southern Ohio east were heavy despite its deplorable condition, especially in the winter months. In 1798, United States mail service was established over the road, and stagecoach service was begun in 1805.

Wednesday, March 14, 1798, was the day set for the Worthingtons' departure, but preparations for moving had been going on, it seemed, all winter. It took the Tiffin family three days to prepare food and finish packing for the journey. The Worthingtons had collected their furniture, including two lovely pier glasses inherited by Eleanor from her mother, and, in addition, had gathered together the family silver

---

[34] Worthington to Massie, November 29, 1797, in Massie, *Massie*, 137. A Mr. Lynn also purchased a portion of Worthington's property. See Lucas, "Thomas Worthington of Virginia," 141. Abraham Shepherd seems to have bought from him a farm of about 250 acres called Rocky Fountain. A. Shepherd to Worthington, November 24, 1800, and June 28 and November 27, 1801, in WM.

[35] Worthington to Massie, September 9, 1797, and November 24, 1797, in Massie, *Massie*, 132, 134-35.

and linen, farming implements, pots and pans, chickens, fruit trees, shrubbery, and seeds of every kind. The traveling party consisted of Worthington and his wife and daughter; his brother Robert and his wife (Ann E. Whiting) and their three children; Mrs. Worthington's two brothers, James and Samuel Swearingen; Dr. Tiffin and his family, which included his wife, his parents, two brothers, and two sisters; a Mr. Woods and his family, including several big boys who were millwrights; and a group of free Negro servants. Paradise, the Tiffin home in Charles Town which had recently been sold to James Wood, was the first stopping place for the pilgrims. Thence they moved across the valley of the Opequon to Martinsburg, where they rested a day while the wagons went ahead a day's journey on the trail around North Mountain and across the Cacapon through Bath (Berkeley Springs) to Paw Paw Ferry. There the company crossed the Potomac and followed the crude road to Cumberland by way of Cresaps (Old Town). At Cumberland they took Braddock's Road across the mountains to Pittsburgh.[36]

The next stage of the journey was three hundred forty-five miles by Ohio River flatboats to the mouth of the Scioto. The immigrants were delighted with the scenery along the Ohio, which the French had called *la belle rivière*, and which Elbridge Gerry, Jr., one of Worthington's contemporaries, thought "the most beautiful river in the world."[37] Its "elegant banks" were tree-covered, and its many islands were most picturesque. Grapevines "8 inches or more in diametre" hung from the giant trees. Down past the villages of Beaver, Steubenville, and Wheeling, which they reached April 3, they drifted, sailed, and poled. The valley appeared to be very rich, and at the confluence of the Ohio's many tributaries other fertile valleys stretched invitingly. Four days of alternate shade and sunshine brought them to the village of Marietta, at the mouth of the Muskingum. There they viewed the forty acres of ancient fortifications—prehistoric Indian earthworks—looked over the projected right-angled streets, which gave future promise of "a Town of great magnitude," and admired the beauty of the placid Muskingum. Again embarking, they spent five more days sailing the one hundred ninety-three miles to the site of the old Shawnee village at the mouth of the Scioto River, another placid, but much smaller, stream flowing from the north into the Ohio. This part of the trip had been easy and pleasant compared with the arduous horseback journey now facing them. Perhaps the women recalled how, forty-

[36] Tiffin to Worthington, March 10, 1798, in WMOSL. Some details are added to the account in the *Private Memoir*.
[37] Annette Townsend and Claude G. Bowers, eds., *The Diary of Elbridge Gerry, Jr.* (New York, 1927), 110.

three years earlier at this very place, their athletic fellow Virginian, Mary Draper Ingles—she could leap on her horse from a standing position—had been held captive by the Shawnee, her life spared chiefly because they learned she could make shirts; here her third child was born, in some measure replacing those the Indians had sold into captivity. Perhaps they remembered, too, how all the captives but Mary had been forced to run the gantlet.³⁸ Such memories no doubt strengthened them for the long walk and ride up the almost indistinguishable river path to Chillicothe. Not until April 17 did the tired though patient company reach that wilderness settlement and welcome the sight of their new homes.

5

The reasons which persuaded Worthington and his party to go to the Ohio country merit a word of explanation. They despised the institution of slavery and agreed with their Virginia neighbor, Colonel Richard K. Meade, that its abolition in Virginia and throughout the South was "the wish of every liberal mind, . . . the mode of affecting it" being "the only real obstacle."³⁹ They were happy that the government established for the Northwest Territory by the Ordinance of 1787 had excluded the evil institution. Too, they had often heard that eminent Methodist circuit rider, Francis Asbury, denounce its wickedness when he regularly stopped in their neighborhood. They would have approved the entry he made in his diary on January 9, 1798, and they acted in conformity with its sentiments when they left Virginia just three months after it was penned:

> Oh! to be dependant on slave-holders is in part to be a slave, and I was free born. I am brought to conclude that slavery will exist in Virginia perhaps for ages; there is not a sufficient sense of religion nor of liberty to destroy it; Methodists, Baptists, Presbyterians, in the highest flights of rapturous piety, still maintain and defend it. I judge in after ages it will be so that poor men and free men will not live among slave-holders, but will go to new lands: they only who are concerned in, and dependant on them will stay in old Virginia.⁴⁰

Yet strong as this feeling against slavery undoubtedly was, it was not the chief factor in the decision to make the move to the Ohio country; Worthington was not a slaveholder in the true sense of

³⁸ Archer B. Hulbert, *The Ohio River: A Course of Empire* (New York, 1906), 58-69.

³⁹ Colonel R. K. Meade (aide-de-camp to General Washington and brother of David Meade), Frederick, Virginia, to Governor St. Clair, May 4, 1789, in William Henry Smith, *The Life and Public Services of Arthur St. Clair* (2 vols., Cincinnati, 1882), II, 113.

⁴⁰ Francis Asbury, *The Journal of Francis Asbury* (3 vols., New York, 1821), II, 306-307.

the word, for his Negroes were servants and members of the household. The pioneer instinct, the economic motive of bettering his condition by moving into a country where land was rich and cheap, and the opportunity to be an influence in building a new country were the true reasons which led to his departure from friends and familiar surroundings. To a young man of ambition, the West, with its promises of adventure, wealth, and opportunity, exerted an almost irresistible attraction. The story of the movement westward has been told over and over again, but an attempt to rationalize it completely is foolish. The wilderness called, and men of spirit, of daring, of imagination, answered. Moreover, third-generation life in the lower Shenandoah Valley had lost much of its excitement and opportunity; the area's shallow soil, its great distance—both geographically and socially— from the center of political affairs in Virginia, and the inability of its inhabitants to get ahead as fast and as far as they desired were important considerations. No such economic, political, or social handicaps existed north of the Ohio; an ambitious man's success was circumscribed only by his personal limitations.

Thus were installed in this new country two men who were to wield an influence matched by no other two, in industry, politics, and service to the community. Edward Tiffin was the first of two licensed medical practitioners in the settlement (Samuel McAdow was the other); Bishop Asbury had made him a lay preacher in the Methodist Episcopal Church; he came to Chillicothe commended to the attention of Governor St. Clair by former President Washington; and from the time of his arrival he was accorded the highest social, professional, and political recognition it was in the power of the people of his community, territory, and state to bestow.[41] Worthington, without Tiffin's schooling, professional recognition, or high endorsement, relied on his enormous energy, sound judgment, dauntless courage, and driving ambition. From the time of his arrival, he set an example of business acumen, political sagacity, and achievement in public service that seldom has been excelled.

---

[41] William E. Gilmore, *Life of Edward Tiffin, First Governor of Ohio* (Chillicothe, 1897), 1-18.

ii

Businessman and Citizen

WHEN IN 1798 at the age of twenty-five he settled permanently at Chillicothe, Thomas Worthington was a man with character formed and habits established. He was amazingly energetic and able to turn a profit in almost any enterprise which he undertook. He recognized and accepted the challenge of the wilderness and established with confidence and skill an extensive and profitable milling, farming, stock-raising, and shipping business. He welcomed every political opportunity with eagerness and never displayed the slightest lack of confidence in himself or his abilities. He was impetuous by nature and had a quick temper, but taught himself restraint and caution. Throughout his career he was constantly irritated by the weakness and indecision of his contemporaries, but experience brought him patience and wisdom.

Almost six feet in height, well built, and robust, this young pioneer might have been considered handsome. His complexion was ruddy, his hair sandy. A long, moderately aquiline nose and dark-blue, piercing, heavy-browed eyes relieved his otherwise rather impassive English countenance. His disposition was on the sober side; he smiled when other men laughed, and chuckled when they guffawed. Quiet for the most part, his eyes could burn with ardor or excitement, and his face flush with zeal or indignation. Usually reticent and short of speech, when aroused he could cut an opponent's argument to pieces with rude eloquence, or with mounting anger and burning invective espouse a cause to rectify a grievous wrong.

Well endowed with property, encouraged by a talented wife, and alive to the political and economic opportunities of his new environment, from the time of his arrival Worthington took a very active part in the life of the community. On his ready acceptance of civic and political responsibilities, but even more particularly on his business enterprise, was founded the noteworthy career of this Ohio citizen.

In the early days of our history most of our public men speculated in land, but the word "speculator" then carried no derogatory connotation. Land speculation was a legitimate means of making money. The great landholders were not such objects of envy as are our agrarian barons or capitalists, and few accumulated large or permanent fortunes. High taxes, Indian wars, lawsuits over titles, and fluctuating economic conditions made the business precarious at best.[1] When it came to selling, each speculator had to compete with the state, the federal government, and other speculators. Wild land increased in value very slowly, and few men lived long enough to enjoy the un-earned increment which actually accrued over a long period.

In the Virginia Military District there were 3,900,000 acres of land which had been reserved by Virginia for her soldiers when she ceded her western land claims to the federal government. Warrants for practically all of this had been issued by 1800. Each soldier, instead of locating and patenting his land, was usually content to sell his warrants to a speculator. Thus by 1800, seventy-five persons owned a third of the District. On this list Worthington stood twentieth, with 18,273 acres. The largest holding was 118,601 acres.[2]

To the east of the Scioto River and bounded by it, by the Greene Ville Treaty line, by the Seven Ranges, and by a line due east from Franklinton, lay the smaller United States Military Tract (or Military District) of some 2,540,000 acres, on which warrants were issued to pay the Continentals for their services in the Revolution. Seventy per cent of this tract was held by one hundred fifteen persons, mostly absentee speculators. Jonathan Dayton owned not less than 64,000 acres, and John Cleves Symmes 36,000, but in general the holdings were smaller than those in the Virginia Military District.[3]

To the south of the United States Military Tract and including all land to the Ohio River except that of the Ohio Company and the Seven Ranges, lay the Congress Lands, an area about the same size as the Virginia Military District. These lands were put up for sale by the Land Act of 1800 through land offices at Chillicothe, Marietta, and Steubenville.[4] The usual procedure of the speculator was to buy up warrants at an average of about forty cents an acre; to have them located, entered, surveyed, and patented; and then to hold the land for a profit.

As early as 1797 Worthington bought some warrants for his friend Nathaniel Massie;[5] whenever he found others for sale he usually pur-chased them if the price was reasonable. He noted in his diary on December 6, 1804, for example, the purchase of warrants for two

[1] Hutchinson, "The Bounty Lands," 201-202.
[2] Ibid., 196-97.
[3] Ibid., 157; Beverley W. Bond, Jr., ed., The Correspondence of John Cleves Symmes (New York, 1926), 187.
[4] The Land Act of 1800 is in Clarence Edwin Carter, ed., Territorial Papers of the United States (22 vols., Washington, D.C., 1934-), III, 88-97.
[5] Nathaniel Massie to Worthington, December 11, 1797, in WMOSL.

half-sections for $500; and on December 12, the purchase of warrants for 1,000 acres for $100. An entry made on November 6, 1812, records a price of twenty-five cents an acre for the purchase of 700 acres. The average price of warrants at this period was about fifty cents per acre. Massie had regular warrant-buyers in the field, but Worthington purchased his own. In June, 1806, he entered into a contract with Duncan McArthur whereby Worthington was to buy warrants which McArthur was to locate for him on the shares, but they never operated under the contract to any great degree;[6] if anything, they were rivals rather than partners. Whenever possible, Worthington purchased his land outright or traded a large tract of unimproved land for an improved or more advantageously located piece. He also participated in the rather good business of locating and supervising the survey of tracts for warrant-holders, whereby he secured a share, usually one-fourth. Warrant fees varied from one-fifth to one-half but usually averaged about one-fourth. Acreage secured in this manner could often be sold for cash, an article all too scarce among land-dealers; thus in March, 1801, Worthington sold, for seventy-five cents an acre, one-half of the 1,700 acres he received for locating some warrants for John Cleves Symmes.[7]

The ethics of the game between speculators were none too good. Worthington's neighbor, McArthur, wrote his partner, Robert Means, on November 16, 1806, that he had sent a warrant to cover by entry a tract already half-covered by Worthington, who awaited more warrants. He concluded, "He will no doubt be much enraged when he hears the news, but I trust you will not let my name be known in the business though it is generally believed he would take the chance if it was in his power. I would not regard it was he not so near a neighbor."[8]

Buying and selling land and paying land taxes for absentee friends took much of Worthington's time. He was land agent for Albert Gallatin for both his Ohio and Virginia land. That Gallatin's holdings were extensive is indicated by the fact that he held 7,115 acres in Ohio in partnership with Savary[9] and two tracts in Virginia comprising

[6] Document dated June 5, 1806, in the McArthur Papers. Hutchinson makes the mistake of referring many times to Worthington as a warrant-buyer for McArthur. It is true that Worthington represented McArthur's interests in the attempt to get the Ludlow Line extended in the Virginia Military District controversy. See McArthur to Worthington, December 27, 1811, in WMOSL.
[7] Worthington's diary, March 7, 1801; Worthington to Symmes, March 11, 1801, in Worthington's letter book, LC.
[8] Letter in the McArthur Papers, I, 171, LC.
[9] Gallatin to Worthington, August 15, 1801, February 7, 1818, August 5, 1825, etc., in WMOSL.

7,956 acres for which Worthington was made an offer of twenty-five cents an acre.[10] He was also agent for Senator James Ross of Pennsylvania (after whom Ross County, Ohio, was named), with power of attorney and "full right and confidence" to sell all his lands.[11] A survey dated December 5, 1799,[12] of 4,300 acres on Deer Creek made for Ross by Duncan McArthur indicates the scope of Worthington's dealings in behalf of Ross. Among other friends for whom Worthington acted as agent were Samuel Cabal, Joseph Swearingen, Henry Bedinger, Nathaniel Macon, Stevens Thomson Mason, John Breckinridge, and Thomas Jefferson. He collected a fee for paying taxes as well as for all other services; for instance, he paid taxes of $82 for Abraham Baldwin, for which he received a fee of one-sixteenth;[13] in 1802 he paid a tax of $69.84 for Bailey Washington on the Washington lands on Paint Creek.[14]

In his own land-buying he was wise enough to secure mill sites, and very early he had mills constructed on the north fork of Paint Creek (built and run by his brother Robert), at the falls of the Hockhocking River, and on Kinnickinnick Creek. His Kinnickinnick mill, situated a few miles north of Chillicothe, did so well that on October 12, 1802, he could confide to his diary, "Find my mill grinds for ⅔ of the people in Fairfield and Ross Counties." This mill was equipped with four-and-one-half-foot stones, first secured at Redstone, Pennsylvania, a town on the Monongahela above Pittsburgh. An early set made for him in 1802 at Baltimore cost him £96 in Pennsylvania money ($256) undelivered. He later used Ohio stones exclusively. During the next few years he built sawmills and other gristmills on Paint Creek and on the Mad River in Logan County. In 1811 he had three sets of stones operating in his Chillicothe mill. Most of the time his mills were rented or let out to managers who, in addition to grinding Worthington's grain, paid a stated amount in kind. Thus the manager of his Chillicothe mill in 1808-1809 paid him one hundred barrels of flour, one thousand gallons of whiskey, and half the hogs.

In 1810 he established a ropewalk and a cloth mill at Chillicothe, thereby inaugurating an attempt at home manufacturing, a project in which he was always much interested. The mill was equipped to weave cotton, flax, and wool, and was managed by Hector Sanford. His

[10] M. R. Thompson of Coalsmouth, Kanawha, Virginia, to Worthington, September 3, 1819, in the Rice Collection, OHS.
[11] Ross to Worthington, November 18, 1802, in the Rice Collection.
[12] In WM.
[13] Worthington to Abraham Baldwin, March 6, 1801, in Worthington's letter book, LC.
[14] Worthington to Bailey Washington, July 20, 1801, ibid.

first cloth was chiefly linsey, cassimere, and flannel. At the same time he went into sheep-raising on a considerable scale to provide wool for his mill. He paid $250 for a full-blooded Merino ram, which he secured, together with several ewes, from the farm of his friend General John Mason, of Georgetown, Maryland. In this connection it may be noted that he raised part of the flax which his mill processed; cotton, however, he had to secure from Kentucky, Tennessee, and New Orleans. In 1811, he paid twelve cents a pound for cotton in Kentucky; in 1812, he bought several tons in New Orleans at eight cents, but by the time he got it to Chillicothe it had cost him fifteen cents; in 1816 it cost him thirty-one cents a pound, and in 1817, thirty-two cents.

He tried knitting cotton and woolen socks and other small articles of clothing, but they proved unprofitable. He was more successful with cotton and woolen cloth, yarn, and rope. His dyes included navy blue, light blue, yellow, light brown, snuff, drab, green, and black. His fulling mill was a liability, but the process was a necessity. Year after year he persevered, some years making a good profit, sometimes losing money. By 1817, he had invested $7,200 in machinery which included two carding machines, one mule of 204 spindles, two throstles of 108 spindles each, 1,600 wired spools, a 41-skein reel, one loom, a 30-spindle Betty, and a 40-spindle Jenny. His volume of business is indicated by his receipts of $5,845.34 ½ for his finished product in the first six and a half months of 1820—mostly yarn, but including 640 yards of flannel and 289 yards of shirting. In this particular six months his profits seem to have amounted to about thirty per cent.

To enumerate the varied activities of Worthington's private life is to name almost every occupation followed in the Territory. In addition to those just mentioned, he farmed; bought and sold town lots, cattle, horses, and hogs; and prospected for fertile lands, brick-clay, coal, salt, and iron. As early as 1801 he was investing part of his extra cash in six per cent United States stock and other "active bank stock." On March 20 of that year, he wrote Joseph Nourse at Washington to put $5,173.75 in United States stock at once; again on June 6, he wrote Nourse to put $10,000 in bank stock and requested him to choose the bank offering the best returns.[15] The year 1805 was one of his best for this type of venture: in August of that year, his Philadelphia bankers invested $19,104 for him in 8 per cent and 3 per cent bank stock.[16] He occasionally contracted to build a road; in 1804, he was warned by Gallatin that if he took the contract for the road from Lancaster to the Great Miami, "being a public man you must do it on

---

[15] Worthington to Nourse, *ibid.*
[16] McEuen, Hall, and Davidson to Worthington, August 30, 1805, in WM.

monstrous low terms."[17] The same year, Worthington advocated the establishment of a bank in Chillicothe and proposed that the state be made a shareholder.[18] Somewhat later he was an organizer, stockholder, and acting president of the Bank of Chillicothe.

In July, 1810, he purchased at least 405 "good-sized" cattle from the Chickasaw Indians in Tennessee at $13.25 a head. The expense of driving them to Ohio was $780, which, together with the fact that fifteen were lost in the course of the two drives, raised their cost to about $16 a head. On July 25, he had 750 cattle on hand, and on that day branded 205 with his mark, a large TW. It is probable that this venture was not very profitable, for in his diary for November 26 he relates that the Indian cattle were suffering from the cold rains, to which they were not accustomed, and that they remained scrawny because of the fact that they "have never before eat corn and now eat little or none of it & get very poor."

2

Worthington also found time for his lodge, being constantly attracted by the serious objectives of Masonry though impatient with its foolish diversions. While attending the opening session of the first territorial legislature at Cincinnati in November, 1799, he took the first three degrees in Nova Caesarea Harmony Lodge No. 2, of which Jacob Burnet was the Worshipful Master. In November, 1805, he helped organize the first lodge at Chillicothe, Scioto Lodge, No. 6; but the records do not show that he was very active, nor does it appear that the organization had more than a social function.

In June, 1808, he helped organize New England Lodge, No. 48, at Worthington, Ohio, "according to letters for that purpose to him directed, by and from the Grand Lodge of Connecticut." His "friend and brother" James Kilbourne was installed as Worshipful Master, Zophar Topping as Senior Warden, and Josiah Topping as Junior Warden.

Worthington lived for five years in Chillicothe, the only years of his adult life, in fact, when he actually was a city dweller. During this period he improved his lots and home and planted trees grafted by himself. In the spring of 1802, he built a commodious log house on the eminence he called Belle View, two miles northwest of the town. Although the climate was excellent, the valley was none too healthful

---

[17] Gallatin to Worthington, June 8 and September 24, 1804, in WMOSL.
[18] James Findlay to Worthington, December 21, 1804, and January 31, 1805, in WMOSL.

because of floods and swampy backwaters, which caused bilious and intermittent fevers. Moreover, no true frontiersman wished to be crowded. Worthington sold his home in town and the lots containing the Indian mound to Winn Winship. The hill on which he had now erected his log house overlooked the beautiful Scioto Valley and his own noble estate; to the northeast and visible from his front door, rose the wooded hills soon to be memorialized in the state seal, the idea for which is supposed to have originated with Worthington and some friends as they were sitting outdoors east of the house after an all-night political and social gathering.

A traveler who visited Worthington in August, 1802, has left an account of the man and his home. He reported that the house was a "log cabin but neatly furnished"; its owner was "now growing an orchard of about 300 apple trees . . . and a great number of peach trees, plum trees and Lombardy poplars, etc." The visitor was treated with great attention, and reported that Squire Worthington was "one of the best informed men we have met in *all* the country."[19] That summer was a pleasant one for the master of the new house: the Scioto Valley was healthful all the way up to Franklinton; the wheat was the best he had ever seen in his life; the land and milling businesses were good; his first son, James Taylor Worthington, had been born safe and sound on May 21; and on July 26, "Gov. St. Clair [Worthington's political enemy] passed through town and as usual got very drunk."[20]

His home, farm, and business interests were a constant joy to Worthington, and he filled his diary with news of them, of his family, and of his friends. When he harvested thirty-nine loads of clover hay, that was something to record. The currant crop was unusually good that summer, and Mrs. Worthington "made a barrill of wine." In the spring of 1805, Worthington rewarded Jefferson for his kinship of spirit in the soil by sending him some of his finest "Alpine or monthly strawberry seed."[21] He bought two bay horses and a roan colt from William Trimble on May 31. A lover of horses, he was infuriated when Attorney Michael Baldwin "rode down his horse," and threatened to "cain" him if it ever happened again; everybody rode horses, but only a drunken fool would abuse his mount. Business and politics necessitated continuous horseback travel; Worthington spent the equivalent of several years of his life in the saddle. Occasionally he

[19] "Journal of Nathaniel W. Little," *Old Northwest Genealogical Quarterly*, X (1907), 242.
[20] Worthington's diary, July 26, 1802.
[21] Jefferson Papers, LC, 147:25715, March 3, 1805.

carried a gun on these trips, but he confessed that he was a poor hunter and had no inclination to be a good one. More often he carried a book on his long rides; thus, on a trip to one of his farms (The Barrens), he read Seneca the whole of the way, from whose writings, he noted, he "derived much pleasure and benefit."

During the years 1805-1807, Worthington was occupied with building a permanent stone house on the hilltop just south of the log home to which the family had moved in 1802. The new house, "called at the time of its erection . . . the most magnificent mansion west of the Alleghenies," exemplified in its architectural design and in the extensive grounds surrounding it the tradition of eighteenth-century colonial Virginia. When he was in Washington in 1805, Worthington had commissioned Benjamin Henry Latrobe, noted architect and surveyor of public buildings during the administrations of Presidents Jefferson and Madison, to draw the plans.[22]

The house stood about four hundred and fifty feet from the rim of the hill, facing north up the valley of the Scioto and commanding a view of Mt. Logan through a vista cut in the virgin timber to the east. The area about the house was laid out in symmetrical units. Large orchards on the west were balanced by formal terraced gardens on the east. Beyond the gardens and extending to the northeastern tip of the hill was the "grove," an area of fifty-one acres planted with ornamental trees and flowers in a design of circles, triangles, and squares. Seen from without, the grove gave an impression of "natural and spontaneous growth" similar to that of the "wilderness" at Mt. Vernon and the "roundabout" at Monticello. Beyond the cleared and cultivated areas on the plateau at the top of the hill, virgin forests of hickory, beech, walnut, and oak dropped down the slopes to the east. Some of the native trees had been left to shade the lawns by which the house was surrounded. Lombardy poplars lined the drive which approached the entrance gate.

The house consisted of a central unit two stories high, flanked by story-and-a-half wings directly connected with the main structure and forming an open court at the north or entrance side. The court was terraced, its curving front supported by a brownstone wall topped by a wrought-iron fence. A flagstone path led from the entrance gate to the flagged porch before the front door. At either side of the gate stood a crimson Pyrus japonica. The walk itself was edged with pink

---

[22] Latrobe to Worthington, September 3, 1805, and March 25, 1806. Transcriptions at the Ohio Historical Society from Latrobe's letter books and index are in the hands of Mrs. Ferdinand C. Latrobe, Baltimore. See also Talbot Hamlin, *Benjamin Henry Latrobe* (New York, 1955), 199-201.

and white roses. A clipped privet hedge inside the iron fence formed the outer border of the two small plots of turf beyond the rose borders. Flaring stone steps led from the court to the lawn below. A circular driveway in front of the house curved out across the lawn to skirt the rim of the hill and afford panoramic glimpses of hills, river valley, and woods before descending the slope to join the Limestone Road in the valley to the south.

The terraced or falling gardens, situated about twenty feet from the house on the eastern side, were modeled after semi-formal gardens of Virginia and other parts of the East. The terraces were supported by stone walls, stone steps leading from one level to another. The first terrace was planted with rare shrubs and flowers, many of which Worthington had brought from nurseries in the East, as well as with the hardier native flowers. Lilac, syringa, hawthorne, and other woody plants bordered the walks and the formal flower beds, where grew a profusion of flowers—peonies, phlox, asters, verbena, lilies, lupine, and mignonette. Roses, of which the Worthingtons were very fond, were everywhere. Here was the little pink rose which Mrs. Worthington had found in the woods and transplanted—a flower which became known locally as the Worthington Rose. Here, also, were the moss roses, the honeysuckle, and the yellow jasmine which Aaron Burr sent her after his visit to the house. The next two terraces were devoted to vegetables and small fruits which were of special interest to Mrs. Worthington. German redemptioners, employed as gardeners, laid out and cared for the gardens.

To the west of the house beyond the farm buildings were the orchards which Worthington had planted even before the log house was built. So outstanding were his peaches, plums, cherries, and apples that neighbors came from miles around to secure grafts and seedlings.

The house was constructed of sandstone quarried on the Worthington estate. The traveler Fortescue Cuming recorded that the Morris brothers, natives of Virginia, were the masons.[23] The carpentry and cabinet work were done by George McCormick, Conrad Christman, and Hector Sanford of Chillicothe. All the wood used in the construction of the house and the furniture made on the estate—with the exception of mahogany imported from the East—was procured from the local forests and kiln-dried on the Worthington estate. Walnut was used for the baseboards, chair rails, moldings, and mantels. Cherry, as well as walnut and mahogany, was used for the furniture.

[23] Fortescue Cuming, *Sketches of a Tour to the Western Country* (Pittsburgh, 1810), republished in Reuben G. Thwaites, *Early Western Travels, 1748-1846* (36 vols., Cleveland, 1904-1907), IV, 219.

Marble for three of the fifteen fireplaces was purchased in Philadelphia. Glass for the windows came from the factory of Albert Gallatin at Geneva, Pennsylvania, and wallpaper from the Quaker firm of Thomas and Caldcleugh of Baltimore. Silver, china, tableware, textiles, furniture, and other valuables which the Worthingtons had brought from Virginia were supplemented by purchases in the East.[24] The Worthington furniture was chiefly Sheraton and Hepplewhite, with Chippendale, and possibly Queen Anne, heirlooms.

With some exceptions, the general plan of the rooms followed a modified Georgian design known to architectural historians as the federal style. A survey of the buildings on the estate, made in 1821 by John Peebles, agent for the Insurance Company of North America, contains a detailed description of the room arrangement.[25] The traditional hall running through the building had been divided to provide two rooms. The central portion of the main unit was devoted to living purposes. Within the entrance door was a reception hall with a fireplace at the left, and at the right a staircase leading to the upper floor. Immediately beyond the reception hall and opening from it was a spacious drawing room, twenty-four feet by twenty. To the right of these two central rooms were the family and state dining rooms; to the left were three rooms which were the apartment of the Worthingtons: the central room was their bedroom, the smaller one to the south a sitting room, and the one on the north the "little anteroom." The six rooms on the second floor were bedrooms. The east wing housed Worthington's office-library and a receiving room. In the west wing were a pantry, a kitchen, and a servants' room, and flanking this wing on its western side was a flagstoned porch. At the north end of the porch was an excellent well, and close by were a brick washhouse and a stone smokehouse. Beyond these to the north were a barn, springhouse, and other buildings, and the servants' quarters. The upper floors of both the wings were used for storage, and under each wing was a cellar.

When completed, the mansion was a marvel of beauty and luxury to the pioneer people in the surrounding country, who admired its massive walls (twenty-four inches thick); its size (the main unit was sixty-four feet wide by forty-four deep; each wing, twenty-four by thirty-nine feet); the novelties of large glass windowpanes, papered walls, and marble mantel facings; and the charm of its extensive

<hr>

[24] James H. Rodabaugh and Henry J. Caren, "Adena," *American Antiques Journal,* II (May, 1947), 4-5; Ohio Historical Society leaflets entitled *Adena: A Restoration by the Ohio Historical Society,* and *The Furnishings and Interior Decoration at Adena.*
[25] In WM.

grounds. The mansion was seldom without eminent visitors. One traveler, after recording his impression of the house and gardens, has given us a glimpse of the countryside which this "palace in the wilderness" overlooked:

> I ascended to a platform on the roof, to take a view of the surrounding lands, but there is as yet nothing but woods covering the greater part of the country. Fires that were burning in some places were proof of the fact that new settlers were clearing the woods. From this platform the governor can overlook the greater part of his property, containing five thousand acres of land. . . . The ground consists of low hills, and it is only toward the east, in direction of Zanesville, that more considerable elevations are perceived.[26]

Because of the panoramic view which the house afforded, Worthington called his home Mount Prospect Hall until 1811, when, in a tome on ancient history, he ran across the name "Adena"—descriptive of "places remarkable for the delightfulness of their situations."[27] So Adena it has been called ever since.

Exactly one hundred years after its completion, a replica of the mansion was built at the Jamestown Exposition (1907). John W. Bradford of Ohio State University, who directed the work of reproduction, said in his speech at the formal opening: "So far as my study of the history of American architecture goes, there is not another structure possessing the interest, from the historic architectural standpoint, in all the central states. It is well-proportioned, fine in its architectural composition, with simplicity and dignity as strong features."[28]

Adena remained in the Worthington family until 1903, when it was purchased by George Hunter Smith and Clara Boggs Smith of Chillicothe. In 1946, their daughter, Mrs. Elizabeth S. Fetterolf of Meadowbrook, Pennsylvania, presented Adena and the estate of approximately three hundred thirty acres to the state of Ohio as a memorial to her parents. It is administered by the Ohio Historical Society, Columbus, which restored the property, furnished it with rare and valuable antiques in the Worthington tradition, and opened it to the public as a special feature of the Ohio sesquicentennial celebration in 1953. Thousands of persons visit this restoration each year.

3

At a very early time, trade down the Ohio River was looked upon by Ohio Valley settlers as offering an opportunity for the disposal

[26] Karl Bernhard, Duke of Saxe-Weimar Eisenach, *Travels in North America During the Years 1825 and 1826* (2 vols. in one, Philadelphia, 1828), II, 150.
[27] Worthington's diary, September 18, 1811.
[28] "Ohio Day at the Jamestown Exposition," *Ohio State Archaeological and Historical Quarterly*, XVII (1908), 185, 189.

of surplus products. In the first fourteen weeks of 1801, goods valued at $332,000 were entered for export at the custom house at Louisville; some of the chief items shipped were flour, corn, whiskey, pork, beef, lard, butter, and spun yarn.[29] Most of the shipments came from Kentucky, but the farmers, millers, stock raisers, and merchants north of the Ohio saw to it that their goods were not excluded.

Shipbuilding had started early, chiefly for the transportation of settlers but partly for commodity export. Homemade boats had been passing down the Ohio from the vicinity of Pittsburgh in ever increasing numbers since 1786; in the first eleven months of 1788 alone, some nine hundred boats carrying 18,000 passengers had descended the Ohio.[30] In 1793, an ocean-going vessel was built near Pittsburgh by a Dr. Watson, and in 1800, a 45-foot schooner, the "Redstone," was constructed and launched near Brownsville, Pennsylvania, by Sam Jackson. The next year a schooner-rigged vessel of a hundred tons burden called the "Monongahela Farmer" was built and launched by the commerce-minded settlers on the Monongahela. A number of galleys and brigs (up to four hundred fifty tons burden) were built around Pittsburgh between 1798 and 1804. By 1800, ships were being built in the Ohio country for trade with foreign ports. On September 9, 1801, Governor St. Clair granted certificates of citizenship to Commodore Abraham Whipple and the crew of the Marietta-built brig "St. Clair," bound on a voyage to the West Indies.[31] James T. Adams cites two other examples: "In 1803 the 'Duane' of Pittsburgh surprised the authorities of Liverpool by arriving there from a place never heard of, and a couple of years later the 'Louisiana of Marietta' was trading between Italy and England from the small Ohio town as her home port!"[32] A gentleman at Zanesville wrote on April 29, 1802, that the settlement and improvement of the Ohio country were progressing rapidly, that exporting by the Mississippi route would soon be a great business, and that shipbuilding was well under way at Marietta. He voiced a warning that the transfer of Louisiana to France must not be permitted to interrupt trade. "It will behove [sic] our government to have a watchful eye to that object, which is of incalculable consequence to this country *and to the Union* if [the] integrity of the

[29] *Scioto Gazette* (Chillicothe), May 28, 1801.
[30] C. H. Ambler, *A History of Transportation in the Ohio Valley* (Glendale, Calif., 1932), 70.
[31] Leland D. Baldwin, "Shipbuilding on the Western Waters, 1793-1817," *Mississippi Valley Historical Review*, XX (1933-34), 29-44; *Territorial Papers*, III, 529.
[32] James Truslow Adams, *Epic of America* (New York, 1931), 115.

nation may be considered of the least importance, for this country must follow *the fate of the only outlet to the Ocean.*"[33]

When the Spanish closed the port of New Orleans on October 16, 1802, their action struck the Ohio Valley with consternation.[34] Massie wrote Worthington, December 8, "I am told the inhabitants of Kentucky are very uneasy," and "we ought not to be remiss on the subject." In case the action was taken "for the purpose of setting aside our treaty with Spain," he added, "I assure you the consequences will be serious, as I am sure the inhabitants will never submit for the navigation of that river to be stopped."[35] As soon as Worthington, then in Washington, received this letter, he had a conference with President Jefferson, who informed him that everything possible was being done and that the Spanish minister had dispatched a pilot boat to the governor general at Havana; the impression given was that the intendant at New Orleans had withdrawn the right of deposit without authorization.[36] Worthington called on Secretary of State Madison and doubtless helped stir up the debates in Congress over the situation.[37] Promises did not help greatly, however, and Worthington appealed to Postmaster General Gideon Granger for assistance and information. Granger wrote him on March 11, assuring him that orders were being sent that very evening to the intendant which would have the desired effect.[38] The purchase of the whole territory was soon announced, but the negotiations were so unsatisfactory and annexation sentiment was so strong in the West that Secretary of War Henry Dearborn prepared for forcible occupation and wrote Governor Tiffin, October 31, 1803, to raise five hundred volunteers and have them ready to march by December 20 to dispossess the Spanish.[39] By that time, however, the need had passed: on that very day, in pursuance of the treaty of May 2, the American flag displaced the tricolor at New Orleans. No other step could have done so much to popularize Jefferson permanently in the West.

Meanwhile, on Thursday, February 24, 1803, the first Chillicothe-built, New Orleans–bound flatboat cleared for that southern metropolis with a load of pork, and thereafter produce floated down the Scioto

---

[33] *Republican or Anti-Democrat* (Baltimore), June 4, 1802, OHS.
[34] Randolph C. Downes, "Trade in Frontier Ohio," *Mississippi Valley Historical Review*, XVI (1929-30), 488. See his footnotes for sources on this subject.
[35] Massie, *Massie*, 219-220.
[36] Worthington to Massie, December 25, 1802, in Massie, *Massie*, 220.
[37] Worthington to Massie, January 6, 1803, *ibid.*, 222. See *Annals of Congress*, 7th Cong., 2nd Sess., for debates. Hereinafter referred to as *Annals*.
[38] In WMOSL.
[39] *Scioto Gazette* (Chillicothe), November 12, 1803.

River and other tributaries of the Ohio in ever increasing amounts. The embargo and nonintercourse acts of Jefferson's and Madison's administrations curtailed considerably, but did not stop, the trade. Moreover, the influx of people into the states and territories drained by the Ohio River gave a home market that was equally valuable.[40] After the repeal of the embargo (1809), the Mississippi trade boomed, for the continental blockade excluded Russian supplies. The British army in Portugal imported almost 67,000 barrels of flour from New Orleans in the two years 1811 and 1812. New Orleans supplied another 33,000 barrels to states on the Atlantic seaboard during the same period.[41] The falls of the Ohio at Louisville constituted a serious barrier —many a shipper had his goods dumped or his flatboat staved in— but they were not formidable enough to stop the trade.[42] Cattle-driving to the East was another method of getting Ohio produce to market which was tried as early as 1800; drives occurred spasmodically for a quarter of a century, but did not prosper because of competition nearer the seaboard.[43] The Ohio shippers' best opportunity was the Mississippi until the Ohio canal system gave them a cheaper, shorter, and less precarious route to the East; but even canals did not supplant the Mississippi route for produce from the southern half of the state.

4

Before Worthington moved to Ohio, Nathaniel Massie notified him that through his influence Governor Winthrop Sargent had appointed him, Worthington, major of the militia and judge of the court of common pleas for Adams County,[44] which at the time included the area later set off as Ross County. Massie was then a lieutenant colonel of militia and also a judge. When Ross County was established on August 15, 1798, Governor St. Clair made Worthington a judge of the court of common pleas in that county and raised him to the rank of lieutenant colonel in the militia. This put him in command of the Ross County regiment, but the next year it was divided into two battalions, only one of which Worthington commanded. Judge Samuel Finley was made colonel and put in command of the regiment. Worthington had hoped to be continued as regimental commander with the

---

[40] See W. F. Galpin, "The Grain Trade of New Orleans, 1804-1814," *Mississippi Valley Historical Review*, XIV (1927-28), 500-505.

[41] *Ibid.*, 504-505.

[42] Jacob Burnet, *Notes on the Early Settlement of the North-Western Territory* (New York, 1847), 402-404.

[43] Downes, "Trade in Frontier Ohio," 493-95.

[44] Massie to Worthington, July 20, 1797, in WMOSL.

rank of colonel, but St. Clair informed him that he had appointed Finley because of his service in the Revolutionary War and because he believed the militia would profit more from his experience than from that of a commander who had not seen actual combat. He promised to make Worthington a colonel when and if the county had a second regiment. "I have certainly [had] great reason to be satisfied with your activity and public spirit," the Governor concluded.[45] Worthington was not mollified, and resigned his commission.[46]

As a judge of oyer and terminer he sat with Samuel Finley, who presided, and John Cleves Symmes on one of the earliest cases in the region (June, 1798), in which a white man (Thomas Thomson) was brought to trial for the murder of an Indian. The murder occurred in Thomson's tavern in Chillicothe, where a rowdy gang "were singing songs and drinking grog." The Indian's life might have been saved, but his friends would not let Doctors Tiffin and McAdow trepan his skull. They objected, "One white man kill Indian, two come to scalp him." The doctors had to stop in the middle of the operation at the insistence of the Indians, and the victim died. Before the trial ended, Thomson was permitted to escape, and an attempt was made to placate the Indians with presents; but Jack Hot, the victim's brother, killed two whites on Jonathan's Creek for vengeance and then escaped to Canada.[47]

Another murder trial on which Worthington sat was that of John Bowman, who had stabbed one John Bates. Bowman was found guilty in July, 1801, but a new trial was granted, and this time a verdict of manslaughter was returned by the jury. The court ordered that Bowman "be burned in the hand and forfeit his goods to the Territory." Many other cases were handled, over some of which Worthington was the presiding judge. Forgery of bank notes, warrants, surveys, receipts, and other legal papers was common. Horse-stealing by the Indians was a frequent offense, but in those early days, if the Indian surrendered the horse he was usually released with a solemn warning, for the animosity of the man's tribe was not to be lightly aroused.

An important case because of its political influence was one concerning the selection of the seat of government for Adams County.

[45] *Territorial Papers*, III, 512, 513; Worthington to St. Clair, February 26, 1799, in WRHS, *Tract 39*, p. 17; St. Clair to Worthington, April 14, 1799, in the Rice Collection.
[46] *Territorial Papers*, III, 81.
[47] St. Clair to Worthington, June 7, 1798, in WMOSL; Worthington to Isaac Williams, May 28, 1798, in WMOSL. See also Williams Brothers, *Ross and Highland Counties*, 188, for the Rev. James B. Finley's account of the murder.

The problem revolved around the question of whether the governor or the judges had the authority to determine the location of county seats. Both claimed to represent the interests of the people best, and both undoubtedly had personal motives that in some measure affected the integrity of their decisions. Massie owned a great deal of land at Manchester and wanted the county seat situated there, but St. Clair established it at the mouth of Stout's Run and designated the site as Adamsville. Massie declared this to be a most inconvenient spot since it was "only accessible two ways, either up or down the River." Thereupon St. Clair ordered that the county seat be moved to Washington, a town site at the mouth of Ohio Brush Creek. The court met at Adamsville in June, 1798, when the eight judges determined that their chief business was to decide definitely on a location for the seat of government and refused to follow the proclamation of the Governor. After much deliberation they agreed on Manchester because Massie offered the greatest inducements, especially a gift of land on which to erect the public buildings.[48] St. Clair refused, however, to provide the funds for their erection although work on them had begun.[49] Worthington tried to explain that he had moved no action be taken until the Governor had been consulted, and assured him that there were no improper motives. St. Clair craftily replied that he had never meant to impute improper motives. In any event, the September court met at Adamsville and agreed to a removal to Washington.[50] Judge Worthington, meanwhile, had been transferred in August to the newly established county of Ross, but Massie and Benjamin Goodin were removed from the Adams County bench in October for "having Misdemened [sic] themselves in the execution of their office by attempting to disturb the regular administration of Justice by adjourning the sessions of the said Courts of Gen'l Quarter-Sessions of the Peace & of the Common Plase [sic] to meet at Manchester, when they had been duly & regularly appointed to be held thereafter at Washington and fixed at that place by a Proclamation of the Governor."[51] So the burning question concerning which had the power to erect county seats—the governor, the courts, or the legislature—was left unsettled and remained so even after the first territorial legislature had met.

---

[48] "Territorial Executive Journal" for October 29, 1798, in *Territorial Papers*, III, 494, 513; Nelson W. Evans and Emmons B. Stivers, *History of Adams County, Ohio* (West Union, Ohio, 1900), 88.

[49] St. Clair to Massie and other judges, June 29, 1798, in WMOSL. See St. Clair to Massie, June 29 and July 23, 1798, in Massie, *Massie,* 138, 143.

[50] Evans and Stivers, *History of Adams County,* 90.

[51] "Territorial Executive Journal," for October 29, 1798, in *Territorial Papers,* III, 515.

In addition to serving as a judge, Worthington acted as a United States deputy surveyor under Rufus Putnam. His work in that capacity consisted of surveying post roads and county and township lines. He surveyed that portion of the Marietta-Cincinnati road which went through Chillicothe. He made connection to the west at the Hamilton County line with surveyor John Reily, and with Paul Fearing and Ephraim Cutler to the east at the Washington County line. McArthur, who was also a deputy for Putnam, worked with Worthington survey-ing county and township lines. In 1807, Worthington, along with Jesse Spenser, was employed by Jared Mansfield, who had succeeded Putnam in 1803 as United States surveyor general, for surveys of some five hundred miles.

5

Perhaps the most difficult job Worthington ever held and the one which brought him the most trouble was that of superintendent of public sales and register of the land office at Chillicothe. The act passed by Congress in 1800 provided for four land offices in Ohio and for sales of as little as a half-section at two dollars an acre. Presi-dent Adams nominated Worthington to the Chillicothe office, May 12, 1800, and the Senate confirmed him, May 13.[52] He was bonded for $10,000.

Although Secretary of the Treasury Oliver Wolcott sent instructions on the procedure to be followed and on the interpretation of the law, each register had to exercise his own judgment concerning many points which were not covered. Worthington appealed to Governor St. Clair for his suggestions but wrote Gallatin that the "Old Gentle-man" had had nothing to offer on the subject. Moreover, no entry books or other official supplies arrived, and decent paper or books of the proper sort could not be obtained in Ohio at any price. Fortunately, several ledgers were secured by mail order, but Worthington had to wait until mid-June before the official office supplies arrived. The public sales were to open May 4, 1801. Feeling it desirable that the public be informed, Worthington put on an advertising campaign by publishing a copy of the land act and an announcement in the *Scioto Gazette* for three weeks and by getting out twelve hundred handbills. For three weeks lands were to be offered at public sale to the highest bidder for not less than two dollars an acre. At the end of that time the sales would continue privately at that minimum figure. The sales

[52] *Journal of the Executive Proceedings of the Senate of the United States,* I, 353-54. Hereinafter referred to as *Senate Executive Journal.*

commenced at three-thirty on the afternoon of the appointed day (having been held up until that hour in a vain wait for Governor St. Clair's arrival). Worthington supervised, Rufus Putnam, the surveyor general, advised, and a clerk made the entries. Benjamin Miller, hired at two dollars a day as auctioneer, cried the sales for the two hundred prospective buyers. Neither St. Clair nor his secretary, one or the other of whom was required by statute to be present, appeared until the third day, and then only to criticize. Worthington, they objected, was unauthorizedly collecting a four-dollar application-for-sale fee and requiring the buyer to sign the entry in the sale book. Although Worthington had an explicit authorization from the Secretary of the Treasury to make no distinction in the method of his bookkeeping between sales at auction and private sales,[53] and although he showed this letter to the Governor, St. Clair correctly insisted that the act did not authorize any such fee at the sales by auction. Worthington protested to Gallatin that St. Clair had tried to take the conduct of the sale out of his hands and that he had criticized his every action.[54]

This sale of public lands proved to be a tremendous business; the purchases by May 16 exceeded $220,000; by June 20, $360,000; and by June 26, $400,000.[55] When Worthington remembered that lands offered for sale under the act of 1796 at Pittsburgh and Cincinnati in full sections had brought into the treasury only $100,000 over a four-year period, he had reason to feel that his office was doing an unusual volume of sales. The overseeing of the transactions would not have been such a difficult task had he not been called upon to make all decisions on such perplexing problems as whether land claimed by preëmption or by warrant was subject to the same regulations as that purchased at public or private sale (Worthington ruled that it was); whether a floating mill, that is, one on boats anchored in the river, gave preëmption rights to a section in the same manner as a mill actually located on land (he ruled that it did not);[56] whether a mill or a like improvement gave its owner preëmption rights to the fraction of a section on which it was located or to a whole section (he ruled a full section); and whether he was authorized to charge fees or hire clerks to assist him in discharging unauthorized but necessary

[53] Wolcott to Worthington, November 21, 1800, in WM.
[54] Worthington to Gallatin, May 11, 1801, in Worthington's letter book, LC.
[55] Worthington to Rufus Putnam, May 16 and June 20, 1801, ibid.; Worthington to Presley Neville, June 26, 1801, ibid.
[56] See Sec. 16 of the Act of May 10, 1800, in Territorial Papers, III, 96; see also Worthington to Gallatin, September 18, 1802, ibid., 246.

duties.[57] He complained that he had had to pay for printing and advertising because they were unauthorized. Complications of this sort, together with many others of daily occurrence, did not dismay him, and for over a year he interpreted his instructions according to his best judgment—a procedure which was satisfactory to practically all the purchasers. A few disgruntled buyers and critics endeavored, however, to cause difficulty for the register by criticizing many of his decisions. He was accused of discrimination, of unfair practices such as putting tracts up for sale when those most interested in buying them were not present, of ruling out floating mills, of buying the best land himself (a perfectly legitimate action so long as he applied for it through Rufus Putnam, the surveyor general), of depriving the government of revenue to the extent of at least ten thousand dollars by selling at a figure below that which he could have secured, of hiring unauthorized help, and of charging unauthorized fees.[58] Worthington paid himself and his clerks five dollars a day, and his janitor, Edward Sherlock, fifty cents a day. He wrote Gallatin that the fees barely covered his necessary expenses.[59]

Governor St. Clair and Worthington's other political and personal enemies made the most of the situation and tried to discredit him. Deeply injured by the charges they made, Worthington wrote for advice to some of his influential friends, who almost without exception upheld him in everything he had done. Senator James Ross wrote him that it was quite proper for him to charge fees. Gallatin told him that he should use his own judgment in running the business; that he, Gallatin, had originally felt that the charging of an application fee for sales at public auction was unauthorized, and that he had had Levi Lincoln, the attorney general, write an unofficial opinion which corresponded with his. Gallatin stated, however, that in the final analysis it was his own opinion and Lincoln's against Wolcott's and Worthington's. If any dissatisfied buyer or other malcontent wished to dispute Worthington's fee-taking—or any of his procedures—he could take his case to the courts for a decision.[60] Worthington determined to utilize this excellent advice—not by waiting for a suit to be brought but by instituting one himself. In a diary entry for July 13, 1801, he records that he induced the Fairfield County Court to institute "a friendly suit ag't me for receiving fees at the Publick

[57] Worthington to Secretary of the Treasury (Gallatin), July 2, 1801, in Worthington's letter book, LC; Worthington to Joseph Nourse, July 11, 1801, ibid.
[58] Gallatin to Worthington, August 7, 1802, enclosing a copy of charges made by Elias Langham, in WMOSL.
[59] Worthington to Gallatin, July 2, 1801, in W .thington's letter book, LC.
[60] Gallatin to Worthington, June 10, 1801, in WMOSL.

sales of land. The court unanimously determine that I am entitled to those fees and enter a judgment accordingly," this "notwithstanding 3 out of 4 of the judges were interested in the question, having purchased a considerable quantity of land at the sales." At Worthington's request, the decision was immediately appealed to the Territorial General Court then sitting at Chillicothe, which body in October also upheld his actions.[61] The court decision and appeal did not quiet criticism, however; Elias Langham, a militia officer and one of St. Clair's minions, kept the charges circulating and even drew up a two-page indictment which was sent to Gallatin. Thereupon Worthington wrote in his diary that he was through with public office, told Gallatin he planned to resign, and asked for an investigation.[62]

The upshot of the whole matter was that a year later, in the summer of 1802, Gallatin authorized Governor St. Clair to order an investigation before a court. At the same time he instructed Worthington to take depositions from worthy characters in his defense. In the hearing, which closed September 17, Worthington was completely cleared of all the charges, which were shown to have been motivated by jealousy, by the fact that Langham had had a "floating mill" disallowed, and by the fact that Abraham Claypool, another critic, had not succeeded in purchasing the section of the "High Bank Prairie" on which he had lived for two years.[63] William Creighton deposed that another purpose of the charges was "to raise a clamour in this country to injure Thomas Worthington's election for the [constitutional] convention without the most distant expectation of proving anything criminal against him."[64]

It was in 1802, while Worthington was register of the land office, that he was visited by Colonel (the Reverend) James Kilbourne, a leading promoter of the Scioto Company, formed at Granby, Connecticut, in 1801. The two became close friends. In fact, Kilbourne drew his famous map of Ohio from those hanging in Worthington's land office. In 1803, Kilbourne purchased a township in the United States Military District and established the town of Worthington, naming it in honor of his friend at Chillicothe, who had made a "very liberal donation" toward its establishment and had helped him

[61] Worthington to Gallatin, October 29, 1801, in *Territorial Papers*, III, 183.
[62] "Langham's Notice" is in WM. See Worthington to Gallatin, August 21 and September 30, 1801, in Worthington's letter book, LC.
[63] Worthington's diary, May, 1801, and August 26 to September 25, 1802; Worthington to Gallatin, September 18, 1802, in Worthington's letter book, LC; Williams Brothers, *Ross and Highland Counties*, 274.
[64] See Creighton's deposition, in WM.

in many ways. By 1804, twenty families—a total of one hundred New Englanders—were settled there.[65]

While Worthington was head of the land office, another federal position was awarded him. He was appointed supervisor of the new internal revenue district established by Congress in 1801 northwest of the Ohio River. Gallatin offered Worthington the position because he had a "more perfect confidence" in him than in any other person of his acquaintance in the Northwest Territory.[66] Worthington accepted this office and held it until Ohio became a state. Michael Baldwin, a resourceful young lawyer of Chillicothe, was appointed United States Attorney for the district.

A lesser public duty to which Worthington found time to attend was the supervision of the building of the Ross County courthouse. A public square had been dedicated to that purpose by Nathaniel Massie in 1801, when the erection of such a building became essential. Worthington was instrumental in seeing that it was constructed on a corner lot, that it was set well back from the street, and that it had glass windowpanes. Eight hundred panes ten by twelve inches in size were purchased from the factory of his friend Gallatin, which James Nicholson was running. The way the bill was paid illustrates the ordinary financing of the period. Henry Bedinger of Berkeley County, Virginia, owed Worthington some money. Worthington therefore instructed Bedinger to pay it to Joseph Nourse, who was to pay it to Gallatin, who was to pay it to Nicholson.

Worthington demonstrated in the first years of his residence in the West that he was capable, upright, trustworthy, and able to do successfully a prodigious amount of various kinds of work. In other respects, too, he was adept; his finest roles during these years remain to be related. His accomplishments and the vicissitudes through which he passed as territorial legislator, envoy extraordinary, and state-maker constitute the most important chapters in the story of his early life.

6

In evaluating a man's success, it is necessary to examine some of the moral and spiritual wellsprings of his nature. Worthington was profoundly religious, and had prayers morning and evening in his home,

---

[65] Worthington's diary, August 25, 1802; Kilbourne to Worthington, February 7, 1804, in WM; Helen M. Dudley, "The Origin of the Name of the Town of Worthington," *Ohio State Archaeological and Historical Quarterly*, LII (1943), 248-59; Henry Howe, *Historical Collections of Ohio* (2 vols., Cincinnati, 1904), I, 613-14.
[66] Gallatin to Worthington, August 7 and September 11, 1801, in WMOSL.

a practice which he never relaxed and which was maintained by his wife in his absence. His Puritan and Quaker ancestry made him unsympathetic toward the popular vices of his day; by nature he would have been an excellent circuit rider or lay preacher. In Chillicothe he regularly attended the Presbyterian and Methodist churches, to both of which he and Mrs. Worthington contributed, although in true Quaker tradition they did not actually accept membership in either. Nevertheless, in 1823, he taught a Bible class in the Methodist church and participated in the Communion service. He once rode nineteen miles from Tarlton on a very cold Sunday morning in February, setting out before five o'clock in order to meet his class on time. While spending the month of April, 1823, in New Orleans on a business trip, he associated himself closely with a Methodist Bible class; in his diary entry for April 16 he speaks proudly of "our class of 14 or 15 Methodists who are walking with God."

When away from home, whether in nearby Lancaster, Ohio, or in Philadelphia, Washington, or New York, Worthington regularly found time to attend a Sunday morning service. Just as regularly, he recorded his reactions in his diary; thus, on February 8, 1801, he wrote, after hearing the Reverend William Speer of the Presbyterian Church at Chillicothe, "Sermon very good & tending to produce sincere examinations of the heart." Something of a self-taught theologian for his day, he objected in 1810 to the exegetical discourse on predestination delivered by the Chillicothe Presbyterian minister, Robert G. Wilson, holding that that subject was incomprehensible to mortals and "ought never to be meddled with. We know or may know our duties both religious and moral. This is enough. To inquire into the secrets of an omnipotent God is beyond our reach—the attempt imprudent & folly—nay, worse, it is sinful."[67]

In Washington, D. C., on January 27, 1811, he recorded a typical comment on a sermon: "Much gratified, strengthened and edified." He often referred in his diary to his attendance at Quaker meetings, camp meetings, union meetings, and the Methodist Quarterly Conference when it met in Chillicothe. Whenever possible, he devoted a portion of each Sabbath to instructing his family in the tenets and moral teachings of the Christian religion; in his absence Mrs. Worthington maintained this custom. To them both, such a practice was ordinary good sense, part and parcel of the weekly regimen whereby they lived. It was no accident that the children were upright and worthy citizens of the community. Never mawkishly sentimental or overly emotional—in a day, too, when religious emotionalism traveled

---

[67] Worthington's diary, February 25, 1810.

in waves over the state as the circuit riders made their rounds—
Worthington never displayed publicly the religious fervor which per-
meated his life. But he was in deadly earnest when he wrote, "Fine
Day. Spent considerable part of it with my children endeavoring to
show them how much their happiness here and hereafter depends on
walking in the way of righteousness and of the certainty of a happy
old age from a well spent youth."[68]

Three excerpts from the journal of Francis Asbury, eminent frontier
bishop and circuit rider, illustrate his confidence in the religious life
of the Worthington family:

> On Wednesday [August 7, 1808] came into Chillicothe. On Thursday I
> preached in the chapel. . . . I was invited to pass a night under the hospitable
> roof of General Thomas Worthington at Mount Prospect Hall. Within sight
> of this beautiful mansion lies the precious dust of Mary Tiffin; it was as much
> as I could do to forbear weeping as I mused over her speaking grave—how
> mutely eloquent! Ah! the world knows little of my sorrows—little knows how
> dear to me are my many friends, and how deeply I feel their loss—but they all
> die in the Lord, and this shall comfort me. I delivered my soul here; may this
> dear family feel an answer to Mary Tiffin's prayers!
> Sunday 16 [September, 1810] Thursday, I preached at Chillicothe at four
> o'clock. . . . I paid a visit to my much esteemed friend, Governor [Senator]
> Worthington, at Mount Prospect: he requested me to furnish an inscription for
> the tomb-stone of his sainted and much-loved sister, Mary Tiffin; I gave him
> Luke x. 42. second line to the end.
> Sabbath 23 [August, 1814] From the 24th to the 30th we are at senator
> Worthington's. I pay my mite of worship in this amiable family in great weak-
> ness. The kind attentions I receive are greatly beyond my deserts. Mrs.
> Worthington has taught her boys and girls, servants and children, to read the
> holy Scriptures, and they are well instructed: I heard them more than one lesson
> with much satisfaction. O that all mothers would do likewise! I presume the
> worship of God is kept up in this house, though neither of the heads thereof have
> attached themselves to any society of professing Christians; doubtless God will
> bless them, and their children after them.[69]

Karl Bernhard, Duke of Saxe-Weimar Eisenach, noted some years
later that "the father of the family had the laudable custom of making
a prayer before sitting down" to breakfast. He regarded the Worthington family as one of the most interesting he had met in the United
States.[70]

Worthington's domestic life was particularly happy; his devoted
wife was a constant inspiration to him. She bore and mothered ten
healthy children and gave her strength untiringly to their nurture
and her husband's comfort. Although her name seldom appears in
these pages and apparently but one portrait of her was ever made,
her noble influence manifested itself in the household and in the
community.

[68] Worthington's diary, June 6, 1815.
[69] Asbury, Journal, III, 248, 297, 365.
[70] Bernhard, Travels in North America, II, 149-50.

Territorial Legislator and Politician

UNDER THE Ordinance of 1787 as amended, the initial government of the "Territory North-west of the River Ohio" was vested in a governor, a secretary, and three judges, all appointed by the President. These officials were authorized by the Ordinance to adopt and make operative such laws of the original states as were necessary and most suitable for the peace and prosperity of the Territory. Although Governor St. Clair interpreted this authorization strictly, the judges in general took the position that they were authorized to adopt any laws not repugnant to those of the original states, and this was the policy followed prior to 1799, when the Territory moved to a government of the second stage with a representative assembly. Hence, there was friction between the governor and the judges, and also between them and Secretary Winthrop Sargent, who was acting governor during most of the period.

Moreover, the governor appointed all justices of the peace, who constituted the County Court of General Quarter Sessions of the Peace. These county justices, in addition to their judicial functions, administered local government by appointing constables, surveyors, supervisors, clerks, overseers of the poor, and commissioners. Through the constables they controlled assessments and taxes, and they also supervised the laying out of roads, the administration of poor relief, and the granting of tavern, ferry, and trading licenses.

The settlers, who were anxious to establish local self-government, resented the slowness with which laws were adopted and legal procedures established relating to land, Indian policy, local government, and everything else which needed regulation. This was a period of Indian wars, town-making, land speculation, and the establishment of commercial and business enterprise. The settlers made heavier demands on the new government for legislation than it had time and ability to satisfy, and they had little sympathy with the tasks faced by the governor and judges in enacting laws for the enormous area and the many settlements under their jurisdiction. The two objectives almost all settlers sought to reach speedily were an elective assembly which could legislate in conformity with their wishes and a state government with full sovereignty. They wanted the impotent, dilatory, and tyrannical government by governor, judges, and justices of the peace to be replaced as soon as possible by one made up of persons of their own choosing.

The movement calculated to eventuate in statehood for the Northwest Territory had begun as early as 1790, but the Indian wars delayed it for a decade. However, after the Treaty of Greene Ville in 1795, following Anthony Wayne's defeat of the Indians, frontier life was less precarious; immigrants swarmed to the West, and statehood was again agitated. Kentucky and Tennessee had shown the way, and Chillicothe settlers, largely Virginians and true republicans at heart, demanded a government of the people. In Hamilton County, also, the movement was especially strong; as early as 1797, committees of correspondence were organized there to attain the objective of self-government.

It became apparent, however, that in any division of the Territory as authorized by the Ordinance of 1787 all local interests might not be served. For instance, if a dividing line were run from the mouth of the Great Miami northward, Cincinnati would find herself on the corner of a division, a position which meant geographic disability for leadership and for selection as the seat of government. Moreover, the influx of settlers to the Scioto country threatened to make that area the center of political and economic activities to the detriment of Cincinnati and Marietta. The problem of local interests was further complicated by the fact that the divisions must not be too small or statehood would be delayed—although from a purely administrative standpoint, the more divisions the better. Statehood would be postponed if the line were drawn at the Scioto; and if location were the criterion, Marietta, at the mouth of the Muskingum, would be the seat of government for the easternmost division. In addition to delaying statehood, such a partition would destroy Chillicothe's opportunity to become a seat of government because that town would be placed at the extreme edge of the second area. Cincinnati might well be the capital of such a second area if the second division line were run north, not from the mouth of the Great Miami as specified in the Ordinance of 1787, but from the falls (Louisville) or from the mouth of the Wabash or thereabouts. However, political considerations and the confessed inability of St. Clair, the judges, and Secretary Sargent to administer the immense territory to the satisfaction of the people made an early division very desirable.

In the meantime, the republican element demanded a representative government; Governor St. Clair admitted the legitimacy of the claim under the Ordinance, which specified that the Territory might pass to a government of the second class when it had 5,000 "free male inhabitants of full age." This concession was made, the question of division being for the time held in abeyance. On October 29, 1798, St. Clair, therefore, issued a call for the election of a territorial legislature on the third Monday in December.[1] Ross County was allotted only one representative by this order but later was permitted two, and Worthington and Edward Tiffin were elected.

The delegates from the nine counties constituting the Territory assembled in Cincinnati, February 4, 1799, and Governor St. Clair addressed them the same day. He pointed out that in conformity with the Ordinance of 1787 their first duty was to nominate ten persons from among whom President Adams would choose five to constitute the legislative council. He then advised the legislators to appoint a speaker and other officers and to begin the formulation of necessary legislation which, when completed, could await action by the council as soon as its composition was known. He added somewhat sardonically, "You will find, gentlemen, that the business which will come before you is of considerable magnitude." He explained that many of the laws adopted by the judges, including "nearly all the laws relating to crimes and punishments," were probably illegal, for they had not been adopted bodily from the codes of other states as the ordinance had specified but had been created by the judges in an illicit assumption of a legislative power. He had been compelled to acquiesce in their enactment at the time, but he felt sure one of the first duties of the new assembly would be to repeal these questionable laws and adopt new ones. He pointed out that since many members had come extremely long distances, it seemed unwise for them to go back home only to reassemble at an early date to continue the session. He assured them, again tartly, that in legislating for the Territory it would not be difficult to fill any such interval with plenty of hard work.[2] The delegates made their ten nominations and "promptly" adjourned, having agreed to meet again on September 16.

Ross County citizens meantime protested so loudly that they did not have their fair share of representatives that on August 3, St. Clair allotted them two additional seats, and Elias Langham and Samuel Finley were elected to occupy them.[3]

2

The territorial legislature was supposed to meet September 16, but the delegates from Detroit and the Indiana and Illinois country had

[1] *Territorial Papers*, III, 514.
[2] Emilius O. Randall and Daniel J. Ryan, *History of Ohio* (5 vols., New York, 1912), III, 37-38; Smith, *St. Clair*, I, 207 *et seq.*
[3] *Territorial Papers*, III, 521; Burnet, *Notes*, 289-92.

not arrived by that date. Worthington reached Cincinnati on the seventeenth with his wife and baby. William Henry Harrison, Winthrop Sargent's successor as territorial secretary, entertained them in his new home at North Bend.[4] Although the delegates drifted in slowly, on September 23 a quorum was present. Henry Vanderburgh, a former Revolutionary War officer and later a judge of Indiana Territory, was elected president of the council. Tiffin was elected speaker of the house, and a working organization of committees was established, Langham, Worthington, and John Smith constituting the important committee on rules and regulations.[5]

Governor St. Clair appeared before the legislature on September 25 and in a very able speech called the attention of its members to the legislation necessary for the good government of the Territory. He repeated his advice that most of the existing laws of the Territory should either be repealed or reënacted to make them legal. He very properly urged the immediate enactment of revenue laws, establishment of an effective militia system in order that all communities of the Territory might be safe from Indian depredations, provision for the erection of public buildings, and regulation of interest rates. He urged that action be taken to induce Congress to vest in trustees the supervision of lands reserved for schools and places of religious worship; he specifically mentioned that John Cleves Symmes (William Henry Harrison's father-in-law) had not yet set aside a complete township for academies and schools from the Miami Purchase as his contract with the federal government had stipulated; and he stated that if action was not taken on the matter, the state might suffer a great loss. Laws for the repression of "vice and immorality, and for the protection of innocence and virtue, for the security of property and the punishment of crimes" were of particular urgency, and afforded this delegated body a "sublime employment" for the welfare of both present and future generations. Finally, he declared that one of the most important duties of the assembly was to choose a delegate to represent them in the Congress of the United States, where for the first time the voice of the people of the Territory might be heard, their causes pleaded, and their grievances redressed.[6]

The addresses made in answer by the houses were mild and polite; the legislators pledged their attention to the suggested subjects, and peace seemed to reign. They followed the Governor's advice by

---

[4] Peter, *Private Memoir*, 39.
[5] *Journal of the House of Representatives of the Territory of the United States North-West of the River Ohio at the First Session of the General Assembly*, . . . *1799* (Cincinnati, 1800), 5. Hereinafter cited as *House Journal, 1799.*
[6] *Ibid.*, 7-11; Smith, *St. Clair*, II, 446-57.

speedily reënacting a considerable body of legislation which had been in force under the previous government. In addition, it was unanimously determined that Virginia soldiers should not be permitted to bring their slaves with them to the territory.[7] In all, some thirty-nine acts of an ordinary nature were passed and approved.[8] These varied from a tax on land—the chief wealth available for revenue—to one levying a fine of fifty cents to two dollars for hunting, fighting, or indulging in "worldly employments" on Sunday, and another which placed a tax of fifty cents to two dollars on all able-bodied bachelors who did not own taxable property in the amount of $200. In general, the code was an excellent one, combining the best political practice of England and the American states with a generous sprinkling of frontier ingenuity and Puritan morality.

Scanty as are the facts in the official journals, it is evident that there was a clear realization of the opposition of political forces in the legislature. If the representatives had claimed and secured a certain measure of authority in this second stage of territorial government, St. Clair's power had also been increased. The Ordinance elevated him from his position as one of four legislators and executives to a status in which he commanded a third of the legislative power through the unlimited veto formerly exercised by Congress; his executive power was greatly increased, for now he was authorized to call, prorogue, and dissolve at will the representatives of the people. Moreover, he still held control of the patronage, appointing practically all civil and military officers of the Territory and issuing licenses for taverns, marriages, and so on—thus wielding an almost dictatorial power. He was the leader of a very considerable group in the legislature made up of Federalists and supporters of the Adams administration who for personal and political reasons found it desirable to oppose the Jeffersonian Republicans.

The first contest in the Assembly came over the election in joint session of a delegate to Congress. The Republicans nominated William Henry Harrison, while the Governor's party tried to elect Arthur St. Clair, Jr., the Governor's son. Harrison was elected on October 3 by a vote of 11 to 10. Sol Sibley wrote Paul Fearing the same day that if the delegates from Washington and Wayne counties had been there, St. Clair would have won.[9] As things were, the Republican

---

[7] *House Journal, 1799,* 19-20, September 27.
[8] Salmon P. Chase, ed., *Statutes of Ohio and the Northwestern Territory* (3 vols., Cincinnati, 1833), I; Theodore C. Pease, ed., *Laws of the Northwest Territory, 1788-1800* (Illinois State Historical Library, Collections, XVII, Springfield, 1925).
[9] *House Journal, 1799,* 32; Fearing Papers, in the Marietta College Library.

coterie was successful in elevating an able partisan to a position where he could represent their best interests with a Congress which was known to be friendly. Harrison was pledged to work for a new land law which would make it possible to buy Ohio land in quantities of less than a section, to secure from Congress immediate authority for the use of school lands for education, and to obtain a law to set aside for statehood that part of the Territory lying east of a line drawn north from the mouth of the Great Miami—the last in conformity with a provision in the Ordinance of 1787.

The real conflict came, however, over the establishment of counties and the designation of boundaries and county seats. The Republicans held, not without reason, that the power to regulate these matters had passed to the legislature on its organization. They made the location of the seat of government for Adams County a test case. The bill which moved the county seat from Washington to Manchester was presented to St. Clair on December 5.[10] Several new counties were created, and the boundaries of a number of others were changed. Pushing the advantage, Worthington introduced a bill on November 28 for a census of that part of the Territory east of the Great Miami. This was undoubtedly the first official step toward statehood, and the design of the Scioto delegates to make Chillicothe the state capital was evident. Nevertheless, the bill passed and was presented to St. Clair for his approval.[11]

On December 19, the last day of the session, St. Clair sent his famous veto message in which he explained why he had not signed eleven of the thirty-nine bills passed by the legislature. He refused to establish Manchester as the county seat of Adams County because, he said, the majority of the people wanted it at Washington. He refused to sign the bill for the proposed census because it contemplated a division which the legislature had no authority to make. He vetoed several acts establishing new counties on the ground that the legislature had usurped a power which belonged to him alone. Two bills regarding the licensing of taverns and marriages (which incidentally took from the Governor the right to collect fees) were declared invalid because, St. Clair asserted, they were no improvement over existing statutes, and they would permit, in the one case, the marriage of minors, and, in the other, the multiplication of taverns, especially

---

[10] House Journal, 1799, 51, 81, 149, 205, 210; Journal of the Legislative Council of the Territory of the United States, North-West of the River Ohio. . . . 1799, 51. Hereinafter cited as Council Journal, 1799.
[11] House Journal, 1799, 125, 129, 147.

in the country; each of these pieces of legislation, he held, would adversely affect the "industry and morality of the people."[12]

Thus the body of issues between the Governor's conservative party and the popular party of progressives was clearly defined. To Governor St. Clair the major issue was the preservation of the status quo by defense of the national administration, by control of the patronage, and by the maintenance of the aristocratic philosophy of Federalism; to the popular party the major issue involved the overthrow of the Governor's régime, seizure of the patronage, the acquisition of local and territorial control, with almost immediate statehood, and aid to the cause of Jefferson on the national scene.

3

St. Clair took the attitude—a familiar one in the annals of the Federalist party—that the Ohio people were not fit for local self-government, much less for statehood. He particularly disliked the Virginia element and agreed with Winthrop Sargent that they were "very licentious & too great a proportion indolent and extremely debauched" —a striking contrast to the excellent New England settlers or even to the French on the Wabash and the Mississippi, or at Detroit, who were "upright and Docile . . . [the] equal [of the New Englanders] in their mind and manners . . . but not . . . [as] industrious."[13] At the very time the first territorial legislature was meeting, St. Clair characterized the citizens of the area northwest of the Ohio River as

> a multitude of indigent and ignorant people . . . ill qualified to form a constitution and government for themselves . . . [and] too far removed from the seat of government to be much impressed with the power of the United States. . . . Fixed political principles they have none, and though at present they seem attached to the General Government, it is . . . but a passing sentiment . . . and . . . a good many . . . hold sentiments in direct opposition to its principles. . . . Their government would most probably be democratic in form and oligarchic in its execution and more troublesome and more opposed to the measures of the United States than even Kentucky.[14]

When it came to individuals, Republicans (Jeffersonians) were no less obnoxious to St. Clair. James McMillan would do as delegate to Congress, he wrote President Adams on January 27, 1800, for "tho' he has rather leaned toward democracy, I can say with truth he has always been moderate."[15] Regarding militia appointments, he wrote

---

[12] Ibid., 205-206, 209-10; Smith, St. Clair, II, 474-80.
[13] Sargent to Pickering, September 30, 1796, in Territorial Papers, II, 578.
[14] St. Clair to James Ross, n.d., in Smith, St. Clair, II, 482.
[15] Letter in Territorial Papers, III, 75.

Secretary of State Pickering on March 30, 1800, "Nathaniel Massie commands [in Adams County], an active intelligent man, and by far the most wealthy in the County, but a little tinctured by democracy. Next to him stands John Belli, a well informed Man and clear of those prejudices."[16] People "tinctured by democracy" seemed to be plentiful in the Ohio country in 1799 and 1800, and they heartily resented the attitude of St. Clair and his friends. Their resentment was to grow until it finally retired him to his native Pennsylvania. Like the Federalist supporters of John Adams in Congress, St. Clair did not grasp the fact that aristocracy was on the wane and frontier democracy on the rise. When he was defeated for governor of Pennsylvania in 1790 by a ratio of ten to one, he should have realized the trend.[17] In 1798, when he threatened to run for Congress from his west Pennsylvania district, his friend James Ross dissuaded him. Ross reported that there was no Federalist party there; that all the candidates against whom he would have to run were leaders in "the great universal mass of insurrectionary anti-federalism, Jacobinism, or whatever you please to call it." He would not have a chance "unless the Sansculottes should quarrel among themselves."[18] St. Clair was able the same year, however, to support the Federalist cause by writing two pamphlets to combat the spread of democracy and defend the Alien and Sedition Acts; President Adams was warmly grateful.[19]

Governor St. Clair watched the course of that incendiary movement on the Continent, the French Revolution, with trepidation and disgust. For ten years he had seen certain portions of the American people manifesting the same sort of demoniacal tendency. He loathed and feared the Cincinnati citizens who could toast the "San Culottes of France and the cause of Liberty triumphant"[20] or could express the wish that that "old harlot of aristocracy—May she speedily be dunned out to the tune of Ca ira";[21] and he abominated the sentiments of one "Dorastius," who could describe St. Clair's government (before 1798) as "oppressive, impolitical, and altogether improper and . . . entirely opposite to those rights and privileges belonging to free men."[22]

---

[16] Letter in *Territorial Papers*, III, 81.
[17] Ellis Beals, "Arthur St. Clair," *Western Pennsylvania Historical Magazine*, XII (1929), 184.
[18] James Ross to St. Clair, July 5, 1798, in Smith, *St. Clair*, II, 422.
[19] Adams to St. Clair, May 17, 1799, and St. Clair to Adams, June 24, 1799, *ibid.*, 422.
[20] *Centinel of the North-Western Territory*, July 12, 1794.
[21] *Ibid.*, March 28, 1795.
[22] *Ibid.*, January 31, 1795.

4

Plans were now formulated to get rid of St. Clair as the chief obstructor of statehood. Worthington was delegated to go to Philadelphia to help Harrison secure a division of the Territory at the Great Miami. It was hoped that a new governor would be appointed for the projected eastern division. St. Clair was welcome, if a place must be made for him, to continue as governor of the rest.[23] Worthington left Chillicothe on December 30 and, with Harrison, laid plans to push a division law through Congress. Senator James Ross of Pennsylvania, despite his political views, had for some time favored a division of the Territory in anticipation of statehood, for he had helped found Steubenville and had large land holdings in Ohio which would appreciate in value with an increase of population. Harrison and Worthington built on his support and that of their Virginia friends, Congressman William B. Giles and Senator Stevens Thomson Mason. Others who could be relied on to aid their cause included Robert Goodloe Harper of South Carolina, Abraham Baldwin of Georgia, and Joseph Anderson of Tennessee. Harrison was the tactful performer in Congress,[24] and Worthington worked as a lobbyist. Their immediate plan had three purposes: to secure the division of the Territory at the Miami, to make Chillicothe the capital of the eastern division, and to get rid of St. Clair. They were aided in their division plan by a petition from the Illinois country asking that that area be permitted to revert to a government of the first stage with a division at the Great Miami.[25]

Since Governor St. Clair objected strenuously to such a division, he sought to influence Harrison to support a triple partition by means of a line due north from the mouth of the Scioto and another due north from the southern terminus of the Greene Ville Treaty line. He warned Harrison that "almost any division into two parts must ruin Cincinnati."[26] St. Clair's real sentiments were expressed in a letter to Secretary of State Pickering, in which he boasted that he wished to procure a division of the Territory so that no part of it could obtain statehood for a long time because any such state or states would oppose

---

[23] Worthington to Massie, December 27, 1799, in Massie, *Massie*, 154; St. Clair to James Ross, December, n. d., 1799, in Smith, *St. Clair*, II, 480.
[24] Randolph C. Downes, *Frontier Ohio, 1788-1803* (Ohio Historical Collections, III, Columbus, 1935), 174.
[25] *Territorial Papers*, III, 76; Harrison to Massie, January 17, 1800, in Massie, *Massie*, 156.
[26] St. Clair to Harrison, February 17, 1800, in *Territorial Papers*, VII, *Indiana Territory*, 4-6.

the Adams administration.[27] Confusing party pride with patriotism, he asserted in another letter that any state from the Northwest Territory would be "as unfriendly to the United States as possible."[28]

Despite formidable opposition, Harrison gallantly pressed through Congress, May 7, 1800, the Division Act which created the Territory of Indiana west of a line from a point opposite the mouth of the Kentucky River to Fort Recovery, thence due north to the Canadian boundary. The Act also provided that as soon as the eastern division, which retained the name Northwest Territory, became a state, the line should start at the mouth of the Great Miami in accordance with the Ordinance of 1787. The Indiana Territory was allowed to drop back into a government of the first stage with a promise that whether or not it had 5,000 voters, it could have a territorial legislature and government of the second stage whenever a majority of its voters wished. The Act also provided that Chillicothe should be the seat of government for the eastern division and Fort Vincennes for the western.[29] The people of the Scioto country and the Vincennes region favored this division, as did also, probably, a majority of those in the Indiana-Illinois country; but Hamilton County was in large measure offended.[30] Harrison himself was displeased, or at least pretended to be to his Cincinnati neighbors, by the establishment of Chillicothe as the seat of government. He believed that the determination of this matter should have been left to the territorial legislature.[31]

That the Chillicothe party could have obtained this favor over Harrison's objection seems strange. He had been warned by St. Clair that the division alone would ruin Cincinnati. How much worse was the establishment of the capital elsewhere! His appointment as governor of the Indiana Territory and his extraordinary success in securing the passage of the Land Law of 1800 during the same session may have helped him reach his decision, or else Worthington's work behind the scenes was more potent than Harrison had wished it to be. So far as the records show, however, the two were in perfect agreement. The major appointments under both the Division Act and the Land Law went to the Republicans, and Harrison was regarded, at least by un-

[27] Referred to in a letter from Worthington to Jefferson, January 30, 1802, in Smith, St. Clair, II, 570.
[28] St. Clair to James Ross, December [20], 1799, ibid., 483.
[29] Territorial Papers, III, 86-88.
[30] Annals, 6th Cong., 1st Sess., 593; Territorial Papers, II, 578; III, 76-77.
[31] Harrison said he introduced the bill because of the flood of petitions favoring it. Harrison to his constituents, May 14, 1800, in Logan Esarey, ed., Messages and Letters of William Henry Harrison (Indiana Historical Collections, VII, Indianapolis, 1922), I, 12-18, reprinted from the Western Spy (Cincinnati), June 11, 1800.

biased Republicans, as having "come forward very handsomely."[32] Worthington would have preferred the transfer of St. Clair to the Indiana Territory, but he entertained the hope that St. Clair would not be reappointed governor of the Ohio area.

The "politicians of Cincinnati" were greatly disappointed by the loss of the seat of government, the present location of which, they felt, would, as Senator John Brown of Kentucky had written Worthington in May, probably prove permanent.[33] They began immediately to consolidate their forces with those of Marietta and the Federalist party in general to compel a redivision so that Cincinnati would become the natural center, geographic and political, of the area to the east and west of that rapidly growing town. Washington County was promised the delegate to Congress if it would unite in bringing a capital to Cincinnati. Moreover, a new division of the Territory at the Scioto would practically guarantee Marietta the seat of government for the eastern division. St. Clair was to be retained as governor of one section or the other.[34]

5

Such was the situation when the assembly met at Chillicothe, November 3, 1800, Tiffin, Langham, Worthington, and Finley representing Ross County. The members assembled on the first floor of the largest house in town—"Abrams' big house," a two-story log structure erected in 1798 by Bazil Abrams at the corner of Second and Walnut streets—in a room hitherto used as a courthouse, a church, and a singing school. The upper chamber contained a billiard table, and was a place of recreation for the legislators and local worthies who liked to drink and gamble, although they could usually be found in larger numbers at Joe Tiffin's tavern, the "General Anthony Wayne," or at Tom Gregg's "Green Tree." On November 5, St. Clair addressed the legislature. He stressed the fact that he might not meet with them again since his term of office expired December 9. "I well know," said he concerning his reappointment, "that the vilest calumnies and

---

[32] Israel Ludlow to Worthington, May 15, 1800, quoting a letter from Caleb Swan to James Findlay, January 11, 1800, in WMOSL. Mrs. Peter says Worthington secured the passage of the Land Law "through his friend Mr. Harrison." *Private Memoir*, 41. I have been unable to find any direct evidence to support this assertion.

[33] Brown to Worthington, May 2, 1800, in WMOSL.

[34] C. W. Byrd to Massie, August 20 and September 24, 1800, in Massie, *Massie*, 162-63; John Smith in the *Western Spy*, December 31, 1800.

the grossest falsehoods are assiduously circulated among the people with a view to prevent it."[35]

The reply of the house to St. Clair's address was so mild and approving that the Chillicothe party tried to defeat it, but they were outvoted 10 to 7.[36] The amiability of its tone toward one on whom they had declared war enraged the Chillicothe group, but more particularly were they offended by the fact that the response expressed surprise that the seat of government had been moved to Chillicothe by action of Congress. The move was no surprise to Worthington's group.

On November 11, Massie introduced a resolution for the appointment of a joint committee to draw up an address to the Governor. Massie, William Goforth, Worthington, and Paul Fearing were appointed from the house and James Findlay from the council.[37] The address as adopted showed a definite tendency to restrict the governor's powers. It claimed, first, that the establishment of an elected legislative body had transferred to that body the power of laying out counties. Second, it demanded that thereafter the governor return for reconsideration, within ten days, any bills of which he did not approve.[38]

This address was both conciliatory in tone and threatening in spirit. Its aim was to curtail St. Clair's control by taking from him two of his chief powers, the laying out of counties and the absolute veto. It was mild enough to gain the approval of the legislature's moderates, and radical enough in its effect on the governor's authority to satisfy the Republicans temporarily.

St. Clair snapped at the bait. In his reply, November 24, he maintained that the ordinance vested in him the power to lay out *all* new counties. "It may be true, gentlemen, that this power might have been better vested in you. . . . I will not dispute it. I will only observe that the Congress did not think fit so to vest it." The Governor turned a deaf ear to the legislators' request in regard to his veto power and refused to promise that any bills of which he disapproved would be returned for revision and reconsideration. He upheld the right of his "absolute negative" and accused the legislators of endeavoring to convert it into

[35] *Journal of the House of Representatives of the Territory of the United States, North-West of the River Ohio, at the Second Session of the First General Assembly, A.D. 1800, and of the Independence of the United States of America the Twenty-fifth* (Chillicothe, 1800), 9-20. Hereinafter cited as *House Journal, 1800*.

[36] *Ibid.*, 38, 40.

[37] *Ibid.*, 31; *Journal of the Legislative Council of the Territory of the United States, Northwest of the River Ohio, at their Second Session, Begun and Held at Chillicothe, on the Third Day of November, Anno Domini, 1800* (Chillicothe, 1800), 26. Hereinafter cited as *Council Journal, 1800*.

[38] *House Journal, 1800*, 47; *Council Journal, 1800*, 29-31.

"a kind of qualified negative." "You do not require, indeed," said he, "that, should the objections be deemed of little weight, your acts may become laws without the assent of the Governor," but he accused them of having that purpose in mind. He warned them that he would never yield or compromise his veto right until Congress changed the law or redefined the governor's powers.[39]

The first major test of strength between the Governor's party and the group made up of his enemies, sometimes called the Chillicothe junto, was the election of a delegate to Congress to succeed Harrison. Operating according to preconcerted plan, the Governor's coalition party was able to elect William McMillan of Hamilton County for the unfinished term and Paul Fearing of Marietta for the full term.[40] Unfortunately for the peace of the coalitionists, when it came to moving the capital to Cincinnati, Marietta was not willing to agree; until the new division had actually been made, it seemed desirable that no permanent seat of government be chosen. The second significant geographic partisan contest hinged on where the next session of the legislature should be held. A bill passed the council on December 3 providing for the alternation of all future sessions of the territorial legislature between Cincinnati and Marietta, but the house amended it to include Chillicothe. In a bold move, the Federalists offered an amendment providing that the next session and all subsequent sessions "during the continuance of this temporary government" should be held at Cincinnati. The amendment was defeated, however, by a vote of 4 to 14. A motion to rotate the sessions between Marietta and Cincinnati lost 8 to 10. Finally, the house voted to repudiate the whole act by striking out the enacting clause. Since the session was prorogued on December 9, according to St. Clair's earlier announcement, no decision was reached, and the next session met at Chillicothe as Congress had stipulated in the Division Act.

The prorogation of December 9 came about in pursuance of an announcement made by Governor St. Clair on December 2, an announcement which he had threatened to make for some time. He contended that since his commission lapsed on the ninth, legislative action must be suspended; this was one instance in which the Secretary of the Territory could not act in his stead as he had so often done in the past. This was an adroit move on the part of the Governor. Harrison, who had been Secretary of the Territory before he was named the delegate to Congress, had been succeeded by Charles Willing Byrd, a strong Republican and a political enemy of St. Clair; had Byrd

[39] *House Journal, 1800,* 61-67.
[40] Downes, *Frontier Ohio,* 196-98.

been permitted to assume the Governor's duties, as had Sargent and Harrison, the legislature would doubtless have passed a large amount of democratic legislation. Byrd had wrongly diagnosed St. Clair's maneuver, for as early as November 26, he wrote Nathaniel Massie that the threatened prorogation was merely for the purpose of keeping the legislators from petitioning against St. Clair's reappointment. When it occurred, Byrd had no power to oppose it effectively; he was not even in Chillicothe. If the Republicans had definitely planned to circumvent the Governor, he had instead circumvented them. St. Clair's biographer, William Henry Smith, calls it a *"coup d'état* which completely surprised and discomfited the intriguants."[41]

An attempt was made during the final days of the session to authorize a constitutional convention. The effort failed, but on the very last day the Republicans jammed through a resolution by a vote of 10 to 7 that since the federal census which had just been authorized would undoubtedly show that the Territory had the number (60,000), or nearly the number, requisite for admission to the Union under the Ordinance of 1787, the people east of the Miami should instruct their delegates to the next assembly to favor all measures leading to statehood.[42]

The dismissal of the assembly, a good illustration of the power of the Governor to do pretty much as he pleased in his conduct of affairs, still further aroused those Republicans who desired a state government. The Adams-Jefferson conflict in national affairs was being enacted on a smaller scale in the Ohio territory, political power being the chief stake in each case. The Republican party in the eastern division wished to achieve statehood for a variety of reasons. The desire for self-government was probably the strongest motive behind the movement. At the same time, moreover, if this region, then dominated by the Republicans, were to achieve statehood, it would help Jefferson in his struggle against the Adams forces, and in return it would bring to Republicans in the Territory not only offices in the new state government but also political appointments in the national government. The régime in power of course labored to maintain itself. St. Clair struggled as hard locally as Adams did nationally, and Federalists Burnet and Fearing went down to defeat with as little grace as did Griswold and Morris. The Federalists' excuse that Ohio was not yet ready for statehood had some validity, but it was obviously employed for political reasons. The Federalists used their opposition to statehood

---

[41] Smith, *St. Clair*, I, 222. Worthington, Henry Massie, and Thomas Gibson went bond of $20,000 for Byrd when he became secretary. See bond dated January 19, 1801, in the Pengelly Papers, OHS.
[42] *House Journal, 1800*, 105, 124-30.

as a maneuver for control once statehood was achieved. The high-handed independence of St. Clair aggravated a situation in which diplomacy and tact would have won him a longer tenure of office. If he had been more politic, the governorship of the new state might well have been his reward.

Compromise was foreign to the Federalists, who demanded a full victory or nothing. Their machinations when they held up the election of Jefferson in the House of Representatives until February 17, 1801, threatened the very republicanism of the American system; thus Worthington wrote that there was "much alarm in the minds of the citizens of the United States on acc't of the obstinacy of Federal party in opposing the app't of Mr. Jefferson as president contrary to the demonstrated wish of the people."[43] His choice brought an end to a critical situation, and Worthington noted that "this day heard of the election of Mr. Jefferson . . . an event truly happy at the present crisis as the united states are but a step from anarchy should no president have been appointed."[44] Old General Darke put it succinctly in a letter to Worthington, February 27:

> We have little news . . . old dust and Ashes is determined to do all the harm he can before he quits the chair, he has got a number of fedral Judges apointed. 21 was perposed how many there are apointed I cannot tel, as I have not got the last papers, but I expect they will make with their marshalls, clerks an addition of about forty or fifty thousand dollars a year, and are totaly useless. I am informed they are every one tories as has been a constant rule with the late executive, however he will fall in five days never to rise again, let him go to Braintree clothed with infamy to repent of his many crimes in wasting the public money to serve his son and other favorites.[45]

Ohio Federalists were no less blind. They could not read the signs of the times. They put up a good fight, nevertheless, and their defeat was due more to the coöperation of men like Worthington, Tiffin, and Harrison with a national Republican administration than to an inability to match stratagem with stratagem. The aid of Congress was the decisive factor in the victory at Chillicothe.

Petitions for and against St. Clair's reappointment had meanwhile been circulated in the Territory. Stormy feeling rose to such a pitch that in some places the clergy warned their congregations from the pulpit not to sign petitions in the Governor's favor.[46]

On December 22, President Adams laid before the Senate all the papers relating to the Governor, together with his nomination of St.

---

[43] Worthington's diary, February 28, 1801.
[44] *Ibid.*, March 4, 1801.
[45] Letter in WM.
[46] John Gano to St. Clair, November 15, 1800, in Smith, *St. Clair*, II, 524.

Clair. There was little rivalry for the governorship, although Uriah Tracy, Congressman from Connecticut, was willing to run against St. Clair if opportunity offered.[47] Senator Stevens Thomson Mason of Virginia wrote Worthington that some voted for St. Clair only in preference to a rival candidate "more obnoxious . . . such as Tracy," which "would only be exchanging an old and feeble tyrant for one more active and wicked."[48] By January 29, no action had been taken on St. Clair's nomination; the committee to which all petitions and the nomination had been referred had not yet reported. Largely as a result of the good work of Senator John Brown of Kentucky, the Senate committee on February 3 reported favorably on the President's nomination, and St. Clair was approved for a three-year term, though not without opposition. John Marshall, still acting as Secretary of State though appointed Chief Justice some days before, sent him his commission on February 10.[49]

The reappointment of St. Clair was a heavy blow to the Territory's Republicans: "Exceedingly grating to those who have taken an active part agt him," jubilantly wrote Detroit's Sol Sibley to Fearing. He reported that the work of Federalist William McMillan, the Territory's new delegate, was able and effective, supported as it was by a small flood of petitions from loyal Cincinnatians.[50] Kentucky's Senator Brown sought to mollify the Republicans of the Territory by writing Worthington, February 20, 1801, that Adams' nomination had in all justice to be confirmed: "Under all circumstances we could not well do otherwise. The applications from the Territory in his favour were numerous & very respectable, nor could a really better man be found."[51] Virginia's Senator Mason expressed a contrary view when he wrote Worthington, February 5, 1801, that the petitions showed "that he [St. Clair] was obnoxious to a great part of the people and that he ought not to have been appointed."[52] Worthington expressed his opinion of the Governor's reëlection in a letter to Senator Abraham Baldwin, dated March 6: "The reappointment of Governor St. Clair is truly disagreeable to us here but the happy termination of the presidential election in a great measure makes us reconcile ourselves to our fortune. How extremely shameful the federal party have finally made their retreat after sporting

[47] Senator John Brown of Kentucky to St. Clair, December 24, 1800, *ibid.*, 526.
[48] Mason to Worthington, February 5, 1801, *ibid.*, 531.
[49] Smith, *St. Clair*, II, 528, 529, 530.
[50] Downes, *Frontier Ohio*, 194; Sibley to Fearing, April 21, 1801, in the Fearing Papers.
[51] Letter in WMOSL.
[52] Letter in Smith, *St. Clair*, II, 531.

with the feelings of the people of the United States in the most cruel manner which in my opinion will not soon be forgotten."[53]

By mid-1801, the Republicans in the Northwest Territory had won but half a victory; Jefferson was President, but St. Clair was still in the saddle. Statehood for the Territory seemed at least three years away. In January, St. Clair's supporters in Marietta had come out strongly against it at a mass meeting in which their favorite scheme for securing a seat of government was used to propagandize the Washington County voters against immediate statehood. They maintained that with a division at the Scioto, the people of Washington County could have both the seat of government and also statehood as soon as the population in the smaller division of which they would then be a part was capable of supporting it. St. Clair wrote his Marietta partisans that such a dividing law was already in preparation, the dividing lines being at the Scioto and the falls of the Ohio (Louisville), and that if Congress could be induced to assent to the change, then both Marietta and Cincinnati would be favorably located when the proposed territorial lines should become the permanent state lines.[54]

During the summer, a newspaper war was waged spasmodically in the Territory over the statehood issue. A steady gain in the popularity of the movement was discernible as time passed. Secretary Byrd took a census of the Territory east of the Great Miami and found the population to be 45,365, but he anticipated that by the time statehood could be achieved, it would have risen to the requisite 60,000.[55]

Worthington took counsel with his friends in both parties. Senator James Ross wrote him, April 1, 1801, to proceed slowly and let things work themselves out, "to lessen instead of widening the unfortunate misunderstanding" with St. Clair, and "*to prepare* the country for statehood," on the attainment of which the Governor, if it was desirable, could be removed from office. He asked whether order could be maintained, holding that the greatest responsibility in any state was the protection of property, the "faithful administration of Justice," and the ability to "afford to your citizens the real enjoyment of their rights. All good men should zealously cooperate in promoting the adoption of such a constitution & placing such men in the administration of it as will maintain . . . the great Charter which is to hold you together. A great deal depends upon beginning well & I own that I entertain much fear of that beginning."[56] Federalist Kimberly of Steubenville,

---

[53] Letter in Worthington's letter book, LC.
[54] St. Clair to Dudley Woodbridge, January 7, 1801, Illinois State Historical Society.
[55] *Scioto Gazette,* June 25, 1801.
[56] Letter in WMOSL.

although "attached to St. Clair," wrote Worthington, March 10, 1801, that he favored clipping the Governor's wings by judicial process and was willing to finance the case, but he urged "unanimity in our terr'y" at any cost.[57]

The Governor and his party decided that their best means of success was to continue the agitation for a new division of the Territory so that the eastern section would be cut down to the point where it would not have the population required for statehood. Harrison and Worthington had defeated this project in 1800, but Harrison, at least, was now out of the way, and the proposed division might yet succeed. To the Cincinnati Federalists St. Clair could offer the capital now located at Chillicothe. To Marietta he could still offer the seat of government for the proposed eastern division. To his Federalist friends in Washington he could say that this territory should not contribute representatives to augment the strength of Jefferson's revolutionists. He still controlled the patronage. Success was yet possible.

6

The first session of the Second General Assembly opened at Chillicothe, November 25, 1801; for the first time the Assembly met in the new courthouse at the corner of Paint and Main streets. This building, probably the first stone public edifice erected in the Territory, was constructed in 1801 by William Guthrie and William Rutledge under the supervision of Worthington and the three county commissioners. Worthington had chosen the site of the two-story structure and marked off its foundation fifty-nine feet back from each of the two streets, scoured the community to purchase furnishings for it, and secured glass for its windows from the firm of Nicholson and Gallatin at Geneva, Pennsylvania. The glass was shipped by water, but instead of being landed at Alexandria, it was put ashore at Manchester, where Worthington had Nathaniel Massie reship it to Chillicothe. The edifice was surmounted by a cupola, over which was placed a gilt eagle standing on a ball. Fireplaces on the north and south sides of each of the two rooms which formed the interior of the courthouse gave insufficient heat.[58]

With the meeting of the delegates came a renewal of the conflict

---

[57] Letter in WMOSL.
[58] Worthington's diary, February 27, 1801; Howe, *Historical Collections*, II, 496; Massie to Worthington, June 8, in WM; Worthington to Massie, June 13, in Massie, *Massie*, 173; Worthington to I. W. Nicholson, August 7, in Worthington's letter book, LC. James B. Finley, in *Sketches of Western Methodism: Biographical, Historical and Miscellaneous* (Cincinnati, 1854), 273, gives a good description of the interior of the courthouse.

with St. Clair. His address of November 26 warned the legislators against sending him bills at the very end of the session, as they had done the previous year, if they expected him to sign them. He refused to be considered a mere signer of bills: "Be pleased, gentlemen, to recollect that the Governor is a branch of the legislature."[59]

A house committee, headed by Nathaniel Massie, drew up an answer which was short and inoffensive, and seemed to indicate coöperation and unanimity. Its chief significance was not what it said, however, but rather what it failed to say. It did not congratulate the Governor on his reappointment, and in general it lacked the approbative quality which characterized the answer of the Council.[60]

It was apparent to everyone that the Governor's party was well organized and that a real contest was at hand. Worthington outlined the situation for his friend Senator Baldwin of Georgia in a letter dated November 30:

> Several very important questions (as they respect the Terry'y) remain to be discussed & decided—The first in consequence is wheather we shall with the consent of congress become & exercise the priviledges of an independent state or remain under the present arbitrary government, better suited for an English or Spanish colony than for citizens of the United States—In opposition to this question or measure we have all who hold offices (with few exceptions) under our executive, our Governor himself & all good federalists who fear that our state will give three republican votes at the next election for president—send you two republican senators & a Republican representative in congress. I am well convinced that a great body of the people are anxious for a change . . . & feel almost certain that we now have the number of souls (60,000) which will entitle us to a change when we please, but I do hope & trust that congress will not hesitate if we should want a few of the number necessary to receive us into the Union—I am not yet entirely certain that a majority of our Legislature will vote for a state government, but have good reason to believe they will—should they not you will hear from the minority and receive petitions on the subject from every quarter of the Territory. Our Govr. keeps his favorite object still in view, that is another division of the N W Territory by the Scioto to the forks thereof & hence north to the Territorial line as pointed out by his letter laid before congress by Mr. Harrison, this finally to effect a Division of the Eastern State in the Terr'y & thereby prevent for a long time the admission of any state on this side of the Ohio into the Union. We are told by the Gov's friends that an effort will be made in congress at this ensuing session to effect this measure—It will be unnecessary to trouble you with reasons against the measure, they will no doubt appear to you in the clearest point of view.[61]

[59] *Journal of the House of Representatives of the Territory of the United States, North-west of the Ohio, at the First Session of the Second General Assembly, A.D. 1801 . . .* (Chillicothe, 1801), 12-16. Hereinafter cited as *House Journal, 1801.*
[60] *Ibid.*, 29; *Journal of the Legislative Council of the Territory of the United States, North-west of the Ohio, at Their Third Session, Begun and Held at Chillicothe, on Monday the Twenty-third Day of November, 1801* (Chillicothe, 1801), 12. Hereinafter cited as *Council Journal, 1801.*
[61] Letter in Worthington's letter book, LC. See also Worthington's excellent letter of November 10 to William Duane in which he outlines charges against St. Clair, in Worthington's letter book, LC, 91, and Worthington to Secretary of Treasury Gallatin, October 29, 1801, in *Territorial Papers*, III, 183.

The plan of the St. Clair party was made manifest when the council passed a bill, December 3, entitled "An Act declaring the assent of the Territory, northwest of the river Ohio, to an alteration of the ordinance for the government thereof." It proposed to redivide the whole territory by one line north from the mouth of the Scioto and another from the falls of the Ohio to the mouth of the "Chickagua" River.[62] No other measure could have done so much to arouse the antagonism of the Governor's enemies. The success of the scheme would destroy at one blow their plans for statehood, the dream that Chillicothe might be the capital, and any hope that a new state might soon add her strength to the rising tide of Jeffersonian Republicanism. Instead, the Governor and his coalition party from Cincinnati and Marietta would continue to enjoy the patronage until these two towns became the seats of government for states conceived and dedicated to principles scarcely compatible with frontier democracy. In a letter to Baldwin of Georgia, Worthington characterized the bill as "the most extraordinary measure ever attempted by a set of men under similar circumstances."[63]

When and by whom this legislative act was inspired, the records do not reveal. St. Clair disclaimed its authorship.[64] Jacob Burnet seems to have been responsible for it; William Henry Smith, St. Clair's biographer, names him as its creator; we know he introduced it and was its chief exponent. He asked leave to present it to the council on December 3; it was given its first, second, and third readings on that date, and was passed unanimously with only one amendment and sent to the house the same day.[65] The council had expedited business in this instance with the speed and facility that suggested a preconceived plan. While the bill was under consideration in the house, the members were petitioned time and again to exert their influence in favor of a state government, but most of them took no heed, although a motion to receive no more such petitions was rejected. It is strange that a majority in the house persisted in its attempt to thwart the will of the mass of the people in the Territory, but the Federalist party was never opportunistic, and Republicans with local interests at Cincinnati and Marietta combined with them to hold a majority.

On December 18, the bill came to a vote in the house and was passed 12 to 8. Massie immediately jumped to his feet and gave notice

[62] Chase, *Statutes*, I, 341.
[63] Letter, November 30, 1801, in Worthington's letter book, LC.
[64] St. Clair to James Ross, January 15, 1802, in Smith, *St. Clair*, II, 555; but see his letter of December 25 to Paul Fearing, *ibid.*, 549.
[65] *Council Journal, 1801*, 16-18, 36. William Henry Smith, "A Familiar Talk About Monarchists and Jacobins," *Ohio State Archaeological and Historical Quarterly*, II, (1888), 195, 199.

that the minority would ask leave to protest this action. On the twenty-third, he received permission by a 10 to 9 vote to present his protest. It was in the form of a petition which declared the act a violation of the people's constitutional rights granted by the Ordinance of 1787. The petition asserted that the measure was inexpedient in its nature, contrary to the letter and spirit of the territorial constitution, which had by Article V established the line north from the mouth of the Great Miami, and exceedingly undesirable because it would abort statehood in the eastern division without making it possible in any of the other divisions.[66]

This petition was signed by Darlington, Massie, Dunlavy, Morrow, Langham, Worthington, and Edward Tiffin, speaker of the house. A motion was then made to include a certified copy of the protest with the instructions of the territorial delegate, Paul Fearing, but this proposal lost 8 to 11. Thus unwisely the Federalists still further incensed the advocates of statehood. Petitions denouncing the Division Act were circulated by the insurgents in Ross and Adams counties, and at a general meeting at Chillicothe Worthington and Michael Baldwin were appointed to lay them before Congress.

A final attempt was made on January 5 to oppose the projected division by introducing a resolution recommending to Congress that in the event the division was not approved, Congress should authorize statehood for the Territory as at present constituted. This proposal was defeated in the committee of the whole, and the militant minority had to leave the success of their cause to their envoys, Worthington and Baldwin, who had set out for Washington on December 27.[67]

7

Meanwhile, other clashes had occurred in the assembly. The second chief contest with St. Clair was over the power to establish counties. On December 9, Worthington had presented a resolution "for making provision by law for the counties laid off by the Governor since the last session." On December 10, the resolution was given its first and second readings and amended in the committee of the whole. As adopted, it raised the question of the legality of courts established in the new counties and stated that the legislative council and house of representatives firmly believed that the power to create such counties was vested

[66] House Journal, 1801, 68, 80.
[67] Ibid., 43, 88, 93, 114. See St. Clair's letter to Woodbridge, December 24, 1801, in Smith, St. Clair, II, 543, and Samuel Finley to Worthington and Baldwin, n.d., ibid., 505.

jointly in the governor and the legislative bodies. The resolution concluded as follows:

> Resolved, By the Legislative Council and House of Representatives, that it will be expedient to provide by law, for such counties as have been laid out, as aforesaid, by the Governor, and to use the most prompt and proper measures to obtain from the proper authority, an explanation of that part of the ordinance aforesaid.

The original draft seems to have contained a second resolution which was intended to forbid the erection of further counties by the governor. This second resolution had been stricken out in the committee of the whole, and an attempt just before passage to reinsert it failed 5 to 15, only Worthington, Darlington, Massie, Milligan, and White voting for it. Thus another effort to curb the governor's power was defeated.[68]

8

The third major contest of the session was over the seat of government. Jacob White of Hamilton County introduced a bill on December 17 for its removal from Chillicothe to Cincinnati. Worthington and six others voted against permitting him to present the bill, but thirteen favored it. The next day a motion to reject the bill failed, 8 to 12.

On December 19, the opponents of the Cincinnati group attempted to amend the bill by inserting "Marietta" for "Cincinnati," but the vote was again 8 to 12. The insertion of "Franklinton" met a similar fate by a vote of 8 to 12. In desperation, one of the minority substituted "Steubenville," but the proposal was defeated 5 to 15. When some wag offered "Detroit" as a last resort, the Detroit delegate, Jonathan Schieffelin, was the only yea. Thus the contest resolved itself into an out-and-out fight between the Cincinnati-Marietta group and the Chillicothe bloc. This series of events furnishes the key to the motivating factor in the whole controversy in the Territory over statehood. Local rivalry had submerged the higher issue.

Once again, on Monday the twenty-first, when the engrossed bill came before the house for passage, a final attempt was made to amend it by inserting "Lancaster" for "Cincinnati"; but the best the opposition could do was to retain their minority of eight, while the majority held their twelve. This was the final effort, and on the question, Shall the said bill pass? the same division of twelve to eight held. The bill

---

[68] House Journal, 1801, 45-46. Worthington had predicted an open rupture with the Governor over this issue in a letter to Joseph Nourse, November 18, 1801, in Worthington's letter book, LC.

was sent to the council and approved the same day. Governor St. Clair signed it on January 1.[69] Thus the Hamilton County–Washington County coalition was successful all along the line. St. Clair wrote as follows to Dudley Woodbridge of Marietta, December 21: "It is perfectly understood that tho' the next session is to be held in that place [Cincinnati] the succeeding session is to be at Marietta, and for the success of that measure, a sufficient number of members are pledged."[70] This was specious reasoning at best, for if the Division Act which he had just signed had been assented to by Congress, the seat of government would not have been moved from Cincinnati to Marietta, but rather each would have been the capital city of its respective division.

The decision of territorial Republicans to send Worthington and Michael Baldwin to Washington to oppose ratification was a wise move. Moreover, couriers were sent to all portions of the state to hold meetings and secure petitions protesting the action of the legislature and asking for statehood rather than the continuation of the "monarchic system" and the "craftiness and intrigue of the Aristocratic party." William Ludlow reported that even in Hamilton County the great majority of the people were against the division since it would mean "six or seven years additional bondage" when our "necks are already considerably galled in sustaining the yoke." He said that the division party was also circulating petitions in Hamilton County and had secured five hundred signatures; the one petition he had seen bore forty-eight names, twenty-four of which were signed with a cross, and he offered the opinion that "so many unlettered characters implies that children must have subscribed to it."[71]

9

Before Worthington and Michael Baldwin left for Washington, the Republicans, enraged by their opponents' attempt to redivide the Territory and move the seat of government to Cincinnati, rioted in Chillicothe. Some of the younger townsfolk, incited by Baldwin, their own representative in the house and a bibulous firebrand of the community, held an indignation meeting on Friday, the twenty-third, and proposed to raid the Governor's boarding house and bring him out to see himself burned in effigy. Baldwin's electioneering gang, which he affectionately called his "bloodhounds," was a band of cursing, quarreling, fighting rowdies who looked to him as their leader in all contests, political or

[69] *House Journal, 1801,* 62, 65, 67, 71-73, 77; *Council Journal, 1801,* 33, 44.
[70] Letter, Illinois State Historical Society.
[71] Ludlow to Tiffin, December 22, 1801, in WMOSL.

otherwise. They were obnoxious to the law-abiding element of Chillicothe but very effective in tavern and grogshop circles; boisterous and rollicking, they had no compunction at breaking their leader, or a friend, out of jail, and they were the darlings of the rabble.[72] To throw the fear of God into the old Governor or any of the "Feds" at the suggestion of their leader was completely to their liking. Fortunately, Worthington caught Baldwin at the head of his gang, took him aside, and talked him out of the proposed demonstration. St. Clair some days later admitted that violence was that evening aborted by "the splendid exertion of Mr. Worthington," who was obliged to threaten to shoot Baldwin if he persisted in his purpose.[73]

Nothing serious occurred until the next night, Christmas Eve, when William Rufus Putnam's toast at supper to his fellow Federalists at the Gregg House, "May the Scioto lave the borders of two great and flourishing states," rearoused the angry passions of the indignant Republicans, who decided to carry out their designs of the previous evening. Several riotous groups of Baldwin's boys were assembled, and, fortified with a few drinks, they stomped down the street to the Governor's tavern. Michael Baldwin and others forced their way into the Gregg House, struck at Schieffelin, the delegate from Wayne County, and then collared him; whereupon the latter drew his dirk and would have used it, had he not been forcibly restrained. Breaking loose, he grabbed a pair of pistols off the mantel and ordered the rioters from the house.[74] Insults flew thick and fast between the two groups. St. Clair, who had been in his room writing, hurried down and sent in haste for the sheriff and the justice of the peace. He then helped eject the rioters from the tavern and warned them of the serious consequences of their actions.

To Samuel Finley, the justice of the peace who had been summoned, we are indebted for the best account of what happened after the initial clash. (It should be noted, incidentally, that the sheriff was out of town.) Finley says that on Saturday night the Governor ordered his "immediate attendance at his quarters and assistance in quelling a riot." He "hastened to the place expecting to have met with nothing but uproar and confusion," but found St. Clair trying to dissuade Dr. Samuel McAdow from resenting the insult of Representative Schieffelin, who had cast reflections on him and his immediate ancestors. The argu-

[72] Williams Brothers, *Ross and Highland Counties*, 73; "Memoir of the Hon. Thos. Scott by Himself," dated July 19, 1852, RCHS.
[73] St. Clair to James Ross, January 15, 1802, in Smith, *St. Clair*, II, 556.
[74] Julia Perkins Cutler, *Life and Times of Ephraim Cutler, Prepared from His Journals and Correspondence* (Cincinnati, 1870), 55; Burnet, *Notes*, 333.

ment which took place between St. Clair, McAdow, and Schieffelin had drawn a little crowd, but according to Finley, "there was not a weapon to be seen nor did I hear an insulting or angry word by anyone." A representative who lived in the same house with the Governor said he had heard rumors of an intended riot but that nothing much had developed. Finley relates that he "went up to the people and requested them to retire which they instantly did. Dr. McAdow, though considerably irritated . . . left the place and walked with me to Mr. [Joseph] Tiffin's tavern."[75]

Unfortunately, Finley does not disclose what passed between them on their walk or after they arrived at Tiffin's tavern. Nor did the *Scioto Gazette,* a very good paper for its day, reveal any details or print anything but the guarded depositions which were taken some days later. It would appear that the editor, Nathaniel Willis, although a friend of Worthington's from Berkeley County, Virginia, and a sympathizer with the Republicans, took a strictly neutral position on the subject of the fracas.

St. Clair, extremely angry at the demonstration, furnished Justice Finley with the names of Baldwin, Stephen Cissna, and Reuben Abrams as the ringleaders of the plot, and of certain others who had seen the affair and could testify as to just what had happened. He insisted that they be put under bond and bound over to the next session of court.

On Monday, December 26, Finley examined the accused but dismissed them when they swore they had neither meditated nor done anything of a riotous nature. Yet a real demonstration undoubtedly had been in the making, and Worthington had had to exert himself forcefully to avert it. He had expressed his fears on Friday evening to Jeremiah McLene, the Ross County sheriff, who pledged the strongest action to prevent a riot; but it will be noted that McLene and Worthington were both out of town Saturday night when the attack occurred. Baldwin was the logical leader; according to the deposition of William Rutledge, Worthington was keeping close watch both Friday and Saturday nights and had asked him to use his influence to prevent any disturbance.

Sheriff McLene testified that on Friday night he heard Worthington make Baldwin swear he would not again molest the gentlemen at the Gregg House; that Worthington said "he would not suffer any such thing to take place and would prevent it at the risque of his life, and would go and fetch his weapon, and if said Baldwin went there, he would kill him the first person." Baldwin told him not to make any

---

[75] Depositions in the *Scioto Gazette,* January 2, 1802.

threats for fear he might need his weapon, but Worthington argued with him until Baldwin swore "he would engage in no such business." Unquestionably there was much bad feeling between the hotheads of the two political factions, and Worthington, knowing who the leaders were, had done his best to suppress it. As head of the Chillicothe party he could clearly see that the advocates of statehood and democracy dared not discredit themselves in the eyes of the Territory and the nation by any disgraceful action. No man cared less for St. Clair than Worthington, but none saw more clearly that party spirit must not manifest itself through a mob or permit the lowest methods of retaliation to triumph. There was a better way.

St. Clair was so incensed at Finley when he found nothing had been done to punish the leaders that he denounced him for malfeasance and nonfeasance in office. Five letters[76] passed between them on Monday, the twenty-sixth, and the dispute ended by Finley's tendering his resignation. St. Clair laid the matter before the legislature on the twenty-ninth, submitted to them the correspondence with Finley, and asked an investigation of this attempt "to maltreat certain members of the legislature." The next day the house voted an investigation and elected Darlington, Kimberly, Paine, Putnam, and Ludlow to the committee; the council appointed David Vance. There is no evidence that this committee took any action. It reported on January 18 that a few intoxicated citizens had caused the furore[77] and that there was no cause for alarm.

10

The assembly was dismissed on January 23, 1802, after a session which had produced a great deal of good legislation. St. Clair vetoed only one act, which sought to transfer the right to issue marriage licenses from the governor to the prothonotary of the court of common pleas.[78] Although he was poor and needed the fees, it would have been the part of wisdom to avert continued criticism by sacrificing them. Later, Worthington made the Governor's fee-taking in defiance of the legislature one of the major charges against him in his memorandum of February 20 to President Jefferson, and Secretary of State Madison warned St. Clair on June 23 to discontinue the practice.[79]

The Governor's announcement that the next session of the legislature

[76] The letters were printed in the *Scioto Gazette,* January 2, 1802.
[77] *House Journal, 1801,* 102; *Council Journal, 1801,* 41.
[78] *House Journal, 1801,* 176-78.
[79] *Territorial Papers,* III, 213, 231. See St. Clair's letter of defense to Jefferson in Randall and Ryan, *History of Ohio,* III, 96-98.

would meet at Cincinnati was a mistaken prophecy; the Republicans of the Territory and in Congress were to see to that. Outvoted as they were in the assembly by a combination of Federalists, St. Clairites, and zealous citizens of Marietta and Cincinnati, they had time and the forces of change on their side. They knew that by and large the people were with them, and that the national sentiment which had swept Jefferson and Burr into power must soon rob St. Clair and his satellites of political power in the Northwest Territory. Patience, energy, and tact were the immediate virtues needed. Riots and violence had to be avoided; and the confidence, respect, and favor of the people must be marshaled in support of the Republican leaders. In the next chapter we shall see how Worthington's forbearance bore fruit.

State-Maker

On December 27, 1801, Worthington and a Negro servant set out on horseback for Washington. Their route was by way of Lancaster, Zanesville, Wheeling, Cumberland, Shepherdstown, and Fredericktown—a leisurely journey of sixteen winter days which they completed on January 11. Worthington secured board and room for himself and his servant "at 12½ and 5 dollars" a week respectively at Mrs. Wilson's, near the Capitol.

The petitions against the territorial Division Act which Worthington's supporters at home had promised to send him flowed in at an astounding rate. Edward Tiffin mailed him a thousand names from Ross County on January 18 and promised as many more from Hamilton County in a few days. The people of the Territory, he wrote, would not only be pleased with the rejection of the act but would welcome statehood.[1] Massie mailed him three petitions on January 7, and William Creighton reported a thousand names from Hamilton, and seven hundred from Adams, counties on January 30, with many more soon to come. Creighton specified that those he was mailing were not only against the Division Act but also in favor of statehood: "You and Baldwin," he wrote, "can say that statehood is one of the chief objects of the petitions."[2] Sam Finley informed him from Chillicothe that he had one thousand signers in Ross and Adams counties of a petition specifically pleading for admission to the Union.[3] James Caldwell and David Vance wrote from St. Clairsville in Belmont County that a mass meeting had almost unanimously approved the statehood project.[4] Similar reports were received from Clermont and Jefferson counties during the ensuing month.[5]

Meanwhile, Worthington and Baldwin had been busy lining up their friends in Congress. William Branch Giles, a rabid Virginia Jeffersonian

---

[1] Tiffin to Worthington, January 18, 1802, in WMOSL.
[2] Creighton to Worthington, January 30, 1802, in WMOSL.
[3] Finley to Worthington, February 22, 1802, in WMOSL.
[4] Caldwell to Worthington, March 8, 1802, in the Rice Collection; Vance to Worthington, March 20, 1802, in WM.
[5] *Scioto Gazette*, March 13 and 20, 1802; J. Pritchard to Worthington, March 23, 1802, in the Meigs Papers, OSL; John Smith to Worthington, March 26, 1802, in the Rice Collection.

and an old friend of Worthington's, was to manage their affairs in the House. As William Gilmore, biographer of Edward Tiffin, so neatly put it, Worthington had "secured the very active and zealous support of . . . [this] able, influential and exceedingly energetic member of Congress. . . . And no doubt—indeed it is certain—the President quietly and privately assumed the guidance of the state project through [him]; . . . for, would it not most probably strengthen his party, and secure to himself three more electoral votes?"[6] In any event, Worthington found everything promising for the defeat of the territorial law and the admission of the Ohio territory into the Union, with its west boundary at the Great Miami. Three days after his arrival, he could write Massie, "So far as I can determine have reason to believe we shall obtain our utmost wishes."[7]

In the Senate, Michael Baldwin's brother Abraham was the chief representative of the Republicans, but he had able supporters, among whom were Stevens Thomson Mason of Virginia and John Breckinridge and John Brown of Kentucky, all old friends of Worthington's and aware of the situation in the Territory through correspondence with him. Worthington had written Brown and Baldwin in November that a great many members of the territorial legislature were in favor of immediate statehood if Congress would only make admission possible; he had sent Baldwin a copy of the dividing law as concrete evidence of the scheme hatched by the Federalist opposition to delay statehood for a long time.[8] Even earlier (November 10), looking toward the work of the legislature, which was to assemble late that month, he had written William Duane, editor of the Philadelphia *Aurora*, the official Republican organ, complimenting him on his criticism of the arbitrary government in the Northwest Territory in his issue of October 26, and seeking his aid in supporting statehood for it. He recounted St. Clair's tyranny, especially his veto of eleven laws at the last session of the legislature in opposition to the will of the people. Worthington argued that if Congress were fully informed of the situation, its members would not withhold their consent provided the impending legislature petitioned for statehood. He urged Duane to make his paper the Territory's vehicle for the enlightenment and leadership of Congress, and promised him that the Chillicothe Republicans, including himself, would keep him furnished with information for that purpose. Just before Worth-

---

[6] Gilmore, *Tiffin*, 40-41. See Worthington's diary, January 17.
[7] Massie, *Massie*, 179.
[8] Worthington to Brown, November 15, and Worthington to Baldwin, November 30, 1801, in Worthington's letter book, LC.

ington arrived in Washington, Duane came out with a well-timed blast and followed it with another, eight weeks later.[9]

Worthington and Baldwin found Congress exceedingly busy debating the repeal of the Judiciary Act of 1801 and the Adams excise taxes, and not inclined to attend to minor affairs until major issues had been disposed of. Moreover, their business could not be undertaken until Paul Fearing introduced the dividing law to Congress for action. Hence their activities were limited to personal contacts with the men who must act for them.

Baldwin wrote Massie on January 19 that he and Worthington had been presented to President Jefferson the previous day by Senator George Logan of Pennsylvania; that the President "was very particular in his inquiry respecting the territory . . . , extremely anxious to know the real state of political parties with us"; and that he had indicated that he was disposed to remove St. Clair.

Baldwin reported that he had conferred with many members of both houses of Congress, and that without exception they had expressed strong disapproval of the dividing law and promised their most cordial support in defeating it and in removing St. Clair from the governorship; he wrote that Gallatin, Madison, Logan, his brother Abraham Baldwin, and many others felt that President Jefferson would "snap him." He assured Massie he need have no fear of any disagreement between himself and Worthington; that they had "so far agreed in every point. . . . Our business goes on to our wish. . . . I will stay on here until our fate is known."[10]

Baldwin actually left Washington on January 29, missing much of the action of the next three months. Fortunately, the many diary entries Worthington made during this period help piece out the narrative which follows.

On January 18, Worthington made the following note in his diary: "Waited on the president in company with Doctor Logan & Mr. Baldwin. . . . He is plain and simple in his manners—opposed to extravagance &c. . . . Informed him of the Situation of the Terr'y." The next day he "attended the debates in the Senate," where the expediency and constitutionality of the repeal of the Judiciary Act were being argued under the roving eye of Vice-President Burr.

On January 20, Paul Fearing presented the division law to the house, pointed out that it incorporated an alteration in the boundaries for states as planned by the "Old Confederation" (1787), and moved that

[9] Worthington to Duane, November 10, 1801, in Worthington's letter book, LC; the *Aurora* (Philadelphia), January 9 and March 2, 1802.
[10] *Annals*, 7th Cong., 1st Sess., 427. Uncatalogued letter, No. 15105, OHS.

it be referred to a select committee for consideration. Senator Giles immediately rose to voice his objections; such a law would place the people of the Territory in a very disagreeable situation by perpetuating in office an unpopular governor and an unpopular territorial legislature. He had in his hands petitions against the law signed by more than a thousand citizens from the Territory. He favored action on it at the earliest possible moment. Thomas Davis of Kentucky, another Worthington ally, moved that the law be ordered printed and referred to the committee of the whole for action the next day.

Worthington watched with satisfaction and used all the influence he could bring to bear during the next few days. On January 21, he talked with Jefferson on political subjects which must have included no little discussion of the situation in the Territory and of the prospects of securing statehood. Four days later, the house still being too concerned with the tax debates to consider the territorial business, he noted in his diary, "dined with Mr. Jefferson with whom easy and friendly mode of entertainment. I was much pleased—no formality more than true politeness dictates—easy of access and communicative to all—plain in his dress and acting the true part of the first citizen of the Republick." The same day he wrote Nathaniel Massie that Congress seemed determined to defeat the division law and favored admitting the Territory to statehood; already victory was in sight.[11] The next morning the House of Representatives in committee of the whole discussed the proposed law and the petitions against it referred to the committee on January 20 and 25 but "rose without a question."[12]

This same day (January 26), President Jefferson received a long letter from William Goforth of Cincinnati which perhaps strengthened his determination to aid Worthington and his group in securing statehood for the eastern Territory. Goforth denounced the rule of St. Clair as a truly English one, in which the governor, "with all the power of a British Nabob," could "convene, prorogue and dissolve our legislature at pleasure," and could make practically all appointments at his will and thus maintain a "government highly tinctured with Aristocracy and monarchy." He pointed out that a census of the Territory east of the Great Miami showed over 42,000 population, even excluding Detroit, despite the fact that the census-takers had missed many persons and that there had been a large increase since the census was taken early in 1801. He implored the President to use his influence in supporting statehood for the people of the Territory and in rescuing them from a delimitation of territory which would

[11] Massie, *Massie*, 187.
[12] *Annals*, 7th Cong., 1st Sess., 462; Worthington's diary, January 26, 1802.

postpone it and leave them under a despotic and unrepublican régime for many years.[13]

There is little likelihood that the receipt of this letter had much bearing on the defeat of the territorial law, but it added another eloquent voice to the clamor against the division of the Territory at the Scioto and in support of immediate statehood. In any event, the next day more petitions opposing the law were received and referred to the committee. When, in the course of the day's business, the law was considered, Fearing moved that it be accepted, but a debate of some length ensued over its constitutionality, in which Fearing and Roger Griswold supported its validity while Giles, Davis, and James A. Bayard opposed it. Giles finally moved that the law not be assented to by Congress; the committee of the whole agreed and framed a resolution to that effect which the House immediately considered and overwhelmingly adopted.[14] Worthington triumphantly noted in his diary, "Jan. 27.—This day the question on the Territorial law was decided after some debate 81 ag't it, 5 only for it."

Worthington was delighted with this victory and with the way the Chillicothe program was progressing.[15] He wrote William Goforth on the twenty-eighth that the division law had been defeated, that a resolution preliminary to an enabling act had been introduced, and that in his opinion a bill proposing it would be introduced and passed. "You know," he wrote, "I have been uniformly a supporter of the measure ever since I had the pleasure of first seeing you, and that our feelings on this subject have been perfectly coincident."[16] That same day (January 28) he had heard Giles introduce a resolution for the appointment of a committee to take the necessary steps pursuant to the introduction of an enabling act for the Territory. The resolution was adopted the next day, and Giles was appointed chairman of the committee. A number of petitions favoring statehood were also received, read, and referred to the committee.[17]

2

John Fowler, Congressman from Kentucky, was so impressed with the defeat of the division law and the appointment of Giles's com-

[13] Goforth to Jefferson, January 5, 1802, in *Territorial Papers*, III, 198-201.
[14] *Annals*, 7th Cong., 1st Sess., 465-66. The dividing law was printed in the *National Intelligencer*, January 27.
[15] Downes, *Frontier Ohio*, 201-16, is an excellent account of the Chillicothe program and how it developed.
[16] *American Pioneer*, I (1842), 439. The letter as printed is misdated 1801.
[17] *Annals*, 7th Cong., 1st Sess., 469-71.

mittee that he wrote Massie on January 29 that Worthington had worked a revolution in the government of the Territory with courage as bold as that of Bonaparte in crossing the Alps. He regarded the appointment of a committee to report an enabling act as a victory for Worthington and the Chillicothe party since he believed such an act would be unanimously adopted. He anticipated, moreover, that St. Clair would soon get his "marching orders" if plenty of petitions continued to pour in: "You have not furnished your delegation with materials so promptly as they have executed their mission. . . . It behooves you to be active," he enjoined.[18]

What Worthington perhaps did not appreciate, nor Fowler either, was that in Ohio most of the proponents of the division law had been preparing as early as late December for just such an eventuality as an enabling act, and were ready, if necessary, to swing over to support statehood not only for a state east of the Scioto but for one to the west of it as well; all they asked was that the divisions be left as newly established by the territorial legislature's dividing act, preferably as territories but at worst as states. Statehood was not a matter to be undertaken except as a last resort; but when they learned with what speed Worthington and Baldwin were working, a majority of them changed their tack. At the urging of the local Cincinnati politicians and unaware that the division law had already been rejected, Burnet and McMillan wrote Fearing in early February to approve the erection of two states if the division at the Scioto could only be maintained. If statehood was what the members of Congress favored, and if they were convinced that the people of Ohio insisted on being so organized, opponents of such a step would yield in order to salvage the seats of government for Marietta and Cincinnati.[19]

When it was learned that the division law had been defeated, there were many long faces in Cincinnati, especially since the Federalists had raised five hundred dollars to send McMillan to Fearing's aid and he was ready to leave when the unwelcome news arrived. Two meetings were immediately held, and presumably a decision was reached to accept statehood if necessary but to fight for the restoration of the dividing line at the Scioto and hope for the erection of two states instead of one.[20]

In this connection it is interesting to note that George Tod, a

[18] Massie, Massie, 188-89.
[19] Burnet to Fearing, February 4, and McMillan to Fearing, February 12, 1802, in the Fearing Papers.
[20] John Armstrong to Tiffin, February 13, 1802, in the Comly Collection, OHS. See also Tiffin to Worthington, February 1, 1802, in Smith, St. Clair, II, 571-72.

twenty-eight-year-old Federalist lawyer from Trumbull County and a diviner of political portents, had figured out, erroneously in this instance, that the division law would stand but that Congress would undoubtedly also pass an enabling act for the division east of the Scioto. He wrote Samuel Huntington, his choice for first governor of the eastern state, to get busy, since Rufus Putnam had been selected for that office by the Marietta Federalists. He also informed Huntington that Putnam's neighbor, Return J. Meigs, had already departed for Washington in an effort to forestall both of his rivals for the office.[21]

Meantime St. Clair, another interpreter of the signs of the times, realized that the turn of events probably spelled retirement for him, and on March 1 passed through Chillicothe on his way to Washington with Squire John Browne of Cincinnati, armed with depositions in his favor calculated to nullify the effects of the campaign Worthington was waging so successfully against him.[22]

A real celebration was held in Chillicothe on February 9 when word arrived that the division law had been defeated. Baldwin's "bloodhounds" led a shouting parade all over town, with stops for free drinks at each tavern. Sam Finley wrote Worthington on February 12, 1802, that he could not "describe the ecstatic emotion excited in the minds of our inhabitants." He reported that nothing was to be seen

> but smiling countenances—nothing was to be heard but congratulatory salutations. At night the Town was illuminated—The bells would have been rung if we had had them; many a conduit . . . ran with grog. . . . [yet] the festive occasion was conducted with much decorum; and all parties retired to their homes about 10 O Clock.[23]

3

On February 1, 1802, Worthington "waited on the president and delivered to the Sec'y of state charges ag't Gov'r St. Clair." A sample of the type of charge that had been used by the critics of St. Clair has already been presented in Goforth's letter of January 5 to Jefferson. Another excellent example was the letter of January 23 which John Cleves Symmes, undoubtedly at the request of Worthington, had sent to President Jefferson. The President received it on the twenty-fifth, and must have been somewhat influenced by its contents. Symmes indicted St. Clair as "by constitution a despot" and

[21] Tod to Huntington, January 14, 1802, in the Huntington Papers, WRHS.
[22] Tiffin to Worthington, March 1, 1802, in Smith, *St. Clair*, II, 574; *Scioto Gazette,* March 6; Massie to Worthington, January 18, in Massie, *Massie,* 183.
[23] Letter in WMOSL.

"unsufferably arbitrary" from "long imperious habits of commanding."
He alleged that the prosperity of the Territory had always been a
secondary consideration with St. Clair, who had consistently opposed
all measures which did not "concentrate their good effect, in his
family or among his favorites." Symmes asserted that although St.
Clair was of "courtly exterior," his heart was "illiberal beyond a
sample," he was "destitute of gratitude," wise in his own conceit, a
wanton deceiver of the people, and a perpetrator of "pious frauds,"
so that "many detesting him, have fled the territory." In extravagant
terms he concluded,

> Do these imputations need proof?—let fetters, prisons, flames, human-
> bones and tears bear testimony; while neglected french-rights, imbecility of
> Magistrates of his appointment, executive deception, unequal tenures in office,
> his Usurped prerogatives, and ill placed patronage, fill the North western
> territory with murmurs, deep—awful—dangerous; while his distracted govern-
> ment totters to its foundation.[24]

Thus when Worthington waited on the President on February 1,
the way had been prepared for his oral and written denunciation of
the old Governor. What he said we do not know, but in his long
letter (summarized and substantiated for the President in ten explicit
charges, February 20) he reviewed the case for Jefferson's consideration. He disclaimed any personal malice toward St. Clair; rather he
viewed him with "an eye of pity." Yet, as spokesman for the inhabitants
of the Territory, he felt obliged to impeach him as "unworthy of so
high and confidential a station in the government of a free people."
He repeated the charges made by Goforth and Symmes, particularly
specifying that St. Clair was interested only in gratifying his selfish
ambitions and pecuniary interests; that he had "wantonly rejected
laws passed . . . for the good of the people"; that he had appointed
his favorites to the best offices in newly established counties even
though they were not residents; that he had collected unauthorized
license fees and sought to control the courts by removal of justices
who did not render decisions in conformity with his opinions; that
he was "an open and avowed enemy to a republican form of government, and an advocate for monarchy"; and, finally, that he was the
author of the dividing law, whereby he hoped to avert statehood as
long as possible for any part of the Northwest Territory.[25]

This was neither the first nor the last interview Worthington had
with Jefferson regarding St. Clair's removal, but the President was not

[24] Letter in *Territorial Papers*, III, 205-207.
[25] Worthington to Jefferson, January 30, 1802, in Smith, *St. Clair*, II, 565-70.
A summary of the charges is to be found in *Territorial Papers*, III, 212-14.

to be hurried. Yet Worthington found many Congressmen who were sympathetic and willing to accept his interpretation of the need for forthright action. He desired an immediate change and hoped that St. Clair could be replaced by Nathaniel Massie, who, "with one exception only," Tiffin, was the "most proper man" in the Territory for the position. Massie was not in the least interested in being governor; he wrote Worthington, February 8, that "under the circumstances in which I at present stand, nothing on earth would induce me to accept of the office." Yet he despised St. Clair and sent Worthington material to be used against him, including petitions, charges, and depositions.[26] Without the active support of Massie and Tiffin as leaders of the opposition in Chillicothe, most of the ammunition Worthington needed in Washington would not have been forthcoming.

4

St. Clair's removal was an important item of business with Worthington, but he did not let it interfere with his major objective, namely, an enabling act. During February, therefore, he spent most of his time lobbying and furnishing his allies with information, oral and written, for use on the floors of Congress. Thus on February 8 he "set up until 3 o'clock making a statement for Mr. Giles Chairman of the N W Committee." Once again, on February 14, he called to see the President to keep the iron hot. On February 27, he listened with great satisfaction as another petition pleading for statehood, this one from Fairfield County, was read in the house.[27]

During the last days of February, Giles, Worthington, and Gallatin drew up a long report justifying the legal, economic, and political desirability of admitting the eastern portion of the Territory as a state with boundaries almost exactly as they are today—a report covering three columns of fine print in the *Annals*.[28] On March 1, Worthington recorded in his diary, "Engaged in copying Report for Mr. Giles for our admission as a state into the union."

This report was read in the house on March 4 by Congressman Giles. It related the great disquietude felt by the inhabitants of the Territory, especially "in consequence of the act lately passed for altering the boundary lines of the States in the Territory, as established by the

---

[26] Massie, *Massie*, 180-205; Massie to Worthington, February 8, 1802, in Smith, *St. Clair*, 572-73.
[27] *Annals*, 7th Cong., 1st Sess., 814.
[28] *Ibid.*, 1097-1100.

ordinance of the 13th of July, 1787." The committee was of the opinion that it was expedient to make provision for enabling the people in the eastern division of the Territory "to form for themselves a constitution and State Government, [and] to be admitted into the union . . . although the number of inhabitants may not amount to sixty thousand." Four resolutions were recommended for adoption: these called for a law which would empower the people to establish a state government, delimit the new state by a western boundary at the Great Miami, provide for the calling of a constitutional convention, and authorize representation of the new state in Congress. The report was tabled.[29]

A period of three weeks ensued in which no action was taken on the Giles resolutions. The House was busy debating the repeal of the excise taxes of the previous administration and the settlement of the French spoliation claims. Worthington chafed at the delay because he was confident of the outcome and anxious to get back to his home and business. On Tuesday, March 23, he noted in his diary,

> *Expected the territorial business would be taken up but disappointed— He who expects to have business done in a publick body which depends on right abstractly must have more patience & self denial than is the portion of man generally. When it does not tend to promote the popularity of the body or a considerable portion of them or to promote their interests directly or indirectly, there are almost insuperable difficulties to obtain success. This my constant observation in life.*

On Friday, March 26, the business was considered by the committee of the whole, but Paul Fearing was ill—or so Congressman Seth Hastings of Massachusetts intimated—and debate was postponed.[30] Worthington's diary comment, under the date of March 28, was as follows:

> *Nothing of consequence done in this business of the Territory. Was called up on friday and postponed because Mr. Fearing was not present. . . . Called up on Saturday again. Mr. Fearing in the entry . . . yet the business postponed by his absence—his object being delay [which he admitted when I] called on him.*

Finally, on March 30, the House took up consideration of Giles's resolutions and after considerable debate passed the first one, providing for the introduction of an enabling act.[31] Here are Worthington's comments on the debate:

> *Mch. 30—This day pleasant the business of the Territory taken up and discussed. Mr. Fearing opposed to the admission on constitutional grounds, but if it*

---

[29] *Ibid.*, 985-1093; *American State Papers, Miscellaneous*, I, 325-29.
[30] *Annals*, 7th Cong., 1st Sess., 1086.
[31] *Ibid.*, 1097-1118.

*appears expedient to his friends who are to write to him by next mail he will
cease to oppose it. If he had a vote he cannot say he would vote against the
measure—yet he believes it unconstitutional—he has never paid any attention
to the petitions from the Territory on this subject except hearing them read from
his seat, nor can he tell from what part of the territory they come but believes
from the counties of Ross & Adams only. It has been said that the minds of
the people are in an unsettled & disturbed state. Mr. Fearing believes this is
not the fact & asserts they are entirely quiet & have been so except in the town
of Chillicothe where there was some disturbances. [He] hoped the house would
not agree to the measure. Mr. Griswold & [Tracy] of Connecticut aided him,
opposed by Mr. Nicholson, Williams, &c the first resolution in the report was
agreed to in a committee of the whole—47 republicans for & 23 Aristocrats
against it.*

On March 31, the second resolution, which concerned the territorial
boundaries, was considered. Fearing argued that Congress had no
right to form only a part of the Territory into a state without the
consent of the whole; that the state so formed would not touch Lake
Erie (manifestly a misunderstanding or misstatement); and that the
Detroit population would be greatly inconvenienced by being thus cut
off and added to the Indiana Territory. His only supporter was Bayard
of Delaware, and Giles answered their objections very ably. Three
obstructive amendments were defeated, and the resolution passed
with 42 ayes. The third resolution was adopted by the same vote, and
the fourth without a division. Some further debate took place over the
provision that 10 per cent of the net sales of government land in the
new state be appropriated for a road to and through it. Griswold felt
that this amount should be cut in half; but Fearing supported Giles
on the point, the full report without further amendment was agreed
upon, and a bill was ordered in conformity thereto.[32] Worthington
makes these comments on the debate:

> *Congress (H. of R.) again took up the same business—Mr. Fearing still
> opposing it as well as every one of his federal friends whilst every republican
> supported the measure. the whole report of the committee was agreed to and
> referred to a committee to bring in a bill or bills. Mr. Fearing did state a few
> days since to Gen'l Bailey of N. York that if the Territory was admitted in
> to the union the people would lay their hands on the publick lands in the
> Terr'y—Gen'l Bailey told T. W[orthington] of this in the presence of John
> Fowler.*

Worthington's diary is, unfortunately, silent about the next few
days; perhaps its author was too busy to think of it. The enabling act
was prepared on April first, and Giles introduced it in the house on
Friday, the second, when it was read twice and passed to the third
reading. On Wednesday, April 7, it was debated at considerable length.
Fearing, John Randolph, and a little group of Federalists opposed the

---

[32] *Ibid.*, 1119-26.

exclusion of the three thousand to five thousand persons north of the proposed northern boundary line, but an amendment offered by Fearing to include them was defeated. Randolph explained that he did not oppose the bill but wished to avoid the admission of too many small states into the union. Fearing then introduced another amendment to permit the new state to choose its own name, which was agreed to.[33]

The next day the bill was again debated, one amendment was adopted, and it was ordered engrossed. Worthington wrote in his diary, "This day and yesterday taken up in the discussing the Territorial law—opposed by Mr. Fearing. Nothing of consequence happened last week." On April 9, the engrossed bill was brought to a vote and adopted, 47 to 29. The same day, it was sent to the Senate and given its first reading.[34] Worthington laconically noted in his diary that "this day the bill passed the House of Representatives and went to the Senate—was read once."

On April 12, the bill was given its second reading and referred to a committee consisting of Senators Franklin, Dayton, Bradley, Brown, and Baldwin. (Breckinridge replaced Baldwin on April 17, when Burr left the capital, and Baldwin was elected as speaker *pro tempore*.)[35] During the nine-day delay which ensued Worthington waxed impatient. On the twenty-first and twenty-third, several amendments were reported and debated, but major action on them was postponed. Worthington wrote as follows concerning the debate:

Apr. 26—On Friday [the twenty-third] the bill for admission of the Territory was taken up. Mr. Dayton, Brown & Gouverneur Morris opposed its passage. Gov'r Morris in his place stated as follows as near as I can recollect. Mr. President I am opposed to giving the salt springs to the new state for a reason which no gentleman has assigned. It will be recollected that in the Atlantic States we pay a tax of 20 cents pr. bushel on salt. Why not levy the same tax on the salt made at these springs—It will be a considerable source of revenue to the U. States & I see no reason why the people to the west ought not to pay the same tax with ourselves—
For shame Mr. Morris. Why did you not enquire what the original cost of salt was at these springs—you would have found that instead of 50 cents, the price you pay for your salt exclusive of the duty, the people of the Western country pay from 2½ to 5 dollars per Bushel for their salt.

Apr. 27th, 1802—This day the bill for the admission of the N.W.T. Again taken up and discussed—passed to the 3rd reading. Mr. G. Morris 1st spoke against it. Was opposed to giving Sec'n No. 16 for schools—it was pledged for the payment of the public debt—so was the salt springs & 1/10 of the lands intended to be applied to opening roads. Was opposed to the whole—stated that in europe many Sovereigns derived their revenue principally from salt springs—that the U.S. ought not to give up theirs—that it might hereafter

[33] *Ibid.*, 1128, 1155-56.
[34] *Ibid.*, 1158-61, 258. Duane gave the bill his support in the *Aurora*, April 12.
[35] *Annals*, 7th Cong., 1st Sess., 259, 265; Worthington's diary, April 12, 1802.

be an engine in the hands of the new state which would aid them in opposing the U.S.—if the U.S. retained it, it would always enable them to counteract the measures of the state and that if it was given, an amendment ought to take place preventing the state from deriving any revenue from these salt springs—motion on Lost. Mr. Wright, Mr. Franklin, Mr. Brackinridge spoke in favor of the gift and roads. Mr. Brown & Mr. Dayton against it. Doctor Logan again spoke in favor of the measure—observed he considered the salt water in the Terr'y as much a common stock as that of the sea. Mr. Brackinridge said the same & much more.

Apr. 29th 1802—This day the Bill finally passed both houses. [The vote in the Senate was 16 to 6 on April 28; the bill was signed by President Jefferson on the thirtieth.] [36]

May 2—Started for home.

By the time the Enabling Act had been passed, no great animosity existed between Worthington and Fearing. It is reasonable to believe that they had reached some *modus vivendi,* or at least an understanding. By April 27, Fearing was packing his goods for permanent removal to his home in Marietta. Both as official territorial delegate and as special envoy for the Marietta and Cincinnati Federalists in their fight for a small Ohio, he had been worsted by his Republican opponents. The fact that he graciously consented to take a large parcel of books home for Worthington in his baggage shows that he bore him no ill will.

Worthington reached Ohio on May 11, and was pleased to find during his two-day ride there—from Kirkwood (Bridgeport) to Chillicothe—that most of the people whom he met were delighted with his success. Arriving at his home town on the evening of the thirteenth, he found his family occupying the new log house, Belle View, on the hill west of town.

Such is the short and simple account of the most important period in the history of the eastern section of the Northwest Territory, drawn chiefly from the notes of the twenty-nine-year-old Ohioan who played the largest part in securing statehood for the area. Worthington came back home with a tremendous pride and satisfaction in his heart only to find envy, malice, and falsehood were still alive. His diary relates under entry of May 29 that

notwithstanding I have spent near five months from my family honestly endeavoring to promote the interests of my country and at my own expense, yet I find on my return that malicious envious reports are circulated ag't me without the least foundation—Conclude in my own mind that nothing is to be expected from mortals prone to evil. [I] pity those who possess depraved hearts and feel myself above resentment, having the approbation of my own conscience—the most satisfactory evidence to a mans own breast.

---

[36] *Annals,* 7th Cong., 1st Sess., 268, 275, 294, 295-97, 1252, 1349-51.

5

One of the reports which the Federalists had assiduously circulated against Worthington in his absence was that he aspired to displace St. Clair as territorial governor. With the passage of the Enabling Act, it was rumored that his chief interest in securing statehood was to get St. Clair out of the way so that he could become the first chief executive of the proposed state. Paul Fearing and Ephraim Cutler spread the report early in May that Worthington had secured for himself the office of collector of customs at Marietta.[37] These reports were circulated in Washington as well as in Ohio, but they had little effect there, for Worthington had the ear of the Administration. At home it was different. To scotch the canards concerning him, Michael Baldwin, who had returned from the capital early in February, rallied to Worthington's support and gave an account of his splendid services to the Ohio people in a letter to the *Scioto Gazette* (March 6, 1802). As register of the Chillicothe land office and collector of internal revenue, Worthington had many enemies; Elias Langham, for one, had attacked him both locally and with the federal administration. Fortunately, neither Langham nor St. Clair had much influence in the Territory, and while in Washington, Worthington was kept informed of their efforts to undermine him. One of the infrequent letters written by Baldwin (April 2, 1802), who corresponded with Worthington, is quoted here in full. Both its gossip and its political content show how unfortunate was the loss of this able but reckless young lawyer's correspondence.

> I must return you my thanks for being so good a correspondent. Your letters have all reached me. I sincerely console with you, for the sacrifice of private business, you must unavoidably suffer. But as we are approaching the most important crisis, we shall, perhaps, ever see this side the Ohio, it is necessary that you should persevere. It seems by your last letter, that old Veto [St. Clair] has not come on. I am a little doubtful whether he will make his appearance, in the City. His friends at the present Seat of government, say that he is going no farther than Ligonier. If he is not there before this, he will not be there at all. His conduct on the road from Cincinnati to Wheeling was truly singular. He was entirely alone, or as Creighton says "in a gang by himself," acting as usual the part of a drunken beast, the whole rout. He lay drunk two days at Williamsberg with his son in law, Rob. What a pity Elias [Langham] was not there, to have given the finishing touch to the scene. But out of regard to decency I will quit the dirty subject.
>
> We have already begun to make a little bustle about the convention. It is as yet uncertain how many candidates will offer in this County. Col Finley will not offer. Tiffin, Massie, Grubb & Langham will, to a certainty, & I expect

---

[37] R. J. Meigs, Sr., to Worthington, May 18, 1802, in the Rice Collection.

McArthur may be added. They have began to break ground in the electioneering field. ————— has began to preach, which is generally a symtom of an election, not being far off.

I have declared as your proxy, that you will take a pull with them. I can easily foresee that we shall have two parties in the County. Heretofore, thro motives of common safety, we have been united, but the moment the storm which threatened us blows over, we shall divide. Do you recollect the conversation I had several times with you, respecting the Doctor [Tiffin]? I still entertain the same opinion, & think my remarks were just.—I have determined to stand a poll for the convention, tho I have but small hopes of succeeding. I had determined not to offer, but there are certain circumstances, which was not within my knowledge till lately which has induced me to come forward. Nothwithstanding we shall be competitors, I assure you that, so far from attempting to injure your popularity, I certainly shall do every thing in my power to promote your Election. As for the other candidates, I shall neither advocate or oppose them. My determination is to stand on my own legs, & if I can carry honorably, to do it, if not, to make the best of it. There is but little doubt of your succeeding by a handsome majority, tho the circumstance of your holding a number of offices, will be used as a pretext by those not friendly to you, to shut you out. But had you no office, they would hatch up something else, so that they [might] as well take you upon that ground as any other. These hints respecting all local affairs I make to you, because no other person has. There has been a little sparring between us, but I assure you that they are entirely forgotten, & I feel every disposition to befriend you so far as is in my power, & shall likewise occasionally inform you of those little local views, & transactions, which occur daily, & which perhaps you would not hear from other channels—If I had more room I would write you a little longer.[38]

This letter indicates that early Ohio politics involved real contests, and all public men were severely criticized. Worthington was temperamentally unsuited to accept vituperation with equanimity, but since he was a sure candidate for one of the major offices which would be made available at statehood he could not escape it. As Baldwin's letter indicates, many aspirants had already offered themselves as delegates to the convention even before Worthington got home; his brother-in-law Tiffin wrote Tom Gibson of Cincinnati on May 29, "We are all in a ferment here—numerous candidates; several of them using every means to pull down the reputations of others; to build up their own."[39] Worthington was not only personally vulnerable to attacks upon his integrity and his objectives because of his extreme sensitivity but also politically vulnerable because of his youth, the public offices he held, his numerous political followers, his wealth in land and stock, his apparent indispensability in negotiations with the federal government, and, finally, his control of the patronage, which seemed to put the fate of every aspiring candidate for major office partially in his power. The very respectable gentlemen of the Federalist persuasion

---

[38] Letter in the Rice Collection.
[39] Letter in the Rice Collection.

particularly resented his growing influence, for they could see that it spelled their own political eclipse.

6

With the passage of the Enabling Act the triumph of the Republicans might have been assured had not St. Clair still been in control and had not his Hamilton County friends still been hopeful of making him the first governor of Ohio. He was surrounded by his personal friends, his political adherents, those who opposed statehood, the citizens of Cincinnati and Marietta who hoped to make capitals of their towns, and others who for devious reasons wished to thwart the plans of the Chillicothe party. The universal feeling on the part of the Ohio Republicans was that St. Clair must be removed. Worthington was very bitter about Jefferson's failure to dismiss him from office, and wrote Nathaniel Macon on July 23, 1802, that if Jefferson did not remove St. Clair, he [Jefferson] would

> loose ground with the republicans of the West. . . . The people here have been oppressed for 8 or 10 years past by Sargent & St. Clair alternately. They have complained & not been attended to and now when Congress have enabled them to form for themselves a gov't of their own choice the executive of the U.S. is about to permit a tyrant by his acts & intrigue to destroy the prospects & thwart the wishes of the people. I have stated these things over & over again to Mr. Jefferson & his councellors yet I fear without effect.[40]

Worthington's charges, however, were not without effect, for on June 23, President Jefferson, after having referred the matter to his cabinet for review, had Secretary of State Madison write St. Clair rebuking him for continuing to lay out new counties and county seats after it had been ruled that such functions had passed to the territorial legislature, for giving his son an "illegal tenure of office," and for accepting illegal fees.[41] This reprimand undoubtedly made the Governor decide to be a little more judicious in his official actions. Since he was in Washington at the time, he may have discovered that Gallatin's report from the Cabinet had stated that his removal would be justified, and that the Attorney General had rendered the same opinion. Gallatin advised the President, however, that it would probably be unwise to dismiss St. Clair at that time since he would be automatically removed in the near future when Ohio was admitted to statehood.[42]

[40] Letter in Worthington's letter book, LC.
[41] *Territorial Papers*, III, 231. See St. Clair's answer of June 23 in Smith, *St. Clair*, II, 571.
[42] Gallatin to Jefferson in the Jefferson Papers, LC, 123: 21155 and 21167. Levi Lincoln's opinion, dated May 23, is No. 21260.

Actually, by mid-May the issue was no longer whether statehood would be granted but what state or states should be formed and who should control them. Even before the passage of the Enabling Act— but after Congress had shown its disposition to favor immediate statehood—the Washington and Hamilton county groups had decided, if necessary, to advocate two states instead of one, in the hope of making Marietta and Cincinnati their respective capital cities. Burnet and McMillan of Cincinnati thought this would satisfy the masses.[43] St. Clair likewise swung over to this point of view during the summer months and advocated the two-state solution in a series of letters in the Cincinnati *Western Spy,* signed "An Old Inhabitant of Hamilton."[44] Benjamin Van Cleve of Cincinnati also denounced the Enabling Act and organized an association in Hamilton County to work for the two-state plan. He argued for a constitutional convention under the Ordinance rather than the Enabling Act, which he and his fellow politicians held to be unconstitutional.[45] Fortunately for Worthington's party, St. Clair was in the East—spending most of his time lobbying in Washington to maintain his office—from March 19 until his return to Cincinnati on July 10.[46] The acting governor, Charles Willing Byrd, refused to call the legislature together so that a convention could be assembled, for he was a member of the Republican group that opposed the dividing line at the Scioto, and a bitter enemy of the St. Clair party.[47]

By midsummer, the Federalists had abandoned the plan of a legislature-authorized convention and had decided to yield to the express action of Congress; thus they set out to win enough delegates to the constitutional convention to control it. They hoped that when they had secured control, the Enabling Act would be amended, the boundaries readjusted to conform to the dividing law, and constitutions for two states authorized. Such a program, if pushed, might yet save them from defeat by the Chillicothe politicos.[48]

To the Republicans, the Federalist threat seemed a great deal more serious than it actually was. They failed to estimate properly the strength of pioneer democracy or the effectiveness of their own

[43] Burnet to Fearing, February 4, 1802, and McMillan to Fearing, February 12, 1802, in the Fearing Papers.
[44] August 28, 1802, and September 11, 1802. See Downes, *Frontier Ohio,* 195 *et seq.,* and 232 *et seq.*
[45] *Western Spy,* June 26, 1802; Burnet, *Notes,* 501.
[46] Tiffin to Worthington, March 1, in Smith, *St. Clair,* II, 574.
[47] Byrd to Massie, May 20, June 20, 1802, in Massie, *Massie,* 206, 210; *Territorial Papers,* III, 533, 535.
[48] Downes, *Frontier Ohio,* 237-39; Sol Sibley to Burnet, August 2, 1802, in Burnet, *Notes,* 494.

propaganda. The rejection of the Enabling Act, the formation of two states, the election of St. Clair as governor of one and of some other aristocrat as governor of the second, the eclipse of Chillicothe, and finally the loss of patronage—all were nightmares. They redoubled their efforts to discredit St. Clair and to ensure the election of Republicans to the convention.

Worthington, determined but always cautious, and not overoptimistic because of his recent successes and the strong drift toward democracy, assumed the Republican leadership. On July 5, he issued to the people of the prospective state a report which was widely distributed. He gave them an account of his activities in Washington and congratulated them on the refusal of Congress to ratify the dividing law and on the passage of the Enabling Act. He thanked them for uniting to remonstrate with Congress against the dividing law, which had been "in perfect violation of the rights and liberties of the people of the Territory . . . having for its primary object the postponement of that period which was to emancipate the people of the Territory from a government hostile to their genius." He had hoped that Federalists and Republicans alike in Congress would support an enabling act, but in the final analysis every Federalist had voted against it. He gave this account of what occurred:

> *Every pretext was used to delay and frustrate the passage of the law, whilst their table was filled with petitions from almost every part of the Territory in its favor. Nor was there one solitary counter petition laid before Congress during the whole session. On the other hand the republicans uniformly declared it was their intention to do us that justice they believed we merited and leave us to pursue that political course which we believed would ensure to us the greatest share of happiness. Let us, said they, do to the people of the Northwestern Territory, that justice they are entitled to—let us enable them to form for themselves a government congenial to the feelings of freemen; we believe their present government oppressive and unjust; let us therefore extend a cherishing arm to them in their difficulties; let us put it in their power to participate in the blessings we enjoy, and have a share in the national councils. We are willing to receive them, be their political opinions what they may; it is our duty to do them justice and pursue that course which will in their own opinion best secure their happiness and prosperity. This was the language of the Republicans in Congress and how far the law is in conformity thereto, I leave you, my fellow citizens, to determine.[49]*

This type of propaganda had a pronounced effect: the enthusiasm for statehood grew steadily. On August 12, Francis Dunlavy jubilantly reported that Hamilton County was safe: "We are all Republicans—

---

[49] [Thomas Worthington], *Communication to Those Citizens of the Northwest Territory Opposed to an Alteration of the Boundaries of the States as Established by Congress and Who are Favorable to the Formation of a Constitution* (Chillicothe, 1802), Political Pamphlets, 103, Rare Book Collection, LC.

not a solitary federalist is now seen thro the whole County. . . . A state government is now the universal Cry."⁵⁰ In September, Worthington wrote Senator John Breckinridge of Kentucky, "Politics run high among us here on the eve of our elections for members of the Convention and I am happy to inform you that I have every reason to believe two-thirds of our convention will be republican although every opposition is made against the republican interest."⁵¹

The campaign intensified as the time of the election drew near. Chillicothe was "glutted with hand bills and long tavern harangues."⁵² Massie wrote Worthington on October 1 that he believed the "dividing party" in Hamilton County was "gaining ground, they calculate very much upon the upper counties joining them." He feared that they would try to write their old dividing plan into the constitution.⁵³

There was some popular discontent in Wayne County because of its exclusion from the projected state and its incorporation into the Indiana Territory by the Enabling Act. Detroit and a total of some five thousand settlers were now convinced that they would be denied statehood for years to come. Sol Sibley wrote Jacob Burnet that Ohio's northern boundary line, drawn from the southern end of Lake Michigan to the River Raisin, had been engineered through Congress by "Judges Symmes and [Return J.] Meigs, and *Sir Thomas* [Worthington]" because the delegates from Wayne County would be a "dead weight" politically, particularly in the control of the new state and in the division of the spoils. "But," Sibley commented sarcastically, "the ruin of five thousand inhabitants, when brought into competition with the interested ambition of half a dozen aspiring individuals, whose intrigues have brought us into the present dilemma, can be of little consequence." He was sure the Republicans would control the convention and, after it, the new state.⁵⁴

In reality, the people of Wayne County favored statehood, but their representatives had supported the wrong faction, for the Republicans had outmaneuvered this particular group of their opponents by getting the whole area cut off by the Enabling Act—in strict conformity, let it be noted, with the Ordinance of 1787.

---

⁵⁰ Dunlavy to Worthington, in the Rice Collection. Downes, *Frontier Ohio*, 233-45, gives a good account of this change of opinion in Hamilton County.
⁵¹ Worthington to Breckinridge, September 13, 1802, in the Breckinridge Papers, LC.
⁵² Massie to Worthington, October 1, 1802, in the Rice Collection. The quotation is from Massie, but he is reporting what McArthur wrote him.
⁵³ *Ibid.*
⁵⁴ Sibley to Burnet, in Smith, *St. Clair*, II, 580-81; Burnet, *Notes*, 494-96. Burnet dates the letter August 2.

At a meeting in Dayton, the malcontents called the Enabling Act legislative usurpation and argued that for Congress to authorize statehood without ratification by the people or their representatives was to emulate the action of Great Britain in forcing laws on the colonies.[55] They based their protest on the well-worn Ordinance of 1787. Their wish, they claimed, was to call together the legislature, which body could authorize, or refuse to authorize, a convention, as specified in Article V of the Ordinance. Their true objective, namely to make Cincinnati a capital, was manifested in a further resolution that Congress should be petitioned to change the western boundary of the Territory from the line at the Great Miami to one at the falls of the Ohio (Louisville), and that the territorial legislature should be recognized as the proper authority to decide whether, when, and at what dividing line the Territory should be partitioned into two states. Unquestionably, they still hoped that the Scioto could be made the eastern dividing line. General Rufus Putnam and others of like mind at Marietta took the same position, and contended that parts of the Enabling Act were no better than bribery calculated to force the people to accept statehood despite their wishes.[56] The Federalists in Washington County were particularly infuriated that Worthington had had more influence at Washington than their local favorite, Paul Fearing.

When the Federalists finally found that they could arouse little popular interest in their schemes, they decided as a last resort to try to capture the convention. After all, the "loaves and fishes" had not yet been distributed, nor had state lines been definitely established.

St. Clair, of course, used his influence to get delegates elected who opposed the Enabling Act. If action under it could not be averted, there would be at least a few gentlemen qualified "to discharge that trust with intelligence."[57] In a speech at Cincinnati late in the summer he accused the Republicans of seeking to exclude the most enlightened segment of the people from participation in the convention. He maintained that slavery would be legalized in the state's constitution if they succeeded in doing so. He further charged that the Chillicothe party planned to make their city the capital of the new state and to secure for themselves a majority of the state offices.[58]

The fears of the Republicans were put to rest with the election on October 12, for they were victorious throughout the Territory except

---

[55] Smith, *St. Clair*, II, 581.
[56] Meigs to Worthington, May 18, 1802, *ibid.*, 586.
[57] St. Clair to Huntington, July 15, 1802, *ibid.*, 587.
[58] *Ibid.*, 590.

in Washington County.[59] Worthington was one of the five delegates elected from Ross County, where the election took place "with much order." Apparently, he was not particularly concerned about the local results, for he spent the week before the balloting and the day after it at his mill on Kinnickinnick Creek and did not even learn of his own election until the evening of the day after it had occurred. It was doubtless with great satisfaction, however, that he noted in his diary on the twenty-third, "From the best information all the members of the convention 5 excepted are republicans."

---

[59] William T. Utter, "Ohio Politics and Politicians, 1802-1816" (unpublished dissertation, University of Chicago, 1929), 1-7, gives details of the election. See also Cutler, *E. Cutler*, 65 *et seq.*, and Downes, *Frontier Ohio*, 239-46.

Framer of the Constitution

THE Constitutional Convention met in Chillicothe, November 1, 1802. Worthington analyzed its membership as consisting of "26 Republicans, 7 Federalists and 2 doubtful"—a very excellent working majority.[1] The delegates were for the most part young men—over half of them were under forty. Burnet, one of the seven Federalists elected, reluctantly admitted years later when he published his *Notes* that the thirty-five framers were "with but few exceptions, the most intelligent men in their counties." Ross County was represented by Tiffin, Massie, Worthington, Baldwin, and James Grubb. In a letter to James Ross on January 15, 1802, St. Clair had mentioned the first four, together with James Darlington, as the only enemies he had in the Northwest Territory.[2] It is significant that all five of these men were elected to the Convention and took a leading part in making the constitution a democratic document.

William Goforth of Hamilton County was elected president *pro tempore,* and William McFarland, secretary *pro tempore.* Worthington was immediately appointed chairman of the Committee of Five on credentials and a member of the Committee of Three on rules and regulations. These were the only committees formed the first day; the inclusion of Worthington on both of them indicates his importance in the Convention. The Committee on Rules and Regulations was a very important one, for by its action a body of twenty-six rules was drawn up which determined the entire method of procedure in the Convention. Since Worthington had served in the territorial legislature and had also had the opportunity to observe procedure in both houses of the United States Congress, it seems reasonable to assume that he was the chief architect of these rules of order, although the other two members of the committee, Chairman John Reily of Hamilton County and John Milligan of Jefferson, also had served in the territorial assembly.

Edward Tiffin, who had been speaker in all three sessions of the territorial legislature, was elected president on November 2; Thomas Scott, also of Chillicothe, was made secretary. The rules drawn up by

[1] Worthington's diary, October 31, 1802.
[2] Smith, *St. Clair,* II, 557.

the committee were adopted on the third of the month. They put into Tiffin's hands no little power, especially through appointments and recognitions. They provided for majority rule and, to obviate any minority activity, that "two-thirds of the whole number elected" were necessary for a quorum.[3]

The election of Tiffin signalized the triumph of the state-makers. Although St. Clair had arrived on the first day "1st Consul like" and had intended to organize the Convention, he had been "informed that the members . . . considered themselves capable of self organization." By the third day the outcome was so evident that when he asked leave to address the delegates, his request was granted by a vote of 19 to 14, but he was explicitly recognized as "Arthur St. Clair, Sen., Esq.," a citizen and not the governor.[4]

In his introductory remarks, St. Clair suggested that the new state was to be launched at a time when national catastrophe was threatening. "Party rage," he charged, "is stalking with destructive strides over the whole continent. That baneful spirit destroyed all the ancient republics, and the United States seem to be running the same career that ruined them with a degree of rapidity truly alarming to every reflecting mind. But she is on the waves, and can not now be stopped." He soon came to the main point of his speech, arguing that the Convention was not bound by the Enabling Act, that the people of the Territory needed no such act to form a constitution, and that Congress "had neither the power nor the right" to take such action. "To pretend to authorize it," he declared, "was, on their part, an interference with the internal affairs of the country. . . . The act is not binding on the people, and is in truth a nullity, and, could it be brought before that tribunal where acts of Congress can be tried, would be declared a nullity." He urged the Convention to disregard the Enabling Act as worse than useless, to admit delegates from Wayne County, and to form a constitution for the whole Territory. He believed that senators and representatives elected in conformity with such a constitution would not be rejected by Congress; but if they were rejected, the Territory would still have a government, a government that would "go on equally well, or perhaps better." He pointed out that Vermont had had to wait eight years for admission to the Union and had lost nothing by the delay. But he defied Congress to reject delegates

[3] "First Constitutional Convention, Convened November 1, 1802. Journal of the Convention," *Ohio State Archaeological and Historical Quarterly*, V (1897), 80-153. Hereinafter cited as "Journal of the Convention."
[4] Worthington to Senator William Branch Giles, November 17, 1802, in *Territorial Papers*, III, 257; "Journal of the Convention," 87.

elected under the new government. "We have the means in our own hands," he solemnly declared, "to bring Congress to reason, if we should be forced to use them."[5]

In this speech St. Clair denied the right of Congress to legislate for the territories of the United States; he accepted the authority of the Congress which passed the Ordinance of 1787, but repudiated the idea that a later Congress could maintain, modify, or abrogate the provisions of that act. This was strange doctrine coming from a strong Federalist; it was the argument of rage and despair. Yet it was staunchly supported by other eminent Federalists, such as Burnet of Cincinnati, on the grounds that the Ordinance was a contract. St. Clair could see the handwriting on the wall; he could see the end of his position and his power.

Moreover, his advocacy of a constitution for the whole Territory was revolutionary. Such a stand was not in conformity with the Ordinance of 1787; it contradicted the explicit will of Congress as expressed in the Enabling Act, repudiated the wishes of a majority of the Territory's population, and advocated abstention from the Union unless federation could be had on the Territory's own terms. This was the last feeble gesture of an enraged partisan, made ostensibly for the good of the section but actually calculated to check the rising tide of Jeffersonian Republicanism.[6]

John Smith, delegate from Hamilton County and soon to be one of the two senators from Ohio, has given us the best side light on the first three days of the Convention and the triumph over St. Clair. He wrote as follows to President Jefferson on November 9:

> Governor St. Clair left this [city] for Cincinnati with a few of his friends yesterday and I have no doubt with some chagrin & disappointment. He took the pains to ride to this place unsolicited under the pretext of organizing the convention—On the day of our meeting he entered our chamber, appointed his secretary and requested the members to hand in to him the certificates of their election & the secretary would have them Registered. The measure was not acceded to—Col. Thomas Worthington with a manly intrepidity & his usual firmness in support of political Justice successfully interfered & we proceeded to the choice of a president and Secretary & to our own organization —The second day following his friends from Marietta took their seats & he again appeared and begged leave, not as a public officer, but as a private Citizen to make a few observations—Under this impression leave was granted— The moment he sat down it was determined to take no notice of it—and [a] resolution [was] passed declaring our intention to terminate this government & that he should be requested to prorogue the assembly after which he withdrew and issued his proclamation and ordered the printer to publish his speech.[7]

[5] Smith, St. Clair, II, 592-97.
[6] Burnet, Notes, 362, 338; Downes, Frontier Ohio, 232-36.
[7] Letter in the Jefferson Papers, 21948.

As soon as St. Clair had finished speaking and taken his departure, a resolution was passed declaring it "expedient . . . to form a constitution and state government." The roll call was 32 to 1, Ephraim Cutler of Washington County casting the only dissenting vote.[8]

2

It would appear fitting at this point to give a brief account of the final disposal of St. Clair as a factor in the history of the statehood controversy. When President Jefferson, Albert Gallatin, and others at Washington were informed of St. Clair's speech, which, it was urged, constituted the last necessary proof of the Governor's duplicity and party disloyalty, the Administration decided to act despite the fact that statehood would soon terminate St. Clair's tenure of office automatically. Gallatin, at the urging of Worthington and other friends of the Administration, recommended to the President that St. Clair be removed. He called the address to the convention "so indecent, & outrageous that it . . . is . . . incumbent on the Executive to notice it. He [St. Clair] calls the Act of Congress a nullity—He misrepresents all its parts. . . . He advises them to make a constitution for the *Whole* territory in defiance of the law."[9]

As a result, St. Clair was removed by Jefferson on November 22— insultingly removed, for the notice of his dismissal by Secretary of State Madison was enclosed for delivery in a letter to his enemy, Charles Willing Byrd, Secretary of the Territory. The letter to Byrd included a copy of the notice sent St. Clair and stated that by virtue of this action the functions of the office of governor now devolved on him.[10]

When St. Clair received Madison's letter, he wrote a withering reply, denouncing the administration for its pettiness in notifying him of his removal indirectly through his rebellious subordinate and critic, Secretary Byrd. He pursued the theme of his original speech by characterizing the action of Congress in passing the Enabling Act as a "violent, hasty, and unprecedented intrusion . . . into the internal concerns of the Northwestern Territory . . . indecorous and inconsistent with its public duty." Five thousand people in Wayne County, he charged, had been deprived of self-government by a dictatorial division of the Territory which could have been no more tyrannical "had it

---

[8] "Journal of the Convention," 88.
[9] Gallatin to Jefferson, November 20, 1802, in *Territorial Papers*, III, 259.
[10] Madison to Byrd, November 22, 1802, in *Territorial Papers*, III, 259; the text of dismissal is on page 260.

happened in Germany"; the nation seemed to have fallen under the control of hands which had degraded it, and too many of her people were "abjectly subservient to that domination."[11]

On December 16, St. Clair appeared in Chillicothe and denounced Worthington, Symmes, and Tiffin as his destroyers. Tiffin was both amused and embarrassed by the "poor old Man"—he was now sixty-eight—and asked his friends not to bother pleading his case. On the twenty-third, it became generally known in Chillicothe that St. Clair had been "deposed"; and on the twenty-fifth, the *Scioto Gazette* carried both Madison's letter and St. Clair's reply.[12]

On that same Christmas, St. Clair left the Ohio country forever, cursing the day he had ever set foot in it, and returned to his home, the Hermitage, at Ligonier, Pennsylvania, where he spent the last difficult years of his life. He was never able to get Congress to reimburse him fully for money advanced for the welfare of his troops during the Revolution or for the extraordinary expenses to which he had been put while holding the extremely responsible positions of superintendent of Indian affairs and governor of the Northwest Territory. He gradually lost the remnants of his property, and finally in 1818 at the age of eighty-four he died in a log cabin near Ligonier.[13]

3

Ohio's first constitution, drawn up and adopted in the short time of twenty-nine days, embodied the principles of triumphant western Republicanism. Its chief features were taken from the constitution of Tennessee, the most recently written and most democratic state constitution. Even more democratic, the Ohio constitution provided for a powerful legislature, the lower house to be elected annually, the upper biennially, with one-half retiring each year; the chief executive was to be a vetoless figurehead; the judiciary, like the executive, was deliberately made subordinate to the legislature; suffrage was liberal to a degree, being based on a small tax and exercised by ballot; the militia was to elect its own officers with the exception of majors and quartermaster generals, who were to be elected by the legislature, and the adjutant general, who was to be appointed by the governor; justices of the peace, constables, county sheriffs, and coroners were to

---

[11] Letter, December 21, 1802, in Smith, *St. Clair*, II, 599-601.
[12] Tiffin to Worthington, December 24, 1802, in the Rice Collection.
[13] John Smith to Worthington, December 25, 1802, in WMOSL; Smith, *St. Clair*, I, 250-56.

be elected by the people, and the state and county judges were to be chosen by the legislature for seven-year terms.[14]

Worthington's contributions to this instrument compare favorably with those of any other delegate. Since he and Tiffin were the leaders of the dominant party, they had a unique advantage, which they utilized. Tiffin's position as presiding officer gave him especial power; Worthington was the floor and committee leader.

Briefly stated, Worthington's activity in committee work was as follows: He served on the committee to report a preamble and Article I; the committee to prepare Article II, on the "Supreme executive authority"; the committee on the judiciary, Article III; the committee on Article V, regarding the "manner in which militia officers shall be chosen or appointed"; the committee to "report an article comprehending the general regulations and provisions of the constitution"; and the committee, composed of one delegate from each county, to consider the propositions made by Congress in the Enabling Act.[15]

To trace Worthington's work precisely and in detail would be desirable, but the Journal of the Convention is very sketchy. Although reports of committees embody his activities, the record usually gives only a report of his vote. Thus in Article I, on elections, he not only helped set the voting age at twenty-five but opposed an attempt to lower it. On a motion to make the senate term one year instead of two, as first reported, he approved the motion, but the nays had it. He favored a large senate and voted to keep its membership exactly one-half that of the lower house at all times. By the same token he preferred a maximum to a minimum number of legislators for the lower house; he voted to increase the original schedule to thirty-five, voted against reducing it to twenty-four, and after considerable debate supported the compromise measure which stipulated thirty.[16] He favored a small fixed salary for state officers and a per diem of two dollars for legislators. In general, about two-thirds of the Convention endorsed this proposed compensation, the rest recommending a somewhat larger amount. The Ross County delegation was evenly split on the question, Worthington and Grubb supporting a low pay schedule and Baldwin and Massie a larger one. Worthington voted to fix the governor's

---

[14] Utter, "Ohio Politics," Chap. 1, gives a good summary of the work of the convention in both its general and specific aspects. See also his later redaction in *The Frontier State* (Columbus, Ohio, 1942), Chap. 1.
[15] "Journal of the Convention," 88-89, 92-93, 96, 101.
[16] *Ibid.*, 103.

salary at $1,000 rather than $1,200. On almost all financial items he voted for the smaller figure.[17]

The salaries as finally adopted were experimental and were subject to change in or after 1803; in every case, the provisions fixing the financial responsibilities of the state were cautiously phrased, the amount being maximized—but not minimized—by the saving words "not more than." Actually, the first legislature cut all salaries slightly, and the total budget for 1803 was a modest $10,950, a figure well within the state's capacity to pay, and one which proved the absurdity of the fears of the Federalists, who had predicted financial disaster.[18]

Chairman Massie of the Committee of Fifteen appointed to draw up Article II, on the executive authority, reported Tuesday, November 9, the famous article that gave to the new state a figurehead governor. The Committee of Fifteen was dominated by the Jeffersonian St. Clair-haters—Byrd, Massie, Worthington, and Darlington. The article was adopted with very little opposition, for the despotism of colonial royal governors was still fresh in the minds of the members of the Convention. The extremely limited power vested in the executive illustrates the discredit which Governor St. Clair had brought to the office and the Republicans' determination to keep the whip in the hands of the legislature. The governor could call extra sessions, make temporary appointments until the legislature met, recommend legislation, command the militia, and retain the honorable custody of the "great Seal of the State of Ohio" with which to stamp all grants and commissions, but that was all. He was removable by impeachment.[19]

The Republicans also dominated the Committee on the Judiciary, Federalists Putnam, Gilman, and Wells constituting a minority of three against a majority of twelve, which included Byrd, Massie, Worthington, Darlington, and Smith. After being amended in the committee of the whole numerous times, the article dealing with the judiciary was passed, November 27. It authorized the legislature to elect judges of the supreme court and common pleas court for a seven-year term. The supreme court consisted of three judges, two constituting a quorum. Like the Pennsylvania court, it was to hold its sessions once annually in each county. The court of common pleas was made up of two (or three) county judges sitting with a traveling (or circuit) president-judge; three circuits were established. The

---

[17] Ibid., 105-109, 120, 136.
[18] Beverley W. Bond, Jr., The Civilization of the Old Northwest (New York, 1934), 132. George Ingersoll's letter (in the Fearing Papers) to his neighbor, Paul Fearing, February 20, 1804, is typical of the Federalist fear that taxes would be higher.
[19] "Journal of the Convention," 92; "Constitution of the State of Ohio—1802," Ohio State Archaeological and Historical Quarterly, V (1897), 137-40.

lowest courts were those established in each township and presided over by justices of the peace, who were to be elected by the township voters for a three-year term.[20]

4

The debate on Article IV, concerning the qualifications of electors, precipitated what is perhaps, from the standpoint of national history, the most interesting discussion that took place at the Convention. This debate concerned slavery and the attitude the new state should take toward the Negro race. Article IV, as originally presented, declared that "all white male inhabitants . . . of twenty-one . . . who have paid or are charged with a state or county tax, shall enjoy the right of an elector." An attempt to strike out the adjective "white" was defeated 14 to 19, Worthington voting nay.[21] The vote indicates a strong sentiment for enfranchising the Negroes. An attempt was made to amend the same section (Sec. I) by adding to it the words, "all male negroes and mulattoes now residing in this territory shall be entitled to the right of suffrage, if they shall within ___ months make a record of their citizenship." This amendment was adopted 19 to 15, Worthington again voting nay. Another amendment was then proposed extending the franchise to the "male descendants" of the said Negroes. This was defeated 16 to 17. On this vote, Abbott, Reily, and Smith switched to the nays. On the other hand, Browne of Hamilton joined the ayes, which would have made the vote 17 to 17 except that the Reverend Philip Gatch of Clermont County, who had voted aye on the first amendment, failed to vote at all on the second.

The same day, November 22, another switch in votes took place on the proposal to add as Section 7 to Article VII the following provision: "No negro or mulatto shall ever be eligible to any office, civil or military, or give their oath in any court of justice against a white person, be subject to do military duty, or pay a poll tax in the State; provided always, and it is fully understood and declared, that all negroes or mulattoes now in, or who may hereafter reside in, this State, shall be entitled to all the privileges of citizens of this State, not excepted by this constitution." To this change Worthington agreed. The others who had voted nay on the previous proposal but now switched with Worthington were Abrams, Baldwin, Bair, Caldwell, Kirker, McIntire, Massie, Milligan, Smith, Carpenter, Donalson, Humphrey, and Woods. These fourteen, with four of the 18 ayes on the

[20] "Journal of the Convention," 98, 127; "Constitution—1802," 140-43.
[21] "Journal of the Convention," 113.

former vote, carried the amendment 19 to 16, the nineteenth vote being Edward Tiffin's.

It would seem fair to conclude that the majority of radical Republicans were not willing to go further than to promise the resident Negro equal protection of the laws, freedom from legal bondage, and the right to live in peace if not in equality. Worthington and most of his party opposed slavery, but they also opposed racial equality. They had come to Ohio to get away not only from slavery but also from Negroes and a society based on Negro labor, free or slave. They would not be a party to throwing Ohio open to the free Negroes or runaway slaves who were bound to flock into the state if anything like equality of citizenship were given them.[22]

Four days later, November 26, the provision in Article IV for the enfranchisement of resident Negroes was deleted after President Tiffin broke a 17 to 17 tie vote. Worthington and the rest of the Virginia party, of course, were in favor of the deletion. The same day, Section 7 of Article VII was also deleted by a vote of 17 to 16, apparently in retaliation by the pro-Negro-rights group, since the Chillicothe party voted against its omission and later tried to substitute the provision, "No negro or mulatto shall ever be eligible to any office, civil or military, or be subject to military duty." This substitution was defeated, however, and Article VII was adopted without any mention of Negroes.[23]

Agreement on the status of Negroes in Ohio was finally achieved in Section 2 of Article VIII, the Bill of Rights. This section had been debated concurrently with Articles IV and VII, but since references to Negroes in them had by then been deleted, it was easier to compromise the issue in Article VIII. The committee on this article was made up of seven Republicans and two Federalists. Ephraim Cutler was one of the Federalists and, according to his account written long after the occasion and hence subject to considerable question, he dominated the committee although John W. Browne of Cincinnati was its chairman. The bill was reported, November 11, by Goforth, and was debated the next day, with Worthington in the chair. Several amendments were made.

Cutler's story of how Section 2 was compromised is our only version of the affair. This section, which permanently excluded slavery from the state and did not bar Negroes from legal equality, was, of course, the focal point of the committee's discussion—"an exciting subject,"

---

[22] *Ibid.*, 114, 116. See James H. Rodabaugh, "The Negro in Ohio," *Journal of Negro History*, XXXI (1946), 9-29.
[23] "Journal of the Convention," 122, 125.

Cutler characterized it.[24] He relates that the committee met with President Tiffin, and Chairman Browne proposed the resolution, "No person shall be held in slavery if a male, after he is thirty-five years of age, or a female, after twenty-five years of age." Cutler had no doubt that Browne's resolution embodied the sentiments of Jefferson. Worthington had told him in Washington at the time the Enabling Act was being passed that the President favored the incorporation of such an article in Ohio's constitution and hoped that no severer limitations would be set regarding slavery, since a constitution containing harsher measures would operate against emigration from the slave states to Ohio. Cutler, backed by several others who were for outright prohibition of slavery in the new state, offered a draft in conformity with the spirit and phraseology of the provision excluding slavery contained in the Ordinance of 1787, which precipitated a warm debate. Cutler expressed the opinion that his Washington County constituents felt very deeply on this subject and stated that so far as his actions were concerned, their wishes must be seriously considered. He proposed thinking the problem over until the next day, to which they agreed.

His account describes the proceedings of the following day:

The committee met the next morning, and I was called upon for what I had proposed the last meeting. I then read to them the second section, as it now stands in the constitution. [There shall be neither slavery nor involuntary servitude in this state, otherwise than for the punishment of crimes, whereof the party shall have been duly convicted; nor shall any male person, arrived at the age of twenty-one years, or female person, arrived at the age of eighteen years, be held to serve any person as a servant, under the pretense of indenture, or otherwise, unless such person shall enter into such indenture in a state of perfect freedom, and on a condition of a bona fide consideration, received, or to be received, for their service, except as before excepted. Nor shall any indenture of any negro or mulatto, hereafter made and executed out of the state, or if made in the state, where the term of service exceeds one year, be of the least validity, except those given in the case of apprenticeships.] Mr. Browne observed that what he had introduced was thought by the greatest men in the Nation to be, if established in our constitution, obtaining a great step toward a general emancipation of slavery, and was greatly to be preferred to what I had offered.

I then, at some length, urged the adoption of what I had prepared, and dwelt with energy on the fact that the Ordinance of 1787 was strictly a matter of compact, and that we were bound either to pass it (the section excluding slavery) or leave it, which I contended would be the law [anyway by the Ordinance], if not so defined by our own action. Mr. Baldwin, the only practicing lawyer on the committee, said that he agreed with me that the ordinance was, in its legal aspect, a compact; and, although many of his constituents would prefer to have slavery continue in a modified form, he would vote in

[24] Cutler, *E. Cutler,* 74-77. See also "Journal of the Convention," 90, 92, 110, 113, 126.

favor of the section as I had reported it. Mr. Browne, who was chairman of the committee, then called the ayes and nays, and his report was negatived, and mine adopted, the ayes being Baldwin, Dunlavy, Cutler, Goforth, and Updegraff; nays, Browne, Donalson, Grubb, and Woods. Several efforts were made to weaken or obscure the sense of the section on its passage, but the Jeffersonian version met with fewer friends than I expected.[25]

On the whole, the Convention was apparently quite satisfied with Cutler's provision. The overwhelming majority of Ohioans were strongly opposed to the legalization of slavery, as were the members of the Convention. The opposition of the Southern element among the delegates was directed only against enfranchisement. It is worthy of note that Darlington's defeat in Adams County when he ran for the first legislature was ascribed to the fact that he had voted with the Federalists to give resident Negroes civil equality, and that James Grubb of Ross County "lost much Credit" by having done the same.[26]

There was a good deal of pro-slavery sentiment in the Territory to the west of the projected state of Ohio. Abel Westfall wrote Worthington from Vincennes that the people there were "almost unanimous" for a limited slavery.[27] Daniel Symmes wrote Nathaniel Massie, February 20, 1803, that Mr. Short, late of Kentucky, "despairs of being able to live among us . . . without his domestics."[28] Benjamin Van Cleve believed that fear of the incorporation of an anti-slavery provision in Ohio's constitution was one of the chief reasons for the opposition of some to statehood and that there was a strong pro-slavery feeling in the "Scioto Country."[29]

It may be noted in conclusion that there is no evidence to substantiate Cutler's allegation that President Jefferson favored a policy of expediency on the question of slavery. Moreover, most of the rumors that the Chillicothe group approved of slavery were party propaganda, and few persons were naïve enough to take them seriously.

5

Worthington's voting record is our only clue to his attitude on a number of other issues. On the resolution to submit the constitution to the people for ratification, the committee of the whole on Novem-

[25] Cutler, *E. Cutler*, 75-76. Gilmore, in his *Life of Edward Tiffin*, 71-79, casts considerable doubt on Cutler's story.
[26] McArthur to Worthington, January 17, 1803, in WMOSL.
[27] Letter, December 27, 1801, in WM.
[28] Massie, *Massie*, 226.
[29] Beverley W. Bond, Jr., "Benjamin Van Cleve," in HPSO, *Quarterly Publications*, XVII (1922), 70.

ber 13 reported disagreement. When the vote was taken in convention, the resolution for reference was defeated 27 to 7. Worthington voted with the twenty-seven who opposed it. This was a party alignment and not a democratic issue; the seven who voted for the plebiscite— Cutler, Gilman, McIntire, Putnam, Reily, Updegraff, and Wells—were making their last attempt to delay statehood. Cutler argued strongly for reference and alleged that the Republicans opposed it because they objected to the delay and expense it would necessitate. In what he called "mad haste," the resolution was defeated.[30]

So far as the people were concerned, there is no evidence that they objected to the procedure. There was nothing really strange about this failure to ask popular approval. The framers of the constitution were Jeffersonian—not Jacksonian—Democrats; government for and of the people? Yes—but not necessarily by them. In any case, ratification was a foregone conclusion. Cutler and the Federalists claimed that this action was more autocratic than any they had ever been accused of favoring; yet nine of the original states had not thought a referendum necessary.

One of the most unwise and patently political resolutions submitted for consideration was the proposal that no member of the Convention should hold office under the new constitution for a year after it went into effect unless elected to an office by the people. The triumphant Republicans were not to be balked by any such stratagem; they defeated the resolution, 3 to 31. After all, the "loaves and fishes" were not to be despised. Moreover, to fulfill its purposes the new government had to be administered by its makers, not its enemies.

An attempt was made on November 20 to amend the third section of the Bill of Rights so that atheists would be barred from office-holding. The proposal was to strike from Ephraim Cutler's contribution to religious tolerance the sentence, "No religious test shall be required as a qualification to any office of trust and profit," and to substitute therefor, "No person who denies the being of a God or a future State of rewards and punishments shall hold any office in the civil department of the State."[31] This motion was probably introduced by Caldwell, Humphrey, or Milligan, since they were the only ones who voted for it; there were 30 nays, including Worthington's. An amendment to the same article making illegal the levy of a poll tax for county or state purposes was adopted the same day, 26 to 7, Worthington voting yea.

When the final vote was taken on the ratification of the constitution,

---

[30] Cutler, *E. Cutler*, 79; "Journal of the Convention," 98.
[31] Cutler, *E. Cutler*, 77; "Journal of the Convention," 111, 126.

Ephraim Cutler's was the only nay. Having opposed statehood from the start and having used every stratagem to delay its achievement, he was consistent to the end, alleging that his action represented his constituents and that he could not compromise them or his own convictions by voting for an instrument of which he did not approve.[32]

6

Worthington's part in the framing of the constitution is evident in spite of the paucity of records and their unfortunate brevity. He was particularly influential in keeping the governor's powers at a minimum. Something of a student of history and government, he was acquainted with the tyranny of the colonial royal governors, and his clashes with St. Clair had confirmed his abiding distrust of a powerful executive. During the summer of 1802, with the convention but a few months away, he wrote Nathaniel Macon, Speaker of the national House of Representatives, requesting his views on the defects in the government of North Carolina, defects which Worthington hoped to avoid in Ohio's constitution. Macon's reply strengthened Worthington's determination to keep the executive branch weak, and furnished many other suggestions that were valuable to him in the writing of the new frame of government. Macon wrote the following letter on September 1:

> In our State governments experience has shown the council to be useless, the governor and council have but very little to do; the executive is however full strong, where ever you find a strong executive, in a country which has any liberty, you will also find violent parties; examine the state constitutions, and by the power of the governor you may very nearly ascertain the general state of party as it relates to state affairs. The same principle produces the same effect in the United States and in the territories; The Executive should not appoint a single officer except as the North Carolina constitution directs; the appointment by the legislature is much better than by the Executive, because it destroys patronage, and prevents sycophants from obtaining offices by the dint of courtship; The representation ought to be according to numbers, and a married man ought to vote whether 21 or not. The militia soldiers ought to elect their officers to captains, the company officers elect the field officers, and the field the general officers; This would leave only the civil officers to the legislature, & by dividing the appointment among several bodies, it in very great measure destroys all attempts to bargain. When the Governor has no appointments to bestow, the election will be made without riot or tumult, nor is it in this case a matter of much consequence whether he is elected by the legislature or the people, I would however prefer the latter; the Judges in every county ought to be elected for a limited time, elections during good behavior are nearly the same as for life, it destroys the desire to to [sic] excel,

---

[32] Cutler, E. Cutler, 68.

in fact it puts an end to industry—every officer in the government should be elected for a limited time, His official conduct should at stated times be under the review of those who elected him. The governor, and the legislature ought to be elected annually—Every cent of the public money paid out of the Treasury and for what paid, ought to be printed and attached to the laws of each session, this will operate against granting money improperly, and greatly curtail what are called conting[en]cies.

These hints will show what alterations I should be glad to have in our constitution, but I would rather have it as it is than to attempt an alteration, because we have hitherto lived happily under it.[33]

On November 29, the delegates finally adjourned, having ratified the constitution and addressed a communication to President Jefferson and to Congress. Worthington was deputized to carry to Washington the constitution and the Convention's message.[34]

7

Worthington left Chillicothe, December 7, in the company of Colonel Samuel Huntington, who rode with him as far as Zanesville. He arrived at Georgetown on the nineteenth and found lodging at Mr. Burch's, where he had stayed the year before. Nathaniel Macon, John Breckinridge, Wilson Cary Nicholas, Willis Alston, and Richard Winn boarded at the same place, and were congenial associates. Worthington wrote Massie on Christmas day that he found "the members [of Congress] very friendly and disposed to do all they can for the state of Ohio."[35] The day after he arrived, he called on President Jefferson; on the twenty-second he delivered to Congress the new constitution and the resolutions of the Ohio legislature accepting, with certain modifications, the conditions of statehood established in the Enabling Act.[36] On the twenty-third, he dined with President Jefferson and his daughters—Mrs. John Eppes and Mrs. Thomas Randolph—and was much pleased to learn that St. Clair had been removed. "This poor Old Man has at length got out of public life dishonorable," was his final judgment. He spent the ensuing days lobbying. He was particularly

---

[33] In WMOSL. This letter is given in Smith, *St. Clair*, II, 590, in garbled form.

[34] "Journal of the Convention," 127, 129; Daniel J. Ryan, comp., "From Charter to Constitution," *Ohio State Archaeological and Historical Quarterly*, V (1897), 78-80, 154.

[35] Worthington's diary, December 20; Worthington to Massie, December 25, in Massie, *Massie*, 221.

[36] Thomas Worthington, *Letter* [December 23, 1802] *of Thomas Worthington, Inclosing an Ordinance Passed by the Convention . . . Together with the Constitution . . . and Sundry Propositions to the Congress* (Washington, D. C. 1802). Also printed in *American State Papers, Miscellaneous*, I, 343. See also Worthington's diary, December, 1802.

solicitous for the people of Wayne County, who, as we have seen, had been excluded from the state by the Enabling Act. He secured assurances from President Jefferson, department heads, and members of both houses that a new territory of Michigan would be created at the next session of Congress.[37] He dined very frequently with outstanding figures, including Albert Gallatin, Tom Paine, Gideon Granger, General Henry Dearborn, James Madison, and President Jefferson.

On February 1, he was pleased to learn that the election in Ross County had been held with great orderliness, and he was not surprised to find that he had led the ticket among the candidates to the General Assembly.[38] He took occasion to attend to a great deal of business during his stay in Washington and resigned his offices as supervisor of internal revenue and register of the Chillicothe land office. On March 1, Congress having accepted Ohio's constitution and passed a bill recognizing the new state, he left for home. He arrived at Chillicothe on the fifteenth, and the next day he took his seat in the state legislature.

8

Meanwhile, plans for selecting the personnel of the new government were under way in Ohio. A caucus of Republicans had drawn up and pledged support to a ticket of state officers before the Convention dissolved;[39] since the constitution had provided for the first election in January, the time was short. Edward Tiffin, postmaster at Chillicothe, was the Republicans' very popular candidate for governor. The Federalists threw their slight strength to Benjamin Ives Gilman of Washington County, or, knowing they had no chance to win, did not vote at all. Bad feeling was so strong in some areas that Return J. Meigs of Marietta could write Worthington, "The Federalists here have grown (if possible) more bitter than ever. They fulminate their anathemas against the administration with unprecedented malice. Such was their obstinacy that (knowing they could not carry a Federalist Governor) they would not vote for governor at all, but threw blank tickets."[40] As a result of the strong Republican organization which Meigs and the Marietta postmaster, Griffin Greene, had built up in Washington County, the Federalists did not

---

[37] Worthington to Sol Sibley, April 20, 1803, in Worthington's letter book, LC.
[38] Worthington's diary; McArthur to Worthington, January 17, 1803, in WMOSL.
[39] "Memoir of Hon. Thos. Scott," RCHS. See also Utter, "Ohio Politics," 26-27.
[40] Letter, January 31, 1803, in WMOSL.

have a chance. The opposition was so slight all over the state that Tiffin wrote Worthington he was glad the Federalists at least had a candidate, for he felt it "would have been an awkward cold race at this very inclement season of the year to have run all over the State of Ohio alone."[41] Jacob Burnet, John Reily, and a few other staunch Federalists tried to organize in Hamilton County, but their plan to split the Republicans failed.[42] Instead, their own ranks were divided. Even on the governorship they could not agree. Gilman of Marietta was the major nominee, but a caucus in Hamilton County agreed to support John Paul of Xenia; and in many of the seventeen counties former Governor St. Clair was prominently mentioned as a fit person to head the ticket of local nominees.[43]

Tiffin and Gilman remained at home rather than ride their horses over the state either together or separately. St. Clair had left Ohio on Christmas day, and interest in him faded entirely during the next month. When the votes were counted by the legislature, Tiffin had 4,564; since none were reported for any other candidate, it appears that the opposition, as Meigs noted, had either refrained from voting or had cast blank ballots. Six months later, 7,793 votes were cast in the Congressional election, a clear indication that the Federalists had accepted the choice of Tiffin in the previous election as a foregone conclusion.

This was the first election in which correspondence societies, organized in 1797, were used in Ohio in every town of any size to co-ordinate the support of candidates. On December 10, fourteen of the Republican societies in Hamilton County met to line up their ticket, and in the same county seventeen meetings were scheduled for December 29.[44]

The Federalists were overwhelmed in the election. Their ticket carried in Jefferson County only. Writing from Round Bottom Mill, January 22, John Smith told Massie of the victory in Hamilton County: "Burnet & Bowers look blacker than ever since the election—I never saw a party so much chagrined as that of the old Governor—I think he will now be forsaken as he has not the loaves & fishes any longer at his disposal."[45]

[41] Letter, January 7, 1803, in WMOSL.
[42] Symmes to Massie, May 9, 1803, in Massie, *Massie*, 225; Burnet and committee to Massie, *ibid.*, 227.
[43] Smith, *St. Clair*, II, 597 *et seq.*
[44] Utter, "Ohio Politics," 53-54; Goforth to Worthington, December 25, 1802, in the Rice Collection.
[45] Massie, *Massie*, 222.

9

The legislature that met in Chillicothe was made up of fourteen senators and thirty members of the house. Of these forty-four, only twelve had been in the Convention. Not only had Chillicothe secured the capital, but her citizens were awarded a fair share of the offices. Governor Tiffin, Speaker of the Senate Massie, Speaker of the House Baldwin, and Secretary of State Creighton were all from Chillicothe. It was in more than one respect a rather close coterie, since Tiffin was Worthington's brother-in-law, Massie and Creighton had married sisters, and the four had been associated in pioneering, business, and politics.

Worthington and John Smith of Hamilton County were elected United States Senators on April 1.[46] Worthington unquestionably deserved one of the Congressional offices in return for his yeoman efforts to secure statehood for Ohio. He was considered by a very large percentage of the Ohio electorate unquestionably the most suitable man in the Territory to represent the new state in Congress.

The legislative records do not reveal any opposition to Worthington's election, but William T. Utter, in his admirable study of early Ohio politics, points out that Samuel Huntington of Cleveland (Trumbull County) was also placed in nomination.[47] Someone had started a rumor that Huntington and Worthington had agreed to lobby for each other, a rumor which grew to such proportions that Worthington in a friendly manner finally asked Huntington to disavow publicly any such bargain. In a cordial private letter to Worthington, Huntington denied that any agreement had been made between them, but neither of the men gave the letter to the newspapers.[48] This incident marked the beginning of a coldness between them and later made them bitter rivals. Worthington had been informed that Huntington started the story,[49] as perhaps he had; but it is impossible to believe that Worthington could have struck such a bargain with an erstwhile Federalist. Huntington and his colleague George Tod had both supported the division law the previous year, and Huntington had had some hope

---

[46] *Journal of the House of Representatives of the State of Ohio* . . . [various places and dates], *1st General Assembly,* 79. Hereinafter referred to as *House Journal.*
[47] Utter, "Ohio Politics," 35.
[48] Worthington to Huntington, October 19, 1803, in the Huntington Papers, WRHS; Huntington to Worthington, October 23, in WMOSL.
[49] Silliman to Worthington, November 20, in WMOSL.

FRAMER OF THE CONSTITUTION 111

of succeeding St. Clair as governor. After the passage of the Enabling Act, both had had the good sense to transfer their political allegiance, but they were justly viewed with some suspicion by their former opponents.[50] The day after the United States Senators were chosen, Huntington was compensated by being made one of the three supreme court judges; Return J. Meigs of Marietta and William Sprigg of Chillicothe were the other two.[51]

A number of nominees entered the race for Ohio's sole Representative in Congress. A legislative caucus of Republicans named Jeremiah Morrow of Hamilton County, an upcounty Republican who lived in what is now Warren County.[52] Other Hamilton County Republicans electioneered for William Goforth. Elias Langham and Michael Baldwin, both of Chillicothe, had some Republican following. Cincinnati Republicans importuned Worthington to support Goforth, but although he respected him and appreciated the aid he had given to the state-makers, Worthington pledged his support to Morrow, the party nominee, and warned Goforth not to split the party and reward the Federalists. The Federalists put several nominees in the field. Jacob Burnet and his associates got out a circular in favor of William McMillan, who "reluctantly consented" to run. The Marietta branch of the party supported Bezaleel Wells of Steubenville. In the June voting, Morrow was elected by a wide margin, receiving almost twice as many votes as his nearest competitor, McMillan. The vote was Morrow, 3,701; McMillan, 1,887; Baldwin, 902; Langham, 615; Goforth, 615; and Wells, 73.[53]

Among other persons to whom political plums were distributed by the first legislature and by the patronage dispensers as part of the spoils of victory were Postmaster Greene of Marietta, who became justice of the court of common pleas in Washington County; Wyllys Silliman, elected to the legislature from the same town, who was appointed president of the common pleas middle circuit; Calvin Pease of Trumbull County, who was assigned the same post in the eastern circuit; and Francis Dunlavy of Hamilton, who was made president of

[50] Tod to Huntington, January 14, 1802, in the Huntington Papers, WRHS. See also Downes, *Frontier Ohio*, 220-23.
[51] *House Journal, 1st General Assembly*, 81; W. A. Taylor, *Ohio Statesmen and Annals of Progress* (Columbus, Ohio, 1899), 37. Huntington wrote his wife on April 2, notifying her of his election, and expressed no regret concerning the senatorial election. In the Rice Collection.
[52] See biographical data and correspondence in Josiah Morrow, "Jeremiah Morrow," *Old Northwest Genealogical Quarterly*, IX (1906), 99-133.
[53] Utter, "Ohio Politics," 173; Josiah Morrow, "Jeremiah Morrow," 101 *et seq.*

the western common pleas circuit.[54] George Tod, who had rather too obviously joined the Republicans along with Huntington, had to wait until 1806 before he was finally appointed judge of the supreme court; Charles Willing Byrd, through Worthington's influence, had already been made federal district judge by President Jefferson. A year later Worthington, as senator, was instrumental in getting George Hoffman of Chillicothe appointed register of public lands at Detroit, and Elijah Backus of Marietta receiver of public monies at Kaskaskia.[55]

Thus ended the long struggle of the Republicans for statehood. To Worthington and his confreres, Ohioans may justly be thankful that their state assumed her place in the Union with broad boundaries and a democratic constitution. We can overlook the selfishness of local politics in the noble achievement of this band of state-makers. Their perquisites of power have perished with them, but the state endures, a monument to their genius.

10

During the summer and autumn of 1803, Worthington built a hay barn and harvested twenty-five acres of wheat and thirty-five of corn. During August, he had a violent attack of bilious fever—in this instance he called it "inflammation of the bowels." He took a trip to his brother's home in Kentucky during the first ten days of September.

Since Mrs. Worthington and the children—Mary six, Sarah three, and James one—were to accompany him to Shepherdstown when Congress convened, a great deal of time had to be devoted to preparations for that journey. Worthington's mills and other business enterprises were placed in competent hands; the care of the house, barns, and stock was entrusted to his white and Negro helpers; and arrangements were made for his financial affairs to go on as usual during his absence. His expectation was that Mrs. Worthington would be back in Chillicothe in about eight weeks and that he himself would not be absent more than sixteen weeks.

The Worthingtons left Chillicothe on September 22 to make the journey of four hundred and twelve miles. Mrs. Worthington and the children traveled in the carriage, a Negro boy driving them, and Worthington rode his horse. Now and then, he and the boy exchanged

---

[54] *House Journal, 1st General Assembly*, 81-87.
[55] *Territorial Papers*, VII, 192, 200-201.

places. Their route took them through Lancaster, Zanesville, Wills Creek (Cambridge), Wheeling, and across the Alleghenies to Cumberland. Their accommodations must have been at least passable, for the only criticism noted by Worthington in his diary concerned the night they spent at Peter Golly's near Laurel Hill, Pennsylvania, where they found "the most dirty, lazy family we had met."

11

Worthington's arrangements for the management of his business affairs during his long absences were of considerable consequence. He was not always so fortunate as in the winter of 1811-12, when Mrs. Worthington's two brothers were in charge: James S. Swearingen lived at Adena and was general supervisor of the estate and the flour mills; Thomas Swearingen managed the textile mill and rope walk in Chillicothe.

Worthington's domestic helpers, especially the Negroes, were not always dependable; James Swearingen reported in 1813 that Nelly, the chief cook, was "fat and lazy," and it was difficult to keep her attentive to her duties, but Mrs. Worthington was very fond of her. Moreover, she was "very impudent to the hands," and tried to run the house when master and mistress were away or out of sight. Worse yet, her young assistant in the kitchen seemed bent on emulating her in every way. Nelly was the ringleader in night visits to neighboring estates. "I can not keep any of them at home at night," reported James. "So soon as I am in bed all off [they go]. . . . They frolic all night." (Perhaps Nelly was not so much lazy as tired during the day.)

Swearingen reported that the Negro boys were good help except Henry, who was not worth much; that he had Peter employed cutting and hauling wood, Jacob tending the cattle, and David and Daniel engaged in lesser duties. Baz was herding the sheep and helping with the cordwood; "Moses is as good a boy as I know."[56] It may be noted in this connection that shepherding the sheep was always necessary, especially during the winter months. As late as November, 1813, Worthington had twenty merinos killed by wolves or so badly injured that they had to be destroyed.[57]

---

[56] James Swearingen to Worthington, December 24, 1811, and January 13 and February 2, 1812, in WM.
[57] James T. Worthington to Worthington, November 16, 1813, in WM.

We may conclude that although Worthington's business and estate interests were fairly well supervised in his occasional absences, they did not flourish as they did when he was home and able to give them his constant attention. There is little question that the master and mistress of Adena paid a price for the public service they performed.

United States Senator

WHEN President Jefferson convened Congress by proclamation on October 17, 1803—a much earlier date than usual—the new thirty-year-old Senator Thomas Worthington from Ohio was there to present his credentials and take the oath. He had arrived at Georgetown on the thirteenth, called on the President on the fourteenth, renewed his acquaintance with friends in Congress, and was ready for work. His friend Senator John Breckinridge of Kentucky had requested that the senators from Kentucky, Ohio, and Tennessee and the representative of the Indiana Territory meet on the fifteenth, prior to the convening of Congress, to determine what policy should be followed regarding the colonization and government of Louisiana.[1] Another reason Worthington was anxious to arrive on time was that he wished to cast a vote for the ratification of the Louisiana Purchase. The treaty providing for the purchase was approved on the nineteenth by a vote of 24 to 7. Worthington's colleague John Smith did not arrive in time to participate in this important action. When he did arrive, they drew lots for the four- and six-year terms, Worthington drawing the lot for the four-year term.[2]

2

The complete control of the navigation of the Mississippi, which was secured by the Louisiana Purchase, was a project which more than any other at the time occupied the minds of the Ohio people. They felt that the whole problem of navigation down the Mississippi, war with France or Spain, and the political and economic future of the country depended on the ratification of the treaty of purchase. As two of Worthington's correspondents put it, "Our people are extremely uneasy" regarding the decision, and "the western people wait with great anxiety."[3] William Creighton wrote Worthington that news of an im-

---

[1] Breckinridge to Jefferson, September 10, 1803, in *Territorial Papers*, IX, *Orleans Territory*, 43.

[2] *Annals*, 8th Cong., 1st Sess., 1-2, 217; Charles Francis Adams, ed., *Memoirs of John Quincy Adams, Comprising Portions of His Diary from 1795 to 1848* (12 vols., Philadelphia, 1874-77), I, 279.

[3] McArthur to Worthington, October 21, 1803, and Creighton to Worthington, October 17, in WMOSL.

pending war with Spain had "agitated the people considerably" and led to action to raise recruits at Chillicothe and other towns in Ohio; for it was believed that General Wilkinson might have to use force to dislodge the Spanish at the time of the transfer, and it was known that the President had instructed him to do so if necessary.[4] Thus, when the good news of the ratification arrived, there was great joy in Ohio. Wyllys Silliman, writing from Zanesville, described the purchase as "an event which I conceive of more real importance to this country than any which has occurred since the declaration of independence and which will more firmly attach the affections of the people of the west to the present administration than any other of its measures."[5]

It is customary to regard the purchase of Louisiana in 1803 as a masterly stroke of state—and it was—but the probabilities are that the consequences would have been the same had we not made the purchase at that time. Peaceful penetration and a treaty of annexation after settlement would have achieved the same result, perhaps without any expenditure of money. A war might have been necessary, but the party in occupation would eventually have been master. It was really the settlers of the West who determined its fate. When the right of deposit at New Orleans was suspended in 1802, some of the Federalists took advantage of the furore this caused in the West to agitate for war, hoping to discredit the Administration. Others approved of the mission of Monroe to settle the vexatious problem by the purchase of West Florida and the Isle of Orleans.[6] The acquisition of the whole territory was not considered; once proposed, however, it offered a way of settling once and for all the question of the navigation of the Mississippi.

In any event, the purchase was made and the treaty hurried through. The fight in Congress came not so much over the purchase as over the subsequent disposition of the territory. The Federalists strongly objected to its incorporation into the Union with the promise of statehood at the earliest possible moment as provided by Article III of the treaty of cession, but they were outvoted on every point. Tracy of Connecticut maintained the treaty was unconstitutional; that the incorporation of Louisiana, first as a territory and then as a state or

---

[4] Creighton to Worthington, November 2, 1803, and Ben Hough to Worthington, December 15, 1803, in WMOSL.

[5] Silliman to Worthington, November 2, 1803, in WMOSL.

[6] Manasseh Cutler to James Torrey, January 15, in William P. Cutler and Julia P. Cutler, *Life, Journals and Correspondence of Manasseh Cutler* (2 vols., Cincinnati, 1888), II, 122; Cutler to Capt. Fitch Pool, January 17, *ibid.*, 123; Rev. Jedediah Morse to Cutler, February 3, *ibid.*, 129.

states, would render the original states "insignificant in the Union."[7]
Manasseh Cutler held it would necessitate separation.[8] Pickering
advocated secession and a northern confederacy. The Federalists as
typified by him were anxious to obstruct any move that might
strengthen the political power of the South and the West. Ever since
1787, the unfair representation afforded the South in the three-fifths
compromise had rankled, and secession had become almost a mania
with Pickering. Every proposal to extend our territory south or west
drove him frantic. His attitude and tactics are a good illustration of
the chief reason for the rapid decay of the Federalist party. Worthington's attitude was unequivocal and definitely western. "Doubt [is]
entertained by some that the treaty does not oblige an incorporation
of the people of the Louisiana Country into the union," he wrote in
his diary. "On this subject I am clear and have no doubt and even if I
doubted I never could agree to have colonies attached to the U. S.
inhibited from the Common rights of citizens."[9]

In December, Senator John Breckinridge brought in a bill for the
government of the Louisiana Territory. It proposed that the vast area
ultimately be divided at the thirty-third parallel. The northern part,
the District of Louisiana, was to be added to the Indiana Territory, and
the southern section was to be called the Territory of Orleans. The
government of the Orleans territory was to consist of a governor, a
secretary, a council of thirteen, and judges—all appointed by the
President. Trial by jury was to be used in all capital criminal cases,
and in all civil and other criminal cases if requested by either party.
Slaves could be introduced only by bona fide owners; none were ever
to be imported.

This bill precipitated a strenuous debate on two points, namely,
whether such an autocratic government should be established and
whether slavery should be so restricted. Worthington felt very deeply
that the territory should be as democratically organized as possible and
that it should have a representative assembly and send a delegate to
Congress, but his motion to that effect was defeated.[10] He renewed the
attack on February 1 in one of his few recorded speeches, summarized

[7] *Annals*, 8th Cong., 1st Sess., 58. See pages 27-74 for the full debate on the
appropriation bill.
[8] Cutler to [J. Morse], October 31, 1803, in Cutler, *M. Cutler*, II, 139.
[9] Worthington's diary, October 19, 1803.
[10] The bill is partly quoted in the *Senate Journal*, 8th Cong., 1st Sess., 143. See
Everett S. Brown, ed., *William Plumer's Memorandum of Proceedings in the
United States Senate, 1803-1807* (New York, 1923), 107-109; see also Brown's
study, *The Constitutional History of the Louisiana Purchase, 1803-1812* (Berkeley,
California, 1920), for the full story on this debate.

in the journal of Senator William Plumer of New Hampshire: "The government contemplated by this bill is a military despotism, & I am surprised that it finds an advocate in this enlightened Senate. The gentleman from Georgia [Mr. Jackson] talks of a *seperation*—Sir, the *western states* will not seperate [*sic*] unless the *eastern States* by their conduct render it absolutely *necessary.*"[11] Worthington fought both friend and foe in his continued effort to secure a liberal government for the new territory. Jackson, on the other hand, maintained that the inhabitants were "too ignorant to elect a legislature" and, being French, despised the jury system. Pickering argued that a "regular government" would "destroy the western states," cause "a *separation* of the union," and "prove our ruin." Worthington's protests bore fruit, however, for the territory was advanced to a government of the second stage the next year, with a representative assembly and a delegate in Congress.[12]

In the matter of exclusion of slavery from the territory, Worthington was willing to permit bona fide immigrants to bring their Negroes with them when they settled there, but he favored their manumission at the end of one year. Thus by law he would have closed Louisiana Territory to slavery just as the Northwest Territory had been closed to it by the Ordinance of 1787. We may conclude that he opposed the extension of slavery even when he must have known that states formed from this particular territory probably would be admitted to the Union as slave states. Finding his position untenable, he voted with the majority to permit the introduction of slaves only by bona fide owners who were citizens of the United States.[13]

3

Perhaps Worthington's most noteworthy contribution to the Louisiana controversy was the resolution he introduced March 6, 1806, providing for the colonization of the territory and for its defense. (Senator William Plumer claimed that John Breckinridge, the attorney general, had told him that he was the author of the proposal.) Two million acres were to be set aside "between the Achafalaya, the Red river, and a meridian line passing by the fort at Natchitoches" to be surveyed and

---

[11] *Plumer's Memorandum*, 134. Hereinafter referred to as Plumer. See also *Annals*, 8th Cong., 1st Sess., 233, 235, 238, 251.
[12] Plumer, 110, 134-38; Adams, *Memoirs*, I, 294; 2 *Statutes at Large*, 283-89, 322-23.
[13] *Annals*, 8th Cong., 1st Sess., 244; Plumer, 111 *et seq.*; Adams, *Memoirs*, I, 292. Worthington voted January 21, 1805, to receive the petition of New Jersey and Pennsylvania Quakers protesting the position of their "degraded fellow-men of the African race." *Annals*, 8th Cong., 2nd Sess., 39.

divided into townships and lots; alternate lots of 160 acres were then to be given to citizens twenty-one years of age not living in the territory who would occupy and improve them, and, with their eighteen-year-old sons, agree to perform military service whenever needed for the defense of the Orleans and Mississippi territories. Plumer noted that Jefferson informed him on April 2 that he considered this bill one of the most important then pending in Congress; that Louisiana was exposed to attack and the militia from the states might not be willing to march there to defend it; and that the bill was designed to induce settlement and at the same time provide protection. Perhaps this plan was dropped because of the Wilkinson-Herrera agreement of November 5 to treat as neutral ground not subject to settlement by either nation the area between the Sabine and the Arroyo Hondo-Calcasieu River line.[14]

That Jefferson was very solicitous for the safety of this extremely important acquisition and entertained serious doubts of his ability to retain it in case of war with Spain is nothing new; but Plumer's account of a conversation with Worthington concerning the President's feeling on the matter is a curious side light on Jefferson. Plumer made this note in his journal:

Mr. Worthington told me, that in a conversation he had with the President —he [Jefferson] told him that none of his favorite measures had been adopted this session—That the bill for classing the Militia had been rejected—That the bill authorizing a detachment from the militia had not yet passed—That this bill for the defense of Orleans territory would not pass—and he then added, with tears running down his face—"The people expect I shall provide for their defense—but Congress refuse me the means."[15]

If Worthington had been facetious by nature, one would suspect he was duping Plumer; but Worthington and Plumer were extremely sober individuals, and both took their senatorial responsibilities very seriously. One can hardly conceive that the extremely correct Republican from Ohio was pulling the leg of the extremely puritanical Senator from New Hampshire.

The proposal was referred to a committee of which Worthington was chairman. He reported a bill on March 21, but after it had been de-

[14] Plumer, 474; Annals, 9th Cong., 1st Sess., 164; Adams, Memoirs, I, 424. For the history of the "neutral ground" agreement, see J. Villasana Haggard, "The Neutral Ground Between Louisiana and Texas, 1806-1821," Louisiana Historical Quarterly, X (October, 1945), 1001-1128.
[15] Plumer, 475. He adds, "This same Mr. Worthington is a strange man. He may deny this [Jefferson tale]—But he has told the same to Genl Bradley—But, he, again, is still more equivocal!"

bated on several occasions and amended, it was postponed until December and thereafter never resurrected.[16]

4

If the purchase of Louisiana brought the Federalists to a position where they were almost willing to destroy their party and the Union in combating it, the proposed purchase of the Floridas gave them another opportunity to implement their policy of party suicide. The successful purchase negotiations in 1803 so encouraged the President that when the dispute with France and Spain arose over the boundaries of Louisiana, and Spain refused to recognize the Perdido as its eastern terminus and sought to establish that boundary at the Iberville, Jefferson decided it would be wise to settle the matter by acquiring all the Floridas. In his message of December 6, 1805, transmitted in secret session, he guardedly asked for an appropriation for this purpose, but John Randolph, chairman of the House Ways and Means Committee, to which it was referred, fought the proposal. The committee wished to bring in an appropriation bill for five million dollars, but Randolph insisted that until Jefferson explicitly asked for that amount and gave an exact explanation of how it was to be used, he should not have it. Despite the obstructionism of Randolph's Quids and the Federalists, a bill passed the house on January 16 providing for an appropriation of two million dollars, ostensibly to permit the President to maintain intercourse with foreign nations but actually to be used as a Florida purchase fund.

The next day, the bill went to the Senate, where it was debated with "great warmth."[17] The Federalists naturally objected to putting such power into the hands of Jefferson, but, having worn the constitutional question threadbare on the Louisiana issue, they now used better tactics by pretending to advocate the purchase of all the territory between the northern boundary of the United States and the St. Lawrence River rather than, or in addition to, the Florida territory. They argued that if the boundaries of the United States were to be extended to their natural limits in the southeast, surely the territories in the St. Lawrence region in the northeast would be the wiser purchase. Of

[16] *Annals,* 9th Cong., 1st Sess., 182, 191, 206, 228; Plumer, 474; Brown, *Louisiana Purchase,* 163.

[17] Plumer, 345-47, 379-80, 384-87; *Annals,* 8th Cong., 1st Sess., 55, 86-88. For Jefferson's message see J. D. Richardson, ed., *Compilation of the Messages and Papers of the Presidents, 1789-1897* (10 vols., Washington, D.C., 1907), I, 388-90; *American State Papers, Foreign Relations,* II, 669-95.

course, the mouth of the Mississippi should be safeguarded, but why stop there? The St. Lawrence needed opening too. Some members of both parties believed that Europe's involvement in a deadly war made the time propitious to purchase or seize what we wanted on both boundaries. To buy was much cheaper than to make war, or, as Senator Robert Wright of Maryland expressed it, it was more ethical to buy than to steal. Senator Sam Mitchell of New York went to the heart of the matter when he remarked, "We have had & still seem to have a land mania. . . . [We now want] all the Globe."[18] Certainly the legislators were wise enough to see that the country could not go to war. They seem to have considered an aggressive war an impossibility, but they were toying with an issue which burnt their fingers six years later. Rounding out the natural boundaries of the country to the southeast at the expense of Spain by annexing the Floridas seemed feasible to many of them. Absurd talk of Canada and the St. Lawrence could not distract those who wanted the Floridas from their serious purpose; now was the most appropriate time to ensure the nation's territorial integrity in the South by acquiring the desired land "by purchase or otherwise."

The matter that most concerned the Ohio senators was whether Mobile Bay could be secured, for, as John Smith pointed out somewhat exaggeratedly, its navigation was "as important as that of the Mississippi."[19] To the senators, Jefferson's plan appeared to be wise whether he secured all the Floridas or just the piece extending to the Perdido. The resurgent discontent of the West which lured Burr to his ruin and rumors of Burr's plans motivated Worthington when he insisted that if purchase was attempted, then surely it was West Florida which must have priority. Plumer jotted down Worthington's observations in his journal as follows:

> My mind is much divided on the subject of this bill—I think I shall vote in its favor.—I believe the President will make a good use of it—The purchase . . . is beneficial to each & every State—The idea of a separation—of a division of the Union is painful—I think of it with horror.—The eastern frontier of the U.S. is strong the South & West is feeble—We want to purchase the Florida's —to remove our bad neighbors further from us—
> I do not feel much confidence that this appropriation will answer the purpose but I am for trying it.
> I see no reason for purchasing in the East [but] The purchase in the west of the Florida's are of as much importance to the eastern States, more so to their commerce, than to the southern & western States.[20]

---

[18] Adams, *Memoirs*, I, 387-92; Plumer, 385, 401.
[19] Plumer, 411.
[20] *Ibid.*, 396-97.

To the objection of Senators Uriah Tracy and Samuel Smith that the money was not available and that the appropriation would necessitate a loan, Worthington impatiently replied, "The Floridas are important & we must obtain them. We shall have money enough—if not we can borrow."[21] In fact, most of the counterproposals and the debate about Canada and the St. Lawrence were largely party politics; the Federalists wished to defeat Jefferson's purpose or else make him openly admit that he intended to use the appropriation as a lever to force Spain's hand. There were, of course, many Congressmen who did not fully grasp the significance of the obstructive tactics; John Quincy Adams characterized the discussion as "one of the most curious debates I ever heard in [the] senate."[22]

On February 7, the bill passed the Senate, 17 to 11, and Jefferson signed it on February 13. The President was thereby authorized to continue his experiments in expansion, an assignment of broad opportunity and great responsibility.[23]

5

Worthington approved of the Jeffersonian foreign policy of conciliation and concession. He recognized that his party chief was bound to maintain peace at almost any cost. He wrote Samuel Huntington, March 4, 1806, that he felt confident Canada would someday be acquired but that to try and get it now at the price of war would be unwise at best, for the country needed peace, and especially peace with England, our most important foreign market.[24] Nevertheless, he believed that if war came, it would be with England and not with France or Spain. "It is against England we have the most serious causes of complaint, and will find the most difficulty to maintain our rights and secure peace," he wrote to one of his constituents on January 17.[25] He was willing to knuckle down to the French with Jefferson in interdicting trade with revolutionary Santo Domingo, for the interdiction was only an empty gesture; it would not actually stop American trade with the island, but it might "inhibit a disgraceful commerce [in slaves]," and it would keep the peace with one of Europe's chief belligerents.[26]

[21] *Ibid.*, 412.
[22] Adams, *Memoirs*, I, 392.
[23] *Senate Executive Journal*, II, 41-42; Plumer, 425, 456, 546, 641.
[24] Letter in the Huntington Papers, WRHS.
[25] Worthington to "A respectable gentleman," in the *Scioto Gazette*, February 6, 1806.
[26] *Annals*, 9th Cong., 1st Sess., 114, 117, 138; Plumer, 379, 387, 435.

In the neutral rights debate of February upon resolutions instructing President Jefferson what policies to adopt toward England, Worthington took an active part. The long series of impressments, confiscations, and interferences with our trade had at last driven the Administration to a position where some effective action short of war was imperative. Unwilling to seek coöperation in the return of her fugitive seamen, too stubborn to arbitrate concerning impressments, and too busy even to negotiate concerning neutral rights, Britain arbitrarily stopped our ships, even near the American coast, and refused to adjudicate our grievances. Since Jay's Treaty had avoided final settlement of these issues and even the commercial clauses of the semi-settlement had lapsed, the United States had no legal position to uphold regarding trade, and England refused to negotiate. Yet dignity, honor, and national pride demanded some action. The Administration, through Andrew Gregg of Pennsylvania, proposed in the House that all importations from Britain be suspended until she agreed to a settlement. This resolution was debated and watered down before passage so as to affect only products which could be secured elsewhere; even then it was not to go into effect until November 15. During the debate, one resolution which was submitted involved the policy which the Senate should ask the President to pursue, the amount of pressure he should bring to bear, and the severity of tone he should employ in urging England to restore the seized property and in forcing her to a negotiated settlement. The resolution recommended that he "demand and insist upon the restoration of the property . . . captured and condemned . . . and upon the indemnification . . . for those captures and condemnations."

Worthington objected to the resolution in that form. He believed that determinations and recommendations of the Senate had great weight and that they should not be made binding upon the President without due consideration. "We are equally responsible with him in our executive capacity," he said, pointing out that the Senate must ratify all the President's engagements with foreign nations. To ask him to "demand and insist" and to make a treaty all in the same breath was rank inconsistency: "The resolution seems to be at war with itself. It is not . . . the bold ground taken . . . to which I object. It is because I fear the resolution . . . will embarrass the Executive in negotiating a treaty to settle our differences. . . . We have no commercial treaty with Great Britain. If, sir, this subject is intended to be embraced . . . let us be more explicit." He argued that a treaty was desperately needed; that without one, the results would be "continual jarrings and probably

ultimate war, with all its concomitant evils." He reminded his colleagues that the President was at the time attempting negotiations on
the matters included in the resolution, and urged a revision of its
present form in order that the Chief Executive's efforts might not be
handicapped by the "demand and insist" clause.[27]

The Federalists fought hard against this proposal, for their purpose
was to maneuver the President into the position that any agreement
negotiated must not interfere with trade; if it did, he must be made
to take the blame. The Administration, on the other hand, sought to
put the responsibility for the arrangement on the Senate. The motion
to strike out the word "insist" prevailed by a single vote, and the
resolution was then passed, 23 to 7. In an effort to make the vote
unanimous, Worthington's colleague John Smith spoke like a true
forerunner of the War Hawks of 1811. In flamboyant terms he declared:
"I deprecate the flames and ravages of war . . . I wish it avoided on
honorable terms; for rather than see the honor and rights of my
country violated, I would wade through rivers of blood and fight until
doomsday in their defence."[28]

Two months later, Worthington voted with the large Republican
majority to adopt the negotiating embargo on various English articles;
Randolph called it a "milk and water bill, a dose of chicken broth,"
because it applied to inconsequential articles and was not to become
effective for nine months. The Senate vote was 19 to 9; Jefferson signed
the bill on April 18.[29]

6

Worthington's most important contribution as a senator was his
sponsorship of a scheme of internal improvements which had been
advocated for two decades, in particular a project for a thoroughfare
to the West. Ultimately, his efforts resulted in the construction of the
Cumberland Road. Washington had seen the necessity for establishing
and maintaining national unity by a system of transportation and
communication facilities, particularly with the West, and so had Franklin. The Spanish Conspiracy in Kentucky, the Whiskey Rebellion
in Pennsylvania, Blount's Conspiracy in Tennessee, and Burr's intrigues
were manifestations of the separative spirit of the western people,
who regarded economic welfare rather than political unity as of

[27] *Annals*, 9th Cong., 1st Sess., 104-106, February 14, 1806.
[28] *Ibid.*, 109-12; Plumer, 433.
[29] *Annals*, 9th Cong., 1st Sess., 851, 240, 1259.

paramount importance. The threatened closure of the Mississippi had been the focal point of western economic interest until 1804. But even before that issue had been settled, there had been an insistent demand that rivers be made navigable and post roads be established. The project of a great artery of commerce from the seaboard to the Ohio over which stock might be driven and wagon caravans pass was the next necessary step. If harbor and lighthouse bills were constitutional, then surely so were bills for improvements of inland commerce.

At the time when Worthington, Albert Gallatin, and Senator William B. Giles were drafting the Enabling Act for Ohio, they decided to incorporate in it a provision for the construction of such a road. The provision specified that one-tenth of the proceeds from the sale of public lands in Ohio should be appropriated for the construction of a national road, but Congress amended it to read one-twentieth, that is, 5 per cent. On petition of the Ohio Constitutional Convention, a provision was inserted in the act of Congress (March 3, 1803) supplementary to the Enabling Act, which provided that 3 per cent of the proceeds from land sales in Ohio should be used for building roads within the new state.[30]

Until November, 1803, nothing was done to realize the objective of the plan. At that time, however, a resolution championed by Congressman John G. Jackson of Virginia and Jeremiah Morrow, sole representative from Ohio in the House, was introduced to secure an appropriation for laying out the proposed road to Ohio. They held that the 3 per cent provided in the act supplementary to the Enabling Act was in addition to the 5 per cent initially provided for, and that 8 per cent was therefore to be appropriated for the road. The House refused to accept this interpretation, and the committee to which the resolution was referred received instructions to bring in a bill providing for the allocation of 2 per cent of the sales money for the road to Ohio. On January 10, 1804, Jackson brought in the 2–per cent bill, which was passed in the House on February 15. Senators Smith and Worthington were on the committees which considered this bill and were successful in getting it passed in amended form in the Senate on March 27. It provided for the appointment of commissioners to explore the route to be followed to the Ohio River. The House considered the amended bill on the last day of the session, when action on it was postponed until the next fall.[31]

---

30 Letter, February 13, 1802, in Henry Adams, ed., *The Writings of Albert Gallatin* (3 vols., Philadelphia, 1879), I, 76-79.
31 *Annals*, 8th Cong., 1st Sess., 254, 263, 273, 298, 305, 631-36, 876, 943, 986, 1012, 1242.

The second session of the Eighth Congress was called for November 5, 1804, but on that day only fourteen senators, including Worthington, were present. (The horse races, which were in full swing, accounted for most of the absentees.) Consequently, Vice-President Burr adjourned the rump Senate. Although a quorum was present on the seventh, little was done until the sixteenth, when, as John Quincy Adams put it, "the races at length are finished, and the Senate really met."[32]

On November 28, Worthington gave notice that in pursuance of the Enabling Act he would ask leave to present a bill making provision for the application of moneys appropriated for the Cumberland Road, but instead, on the thirtieth, he moved that a committee be appointed to consider the Act and draw a bill conformable to it. This motion was adopted December 3, and a committee was appointed with Worthington as chairman. He introduced a new bill, December 28, calling for the appropriation of the one-twentieth part of the proceeds of land sold in Ohio for laying out the road to that state, but the figure was amended, despite his opposition, to read the "remaining 2 per cent."

Worthington wrote his Ohio constituents that Congress had agreed that only 2 per cent should be used in laying out roads to Ohio, but that such a decision was contrary to his opinion as formed at the time of the "compact," that is, the Enabling Act and the supplementary law. His words are significant: "I intended and understood that the three per cent asked by the convention should be in addition to the five per cent before offered by congress." He argued that Ohio should demand a fulfillment of this compact so that the road could be adequately financed. "Our eastern brethren," he wrote, "do not seem to be sufficiently impressed with its importance."[33] John Quincy Adams noted in his diary that "Worthington with his supporters gravely maintained that the modification meant an additional three percent and that congress were already bound to appropriate eight percent to the roads.... It was the merest accident in the world that this stratagem did not succeed." Adams considered the bill "no better than fraud upon the union."[34] The bill was amended January 23 and submitted to a somewhat different committee headed by Worthington. On February 20, further consideration of it was postponed.[35] There the matter rested until December, 1805, when the bill was resurrected and referred to a committee of which Worthington was a member and Tracy of Con-

[32] Adams, *Memoirs*, I, 315.
[33] Letter in the *Liberty Hall and Cincinnati Mercury*, December 16, 1805.
[34] Adams, *Memoirs*, I, 334-36.
[35] *Annals*, 8th Cong., 2nd Sess., 18, 28, 41, 43, 63.

necticut the chairman. On December 19, Tracy announced that $12,652 had accrued for the project as of September 30, 1805, and estimated that it would amount to $20,000 by the time it was needed. In a long and able report he explained why the Cumberland-Wheeling route had been recommended and of what great value the road would be to the nation. The bill he introduced was passed on December 27. The concluding paragraph of Tracy's report merits quotation:

> Politicians have generally agreed that rivers unite the interests and promote the friendship of those who inhabit their banks; while mountains, on the contrary, tend to the disunion and estrangement of those who are separated by their intervention. In the present case, to make the crooked ways straight, and the rough ways smooth, will, in effect, remove the intervening mountains, and by facilitating the intercourse of our Western brethren with those on the Atlantic, substantially unite them in interest, which, the committee believe, is the most effectual cement of union applicable to the human race.[36]

The bill provided for a road four rods wide to be built between the upper Potomac and Ohio rivers, striking the Ohio somewhere between Steubenville and Wheeling, the exact spot to be determined by the committee appointed to draw plans and make a survey.[37] The House passed the bill, appropriating $30,000, on March 24 by a vote of 66 to 50. President Jefferson signed it on March 29. It was not satisfactory to Worthington, Morrow, or Jackson, but Worthington and Morrow were willing to take half a loaf; Jackson was not. The commissioners made their survey during the summer of 1806 and recommended a route from Cumberland to Brownsville on the Monongahela —in general following Braddock's Road—and by a direct line westward to the vicinity of Wheeling.

In February, 1807, Jefferson submitted the report of the commissioners to the Senate, where it was referred to a committee composed of Worthington, Tracy, and Giles. On February 24, Worthington brought a bill from the committee, appropriating $25,000 to start the project, which was adopted February 26. When the bill reached the House, local jealousies arose regarding the proposed route, and on March 3 the bill was indefinitely postponed;[38] however, at least the preparatory steps had been taken in providing for this great avenue of inland commerce and travel.

Meanwhile, the whole subject of internal improvements had come to the front, and Worthington had emerged as their chief spokesman. On February 25, he introduced a motion instructing Secretary of the

---

[36] Ibid., 9th Cong., 1st Sess., 22-25, 26, 42, 43; American State Papers, Miscellaneous, I, 432, 434.
[37] Annals, 9th Cong., 1st Sess., 1236-38.
[38] Ibid., 2nd Sess., 51, 54, 78, 90, 625.

Treasury Gallatin to report on the "usefulness and practicability and probable expense" of the projected Chesapeake and Delaware Canal and on the possibility of an inland waterway between the Southern and Northern states.[39] Various canalization projects, all private undertakings, were under way on the seaboard at the time; Worthington would have nationalized all new ones for the country's benefit. The next day he moved that Gallatin be instructed to study and report on the practicability of a national turnpike to extend north and south from Washington. Two days later he withdrew both these motions and submitted a new one which made it the duty of the Secretary to report on all projected roads or canals and to investigate the expediency of establishing a system of canalization and road-making for the whole nation. This motion, important because it resulted in Gallatin's able report on internal improvements in April, 1808, was adopted March 2.[40]

7

Perhaps the most dramatic scenes of Worthington's first term in the Senate were the impeachments of Judges John Pickering and Samuel Chase. In this instance, it may be said, Worthington is justly subject to criticism for following the lead of demagogic Republicans like Randolph and Giles in their attempt to bring the judiciary completely under the control of the legislative branch. Yet the doctrine of judicial review and the independence of the judiciary were not well established at the time. John Marshall, it is true, had rendered his Marbury decision, but its philosophy had not been accepted. Moreover, one of the causes for the dispute with King George in 1775 had been the British government's attempt to maintain judges in the royal colonies, contrary to the wishes of the colonial legislatures. In the more democratic corporate colonies the judges had been directly controlled by the legislature.

Since impeachment was the only constitutional way to remove the senile and bibulous Pickering, impeachment it had to be; and Worthington voted for it with his party and his friends on March 12, 1804. A century afterward, the eminent historian, John Bach McMaster, wrote concerning the trial that "no act so arbitrary, so illegal, so infamous had yet been done by the Senate of the United States. Without

---

[39] *Ibid.*, 86, 95.
[40] *Ibid.*, 95, 97. Henry Adams refers to Worthington as "one of Gallatin's closest friends" and gives him credit for Gallatin's report. *The Life of Albert Gallatin* (Philadelphia, 1880), 350.

a hearing, without counsel, an insane man had been tried and, on *Exparte* evidence had been found guilty and punished." McMaster was not entirely fair in his denunciation of the judgment in this case since he did not take into consideration the fact that short of impeachment there was no way of removing incompetent or incapacitated judges when they did not retain sufficient intelligence even to resign. Yet, he is entirely right concerning the unfair and heartless procedure used.

The impeachment of Judge Chase was a clear case of persecution because of political differences. Jefferson himself asked for the impeachment because in harangues from the bench—no uncommon practice—Chase had dared attack the sacred principles of democracy and the political theories of the Administration. Instead of impeaching him for his actual attack on the party in power, John Randolph had eight vague charges drawn up against him. He failed, however, to convince the necessary majority of the senators that Chase was guilty of high crimes and misdemeanors on any one of the charges. The trial was a conflict between the politicians and the lawyers, and between the legislative and executive branches and the judiciary. The lawyers and the judges won. Randolph's oratory, far below his usual standard, was in this case feeble and unconvincing. Chief Justice Marshall and his colleagues gave their advice and counsel to the lawyers of the defense. Marshall doubtless gained more from the outcome of the case than any other man, for, had the impeachment of Chase proved successful, he would probably have been the next victim.

As it was, Vice-President Burr and the Senate put on a real display for the audience at the trial. Boxes and chairs in the courtroom were draped in green; the seats of the senator-judges, arranged in a semicircle, were decorated with crimson as befitted the judicial function of their occupants, and the seats of the managers and counselors were covered in blue. After a month of debate and oratory, the senatorial judges voted, each senator voting viva voce once on each charge. Four times did Thomas Worthington rise to his feet and enunciate the word "Guilty," and four times "Not guilty," to the repeated question from Burr, "Mr. Worthington, how say you, is the respondent, Samuel Chase, guilty or not guilty of the high crime or misdemeanor, as charged?" After two hours of this procedure, the figures were totaled, and on March 1 Burr announced Chase's acquittal on every charge.[41]

---

[41] *Annals*, 8th Cong., 1st Sess., 318-67; 2nd Sess., 98-100, 664, 675; Plumer, 230, 272, 311-14; Adams, *Memoirs*, I, 283, 309, 318, 322, 324, 345, 350, 352, 354-64.

Randolph was highly mortified at the outcome of the trial; in the House that afternoon he delivered "a violent philippic against Judge Chase & against the Senate." He proposed an amendment to the Constitution providing that the President might remove any judge from office on the recommendation of a plain majority of each house. Joseph Nicholson of Maryland, another manager of the trial, then moved a second amendment (which Randolph endorsed), namely, that state legislatures be entitled to recall their senatorial representatives at any time. Whereupon, to infuriate the more these frenzied, overheated, and disgusted Republicans, Elliott of Vermont rose, tongue in cheek, to propose for consideration the desirability of referring to the people the revocation of "the Constitution in toto."[42]

The excellent impression that Aaron Burr made as president of the Senate, especially on unusual occasions such as the two trials just mentioned, raised him greatly even in the opinion of those who had hated him for killing Hamilton. On February 28, the Senate had voted him the franking privilege for life, the alignment being, according to Plumer, on the basis of the justifiability of Burr's action. Senator Wright maintained that he deserved the privilege for that one righteous deed alone. Seth Hastings claimed that Burr would have been renominated for vice-president if only he had killed Hamilton six months earlier.[43] A year and a half later the Burr conspiracy that was to ruin the careers of many prominent persons, including that of John Smith, senator from Ohio, was exposed.

However near to Worthington geographically suspicions of treachery came, not one breath of treason touched him.[44] He wrote Massie that Jefferson had confided to him what he conceived Burr's plans to be, and enclosed an outline of them for publication in the Ohio papers. Worthington enjoined all true citizens to use every means to apprehend the authors and executors of the plan, for "one of the greatest curses which could fall upon us would be a separation of these states." He could scarcely believe that Burr had blundered so fearfully. He could not understand how such a patriot and statesman "should form the wild and desperate plan of overturning this government . . . and involv[ing]

---

[42] Plumer, 311; *Annals*, 8th Cong., 2nd Sess., 1213-14.
[43] *Ibid.*, 74-75, 185, 302-307; Hastings to Paul Fearing, December 12, 1804, in the Fearing Papers.
[44] Worthington was not even on the list of suspects compiled by Joseph H. Daveiss, which did include Clay, Breckinridge, John Fowler, and William Henry Harrison. See Daveiss, "A View of the President's Conduct," HPSO, *Quarterly Publications*, XII (1917), 74-75.

it in Bloodshed and ruin." It filled his mind "with horror and astonishment."[45]

8

As senator from Ohio, Worthington was expected, of course, to secure legislation to relieve the economic troubles of his constituents. Purchasers of land were finding it difficult to keep up their payments and meet their taxes. Special legislation was often needed to provide for cases of hardship not covered by general legislation, such as relief for refugees from Canada, cancellation of the onerous contracts of the French at Gallipolis, and the acquisition of school lands for settlers in the Symmes Purchase.

In 1806, in order to make the land laws of the United States uniform, Worthington submitted a resolution in the Senate that a committee be appointed to examine and report alterations in the laws or amendments to them relating to the disposal of public lands. Tracy, Baldwin, and Worthington, as chairman, composed the committee. On December 31, it reported a bill for the uniform survey of all United States lands northwest of the Ohio River which had been laid out by straight lines. The passage of this bill provided for the subdivision of all previous surveys into half- and quarter-sections, and assured the uniformity and accuracy which Ohio's land units have today.[46] In 1807, Worthington pushed through the Senate the Jackson Bill for the relief of purchasers in the Virginia Military District.[47] The northwest boundary of the Virginia Military District was defined by an act introduced and sponsored by him. During the same session he promoted the ratification of several land cessions made by the Indians of Ohio and the Indiana Territory.[48]

As a result, Worthington came to be considered an authority on western lands. His land-office training and his experience in the Senate made him so valuable that Gallatin could write Jefferson, November 25, 1806, "Whatever relates to land cannot be too closely watched. . . . Worthington is the only one in the Senate, since Breckinridge left it, who understands the subject. He has been perfectly faithful in that

---

[45] Letter, January 29, 1807, in Massie, *Massie,* 240.
[46] *Annals,* 8th Cong., 2nd Sess., 28, 30, 32, 39, 41, 1664.
[47] *Ibid.,* 9th Cong., 2nd Sess., 69, 70, 71, 180, 498-99, 1264-65.
[48] *Senate Executive Journal,* II, 4, 9, 15, 25-26; *American State Papers, Indian Affairs,* I, 679, 696; Plumer, 356, 359, 381.

respect, trying only to relieve as much as possible the purchasers generally from being hard pressed for payment."[49]

The erection of the Michigan Territory was another of Worthington's achievements. Immediately after the admission of Ohio, some of the inhabitants of Wayne County who had wished inclusion in the new state and were greatly displeased by the fact that Michigan had been added to the Indiana Territory began to petition Congress through Worthington for separation.[50] Worthington faithfully presented the petitions and on December 14, 1804, introduced a bill for the establishment of the Michigan Territory. The bill passed on the twenty-fourth, and was signed January 11, 1805, much to the satisfaction of the inhabitants of that area.[51]

Worthington was also instrumental in getting school lands for Ohio. By a law passed on March 3, 1803, Congress had given the Ohio legislature the right to choose one thirty-sixth of the Virginia Military District for school lands after the time for the location of Virginia warrants expired, but this law proved a dead letter because the time for making such locations was constantly extended—to 1852, finally. In 1806, the Ohio legislature asked Worthington to petition Congress for school lands in lieu of those in the Virginia Military District. On January 15, 1807, he made the requested petition and secured for Ohio an allocation of public land for school purposes elsewhere in the state.[52]

School lands were likewise secured for the settlers of Connecticut's Western Reserve. They had been promised 50,000 acres from the United States Military District by Congress in 1803, but these had never been set aside.[53] Worthington found Congress disinclined to provide school lands for the Reserve on the grounds that Connecticut herself should be responsible for doing so. Other objections were raised, and he testified that "it required all the exertions which I was capable of making to prevail on the members to agree to make any provision for school lands in the reserve." He was finally successful in getting eighteen quarter-townships and three sections appropriated by the Jackson-Worthington Law of 1807.[54]

---

[49] Adams, *Writings of Gallatin*, I, 323.
[50] Sol Sibley to Worthington, February 3, June 8, July 20, November 6, December 27, 1803, and November 5 and December 4, 1804, in WMOSL.
[51] *Annals*, 8th Cong., 2nd Sess., 16, 20-21, 23-26, 1659.
[52] *Ibid.*, 9th Cong., 2nd Sess., 32, 35, 78; *American State Papers, Lands*, III, 654-56. Tiffin wrote Worthington, January 23, 1807, that speculators were back of the request of this "weak, trifling disorderly" legislature. In WMOSL.
[53] Huntington to J. Kingsbury, March 22, 1803, in the Rice Collection.
[54] Worthington to Elisha Whittlesey, December 9, 1820, in the Whittlesey Papers, WRHS. See also *Annals*, 9th Cong., 2nd Sess., 1265.

In concluding this survey of Worthington's activities during his first term in the Senate, some of his lesser committee appointments and a few of his votes deserve mention. He and Senator Baldwin represented the Senate on the joint committee to draw up necessary Congressional business (March, 1806). He served on a committee of three to consider a bill for the erection of the south wing of the Capitol. He was chairman of the revisionary committee on Clay's bill establishing a circuit court for Ohio. He voted for the Twelfth Amendment to the Constitution, against Wilkinson's appointment as governor of Louisiana, and for the ratification of all Indian treaties. He supported the administration in almost every instance. One exception justifies the belief that he had principles which he would not renounce for anyone: he refused to vote for the ratification of the treaty with the Bashaw of Tripoli until the wife and children of the Bashaw's brother had been returned to him as provided for by Article III of the preliminary treaty.

9

During the years of Worthington's first term in the Senate, he carried on a prodigious amount of private business, particularly for his Ohio friends. Everyone in the state regarded his senators and congressmen as his special agents in matters both public and private. It would appear from Worthington's diary that private affairs took up much more of his time than state affairs; it is filled with entries regarding taxes, patents, subscriptions, correspondence, and trifling duties which he had to fulfill for his constituents.

No survey of his services would be complete without a word regarding the criticisms directed against him and his party associates—statesmen whom Pickering characterized as "a set of men, the greater part of whom have neither the discernment to see wherein lie the real interest, the honor and safety of the country, nor independence and spirit to support them."[55] After John Quincy Adams had worked with Worthington on the Cumberland Road committee, he wrote one of his characteristically uncomplimentary thumbnail sketches of him:

Mr. Worthington is a man of plausible, insinuating address, and of indefatigable activity in the pursuit of his purposes. He has seen something of the

---

[55] Pickering to Rufus King, February 13, 1806, in Charles R. King, ed., *Life and Correspondence of Rufus King* (6 vols., New York, 1894-1900), IV, 492.

world, and, without much education of any other sort, has acquired a sort of polish in his manner, and a kind of worldly wisdom, which may perhaps more properly be called cunning.[56]

It has been pointed out that the Federalists lost most of their influence after 1801. They were replaced in general by comparatively unknown small-town men from the ranks of business and the law who were mediocre but honest, sincere, well-meaning individuals. Republicans of the Jeffersonian persuasion, they deferred to the Administration, and their increasing number, as new states were added, drove the New England gentlemen to despair. The Federalist aristocrats, outnumbered by the Republicans, were constantly on the defensive and were extremely sensitive and irritable; they could not endure what they considered the smirking obsequiousness of their rustic rivals, and came to hate them with the same virulence they felt for Jefferson.

Their positions were constantly jeopardized by the power of the Republicans, as the case of Samuel Allyne Otis illustrates. One of the few remaining Federalists who were still in office, he was in daily fear of losing his post as Secretary of the Senate.[57] He had been in the habit of permitting Senator William Plumer of New Hampshire to take the secret proceedings of the Senate from the office to read and copy as material for a proposed history. Worthington and others criticized the practice. Since Otis was dependent for his position on what he termed "the will of violent men," he insisted that Plumer henceforth do his reading in the office. Although Otis refused to tell him who had complained, Plumer felt sure that it was Baldwin and Worthington. He asked Worthington what his objection was and recorded the answer in his journal:

> *Worthington said every senator had a right to read those records . . . that all he feared was, that possibly incorrect statements might be published from them & the public mind be mislead—That for his own part he really wished, these journals were printed & published—I assured him I should publish no book . . . should take no further minutes—He said he was not dissatisfied with my conduct. But I know the man, his smiles are the smiles of deceit. What course these men contemplated I know not. It may be that they wished to make me desist . . . least I should obtain the knowledge of certain facts which if promulgated would injure them. They will not prevent my reading . . . [though they may plan for] a triumphant majority . . . [to] expell me & give to our democratic Legislature an opportunity of sending a man of different politic's. But I cannot believe, blind and prejudiced as party spirit renders men, that they are prepared for such a course. [These democrats may wish] . . . a pretext to quarrel with Mr. Otis that they may bring in one of*

[56] Adams, *Memoirs*, I, 377.
[57] *Ibid.*, 264.

their tools to be Secretary. Since writing the foregoing, I am informed that Worthington told one of the Secretary's Clerks that he ought to have prohibited me from having access to those journals. *A pretty fellow indeed![58]*

Denunciations of Republicans by Plumer were not confined to Worthington but, like those of Adams, were scattered broadcast. Plumer writes of one of Jefferson's messages, delivered in November, 1804: "It is perhaps, more empty and vapid & wrapt in greater obscurity than any of his previous messages. I know this is saying much, but in this, such is the generality of his expressions & the ambiguity of his style, that they will admit of different enterpretations, & be applicable to events that may hereafter happen as will best suit his crooked policy." Elsewhere in his journal he repeatedly calls Burr a "murderer" because of Hamilton's death at his hands.

The bitter party feeling in Plumer's heart was intensified when the Republicans made fun of the campaign pamphlets which he had issued in New Hampshire and New England under the name *Impartialis*. In an entry dated November 27, 1804, he recounts that one morning, half an hour before the Senate met,

> . . . *General Bradley read aloud to them [a group of democrats], in my hearing, a most insolent abusive attack upon me, as being the writer of Impartialis. Bradley appeared much pleased with the abuse—Worthington looked malignant, & spoke contemptuously—I made no reply.—I will pursue the steady path of duty unmoved by their scurility.—*

Plumer never forgave Worthington, for when he heard the Ohioan was to be succeeded in the Senate by Governor Tiffin, he wrote his final estimate of him (January 16, 1807):

> *Worthington is a cunning designing man—Has more talent than integrity—Tho' his talents are not of the first class—yet he is effective, industrious and intriguing. I always suspect evil from this man—His disposition is malevolent & I rejoice at the decline of his popularity. It is said he will run for the gubanatorial chair at the next Autumn election. He is a native of Virginia—was formerly a deputy sheriff in that State. He is deeply engaged in land speculations—& owns much unimproved land in the western world.[59]*

A contrasting picture is given by Tiffin, who, after being in Washington a little while, wrote Worthington that "I have . . . been extremely pleased to find the high estimation in which you are held by all who knew you, many affectionate inquiries have been made after your health & welfare."[60]

---

[58] Plumer, 201.
[59] *Ibid.,* 203, 209, 576.
[60] Letter, October 26, 1807, in WMOSL.

At the close of his term in the Senate, Thomas Worthington turned with relief from national politics and politicians to the fertile banks of the Scioto, to his family, his farms, and his mills, and to the completion of his new house. He was to find it impossible to avoid Ohio politics or politicians, however, and some of his Ohio critics were to prove even less charitable toward his name and fame than his Federalist critics in Washington had been.

Ohio Politician

By THE time Thomas Worthington returned from Washington in 1807, he was regarded as the outstanding figure in his state. His public services both at home and in the capital had given him a unique opportunity to familiarize himself with the business of government, and he was perhaps the best-informed man in Ohio on national and international politics. He was regarded as the chief personality in the "Chillicothe junto" which was the nucleus of the Republican party in the little Ohio capital.

From the time of his arrival in the Ohio country, he and Edward Tiffin had managed to control territorial and state politics to a great extent. Their names were familiar in every backwoods cabin and village domicile. Tiffin as local doctor, postmaster, lay preacher, president of the Chillicothe village council, speaker of the territorial legislatures, and first governor, had been a very popular figure. Worthington had been county judge, lieutenant colonel of militia, register of the Chillicothe land office, supervisor of internal revenue, territorial legislator, territorial envoy extraordinary, and United States Senator. These two Jeffersonian leaders had had more than their share of political preferment, and enjoyed a primacy in the hearts of the people that was the envy of every ambitious office seeker. When an office was desired, it was necessary to apply to one or the other of them, for in their hands lay that tremendous power called "political pull." When a territorial judgeship was sought, it was they that had the President's ear; when a post office or post road was needed, they had the necessary influence with the postmaster general. Land office jobs in the Old Northwest were not usually filled until the Secretary of the Treasury consulted with Worthington. State offices were at least to some degree dependent on his favor.

Yet by 1807, there were others in Ohio who were becoming skilled in the great American game of politics. The party was the usual avenue to power. As early as 1803, Samuel Carpenter, a loyal Republican of Lancaster, wrote Worthington that the Federalists in Ohio were "clanning together," that is, Federalists appointed Federalists. "These men," he declared, "to a man exert themselves against the Republicans . . . ; a rank Federalist was elected to the assembly in our county." Both

Carpenter and Tiffin wrote Worthington that the Federalists hoped to district the state so as to throw at least a vote or two against Jefferson.[1] Other candidates without party support electioneered for themselves; James Pritchard, former speaker of the senate, in 1807 decided to run for Congress "on his own bottom." Newspapers were being used more than ever for publicity, and an examination of them indicates that everybody was willing to serve the state. Moreover, rotation of office, a sound democratic principle, was being advocated for all it was worth. Certainly, all the intelligent citizens of Ohio—and some not so intelligent—were becoming politics-conscious.

The Chillicothe leaders were popular, but by 1807 their popularity was a two-edged sword. If they had held office—even with credit—so much the more reason that others should now be given a chance. A real necessity for close organization to maintain themselves in power existed among the most popular leaders; a strong political organization was equally essential for those out of office in order that they might get in.

Two groups had formed the first party alignment in Ohio, one favoring statehood and the other opposing it; one group opposed St. Clair, and the other stood by him; one group thought in terms of Jeffersonian democracy, and the other embraced the tenets of the aristocrats. As soon as statehood had been achieved, a new alignment appeared. Practically all Ohio politicians were Republicans, but they were split into two distinct factions. One prided itself on being composed of "pure Republicans" and referred to members of the second group as "Quids," "Feds," "Trimmers," "Aristocrats," or the "High Court Party." The second group was undeniably conservative. By 1807, the two Republican factions were not so unevenly matched as the two earlier groups had been. At the extremes of each party were radicals who brought their respective factions into disrepute and whose wrangling for preferment and power irritated the sensibilities of the party regulars. Governor Tiffin, though a good party man, confessed to Worthington, "When you see what I am compelled to witness you would blush for Ross Counties [sic] representation—but they are kept in countenance by the other counties not exceeding them much."[2]

The disorder in the early legislatures demonstrated beyond the shadow of a doubt that some organization was needed to hold irresponsible partisanship in check. Personal and party rancor also reached a high pitch in Congress. During his term in the Senate, Worthington

---

[1] Carpenter to Worthington, November 7, and Tiffin to Worthington, December 17, 1802, in WMOSL.
[2] Tiffin to Worthington, January 8, 1807, in WMOSL.

had often been tempted to resign his seat and retire to the comparative quiet of business life. The encouragement of true friends like Governor Tiffin kept him in the Senate, but he had refused to enter his name as a candidate to succeed himself and had urged Tiffin to run. When Tiffin returned to Ohio, his immediate embroilment in state politics, where demagogues fought for the daily stipend and for elevation above their fellows, was certainly no improvement on Washington. Two days after he was elected senator on January 1, 1807, Tiffin made the following comment in a letter to Worthington: "The electioneering campaign is over. The intrigues, caucuses, etc. were carried to a length that beggars all description. . . . I have learned on this occasion to know my friends & who I think are friends to this State, which I never before could have the means of knowing—Massie opposed to the last with Dunlap, Shelby & Williams, who I think have nearly disgraced themselves. McArthur & Claypoole were firm."[3] The vote for senator was Tiffin, 25, and Philemon Beecher, 12, 6 votes being scattered.

2

The election in 1807 of a governor to succeed Tiffin brought out all the animosity of the minority Republicans and caused a definite split in the ranks. For months Tiffin had urged Worthington to declare himself a candidate, but he had hesitated. Tiffin had encouraged him to run, as early as March 8, 1806:

> I do think you ought to make up your mind—and explicitly say if you will serve as the next governor—I may be perhaps mistaken if I say you will have no competitor but I am not, I am sure, mistaken when I say you will be elected. . . . I hope you will pardon me if I say I think you are not decisive enough, you can quickly discern how to act with propriety in behalf of the State or the U. States; why then not as quickly determine whether you will serve . . . .
> I know you have many friends who will be grieved at your leaving public life, and will lament the loss exceedingly. but they know not what to think, your declarations are wanted. I could therefore wish that you would make up your mind and let it be known.[4]

Worthington continued to procrastinate, however, and meantime other candidates offered themselves. Lewis Cass, a prominent young Ohio lawyer of twenty-five, wished to support Return Jonathan Meigs if Worthington did not offer to run. When Worthington delayed making a statement, Cass importuned Tiffin to decide what should be done. They agreed that perhaps the assembly's endorsement could wait until

---

[3] Tiffin to Worthington, January 3, 1807, in WMOSL.
[4] Tiffin to Worthington, March 8, 1806, in WMOSL.

Worthington's return from Washington, when he could publicly offer his services. Tiffin assured Worthington that his election was quite probable if he could calmly accept the opprobrium of the envious, as any virtuous public servant must. "Your candidacy," he wrote, "is all important to the State; it is important to the United States."[5]

Meanwhile, a caucus of Republicans outside the junto and Federalists led by Baldwin and Jacob Burnet—Tiffin called the group the "Mongrel Republicans"—met at Chillicothe in January and nominated Nathaniel Massie.[6] This action confirmed the split in the Chillicothe party which had been developing while Worthington was in the Senate. Baldwin was the bitter enemy of Worthington by this time, for Worthington, at Tiffin's suggestion, had recommended to Jefferson Baldwin's removal as federal attorney for Ohio on charges of gross neglect of duty, especially in the Burr affair. As a result, Baldwin had joined with Worthington's old enemy, Elias Langham, Burnet, and other enemies of the junto. Tiffin wrote Worthington just after Baldwin's removal, "He is so abominably vile and his conduct increases his infamy. . . . He is now treating your character in a way that beggars description."[7] The majority of the party, however, wanted Worthington to run and favored Meigs as second choice. The Republicans in the legislature wished to endorse one or the other, but Worthington still refused to commit himself. Tiffin finally wrote him on February 5 that the members of the legislature were "disgusted" with the Massie nomination and that they wanted Worthington and Meigs to get together and decide which of them should run:

> *Washington, Gallia, Athens & Muskingum [counties] will join in favor of Meigs, but if you & he can agree they will cordially support you—We must have war. . . . I am willing to go in front of the battle—for the honor of Ohio & the welfare of this State & the Union—I can not be easy under the awful prospects that lower over us—If you will come forward, first having secured Meigs influence, I shall count on certain victory . . . [but] I will not encounter the dirt and abuse of political war with the opposition without it is for you— as I am fearful a victory would not pay the costs for any other man.*[8]

Despite Tiffin's urging, Worthington refused to take any action. Since he had reason to suspect the friendship and party loyalty of Meigs, who had been critical of his political maneuvering, he let the matter drift. He would serve if elected but would not seek the office.

[5] Tiffin to Worthington, January 25, 1807, and December 8, 1806, in WMOSL.
[6] Tiffin to Worthington, February 3, 1807, in WMOSL. Massie does not seem to have been any more anxious to serve than was Worthington, and was probably nominated against his will. Tiffin to Worthington, February 20, 1804, in WMOSL.
[7] Letter, January 7, 1807, in WMOSL.
[8] Letter, in WMOSL.

Nor would he name a favorite. Meigs was very confident that he could secure any office for which he cared to run, and he believed that both Worthington and Tiffin had nearly exhausted their credit with the voters. He proposed to hold court in the Louisiana Territory, where he was a federal judge, attend one session of the territorial legislature, return to Ohio, resign his judgeship, and campaign for governor. A friend of Tiffin and Worthington, in comparing their merits with those of Meigs, said, "If two Virginians suffer a single Yank to oust them, horseracing must cease & we may hang up the fiddle."[9]

Meanwhile, the adherents of each candidate bombarded the newspapers with articles for their favorite and against the other contestants. The Cincinnati papers carried tickets headed by both Meigs and William Goforth, and the Republican Correspondence Society of the same town held a caucus which nominated Meigs.[10] The independent electors of Hamilton County were urged to support the ticket headed by Massie. The Chillicothe papers were divided in their support of Massie and Worthington, both home-town boys and neither too anxious to serve; each, it appears, was waiting for the other to withdraw before declaring himself a candidate.[11] A Federalist faction in Chillicothe nominated Huntington, and the *Scioto Gazette* struggled to force Worthington down the throats of the voters. At the last moment Worthington threw his influence to Massie and offered himself as one of Ross County's representatives in the legislature. Perhaps the writer in the *Liberty Hall and Cincinnati Mercury* was right when he reminded his readers that since Worthington had expressed a wish to retire from public affairs and attend to his business, "there is no reason to insist on his altering his plan . . . the state abounds with citizens equally capable." He predicted that if the governor's race was run on "fair and honorable grounds" Meigs would get three-fourths of the votes. Actually, Meigs won over Massie by a small majority; the vote was 4,531 to 4,361.

So strong was the feeling of discontent, however, that after the legislature met, a party caucus urged Massie to protest the election on the grounds that Meigs was ineligible because he had not been a resident of the state for the stipulated four years previous to his election; President Jefferson had just recognized him as a resident of Louisiana in appointing him federal judge for the Michigan Territory. As a matter of fact, he and his family had resided in Ohio for eighteen

[9] Quoted in a letter from John Smith to Worthington, June 30, 1806, in WMOSL.
[10] *Liberty Hall and Cincinnati Mercury*, July 7, August 25, September 8, 15, and 21, 1807.
[11] *Ibid.*, September 21, 1807; Creighton to Massie, August 23, 1807, in Massie, *Massie*, 245.

years, and he had been out of the state as federal judge of the Louisiana Territory for only nine months of the preceding three years.[12] Nevertheless, a formal objection was made, and after a spirited conflict in the legislature during which the house supported the protest while the senate opposed it, the election was disallowed. Massie then refused to accept the office, and Thomas Kirker, who as speaker of the senate had filled out Tiffin's term, was continued as acting governor until December, 1808.[13]

3

Worthington, meanwhile, had been overwhelmingly elected to the house, and took a very active part in legislation and politics despite his alleged boredom with public office. After having been elected speaker pro tem, he was denied the regular speakership, which was given to Philemon Beecher, the "rank Federalist" from Fairfield County who had been defeated by Tiffin in January in the selection of a senator to succeed Worthington.[14] This humiliation did not deter Worthington from constructive work or keep him from accepting the adjutant generalship when it was proffered him shortly afterward by Governor Kirker. He was successful in getting bills passed for arming the 2,443 state militiamen,[15] for establishing a state bank,[16] and for incorporating the Chillicothe Academy.[17] In this same session, a bill was passed establishing Worthington Academy (February 10, 1808).[18]

The most interesting business of the session concerned the jurisdiction of justices of the peace. To explain the factors involved, it is necessary to review the judicial history of Ohio prior to 1808. In accordance with the Ordinance of 1787, the statutes for the government of the Northwest Territory were to be copied from enactments in other states. To provide a means of legal process in any case which might arise before the necessary statutes had been enacted in the Territory, the English common law was made applicable by a territorial act of 1795. After Ohio had become a state, this act was reaffirmed by the

---

[12] Worthington to Massie, December 12, 1807, in Massie, *Massie*, 248; *Independent Republican* (Chillicothe), December 13, 1810. There is an excellent statement of Meigs's eligibility in his letter to Brown, July 14, 1807, in the Meigs Papers, OSL.

[13] *House Journal, 6th General Assembly*, 16-17, 21-22, 27, 31-32, 46-56.

[14] *Ibid.*, 4, 11.

[15] *Ibid.*, 12, 34-36, 127-29, 174.

[16] *Ibid.*, 40, 95, 110, 118, 121, 125, 132, 134, 143.

[17] *Ibid.*, 60, 68, 86, 126, 174.

[18] *Senate Journal, 6th General Assembly*, 181.

legislature on February 14, 1805.[19] During the session of 1804-1805, however, under the able leadership of William Creighton of Chillicothe, the criminal code was revised. This revision and the additions to the code made during the session of 1805-1806 were deemed sufficient to justify the repeal of the common law in January, 1806. The Republicans favored the step; the only opposition to it came from the true-blue Federalist irreconcilables, who feared, in the words of Zenos Kimberly of Jefferson County, that it was but another "disorganizing Jacobinical procedure" which would ruin the country. Kimberly must have had the Reign of Terror in mind when he continued, "I am almost glad" that I have "neither wife nor child to increase my anxiety."[20]

In spite of such objections, the great system of jurisprudence to which Jeffersonians had appealed for protection in 1776 against the tyrant George III was abolished, and Ohio Republicans adopted a judicial philosophy and procedure based entirely on specific enactment.[21] The attitude of this same assembly not only demonstrated the desire to escape what Supreme Court Justice Samuel Huntington called the last "disgraceful badge of remaining servitude" to England and English law, but also showed a decisive trend toward legislative supremacy. Common Pleas Judge William Irwin, although ably and eloquently defended by Jessup Couch, was removed from office for neglect of duty; and Judge Calvin Pease declined to be elevated from the circuit to the state supreme court because of the threatened insecurity of a tenure dependent on legislative favor. The removal of Middle Circuit Judge Robert F. Slaughter of Fairfield County the following year for negligence, misfeasance, and nonconformity with legislative enactment, however, made tenure of judicial office just as precarious in that echelon of administration.[22]

The developments of the year 1807 were no less discouraging for the judges. A law passed in 1804 had raised the jurisdiction of justices of the peace in suits at common law to cases involving not more than fifty dollars. This action was in direct contravention of the Seventh Amendment to the United States Constitution, which set the limit at twenty dollars. Judge Pease declared the law unconstitutional in 1806; his decision was reviewed by a committee of the legislature that winter

---

[19] Chase, *Statutes,* I, 190, 512.
[20] Quoted in Milo M. Quaife, "Editorial Comment," *Mississippi Valley Historical Review,* XII (1925-26), 627.
[21] William T. Utter, "Ohio and the English Common Law," *ibid.,* XVI (1929-30), 321-33.
[22] William T. Utter, "Judicial Review in Early Ohio," *ibid.,* XIV (1927-28), 3-24.

and denounced as erroneous. The house could not quite muster a majority for impeachment, however, so no action was taken against him at the time. In August, 1807, a case involving the same law was brought on appeal to the supreme court, and Judges Huntington and Tod declared the law invalid.[23] Since this decision aggravated the difficulty of collecting sums over twenty dollars, when the legislature met in December Governor Kirker directed particular attention to the situation and requested legislative action on the controversy. It would seem that a decision should have been forthcoming immediately since the supreme court judgment had been aired in the papers, but there was no unanimity in evidence.[24] Worthington was put in charge of a committee to report a resolution defining the power of the state's judges to declare null and void acts passed by the legislature. His committee reported as follows on December 25:

> The committee . . . have deemed it their duty . . . to make . . . an enquiry how far the judges of this state, under the provisions of the constitution, have the power to declare acts of the legislature unconstitutional, or null and void; should the house determine the judges have this power, the committee are of the opinion that any further enquiry on that subject, on their part will be unnecessary; they, therefore, respectfully report in part the following resolution for the consideration of the house; the committee forbear to use reasoning in favor of the resolution, in as much as the House will have before them all the information which the committee have had, and will doubtless give the subject, (which the committee believe very important) all the consideration it deserves.
>
> Resolved, That the judges of this state are not authorised by the constitution to set aside any act of the legislature, by declaring the law unconstitutional or null and void.[25]

During the debate on this resolution the senate attempted to force a counterresolution through the house declaring that the courts had the power to declare laws unconstitutional, but it was defeated by the close vote of 14 to 16. The original resolution was then adopted by the house, 18 to 12, only to be rejected in the senate. No clear-cut settlement of the problem of judicial interpretation of legislation was reached.[26]

Thus the legislature's desire to control the judiciary—the same desire that had motivated Congressional Republicans in the repeal of the Judiciary Act and the impeachments of Pickering and Chase—was made manifest in frontier Ohio. John Marshall's dictum in the Marbury case had little weight with Jeffersonian legislators. The lawyers and judges,

[23] Ibid., 8-12; Liberty Hall (Cincinnati), November 3, 10, 1807.
[24] House Journal, 6th General Assembly, 23; Liberty Hall, January 11, 1808.
[25] House Journal, 6th General Assembly, 23, 43.
[26] Ibid., 61.

however, were not asleep and were soon to bring the problem before the people and make an issue of it.

The radical Republicans in this same session were ready to proceed against the "usurpation" of Judges Huntington, Tod, and Pease by the usual process, but division of opinion among other legislators nullified their efforts. The growth of sentiment in favor of the doctrine of judicial review, so well set forth by Marshall in *Marbury* vs. *Madison*, confounded the judges' persecutors; if it were accepted, they had no ground on which to stand. It was probably because of this division of sentiment that convictions were despaired of and the removal proceedings dropped. In any event, Worthington finally threw his influence against the attempt to impeach the judges, and action was temporarily suspended.[27] The next year the charges against the same three judges were resurrected. The first two were acquitted by a margin of one vote in each case, and the charges against Huntington, then governor, were ignored.[28] The Republican majority, lacking the strength to marshal the necessary two-thirds vote for conviction, demonstrated its anger by raising the fifty-dollar law limit to seventy.[29] Thus the doctrine of judicial review triumphed in Ohio, or, more properly, was tentatively accepted with reservations.

4

In 1808, Worthington was induced against his better judgment to make a bid for the governorship in the election to choose a successor to Acting Governor Kirker. The campaign resolved itself into a three-way fight between Worthington, Huntington, and the incumbent Kirker—all Republicans but of different political shades. Worthington was backed by the radicals, who approved his stand against the "High Court Party," as the judges' supporters were called, but their backing lost him the support of many moderates.[30] Even old-time friends like Massie and Creighton, though the latter had always been a conservative, deserted him and supported Huntington, largely because of this issue. Kirker split the radical faction by entering his candidacy after

[27] *Ibid.*, 190.
[28] *Ibid.*, 7th *General Assembly*, 292.
[29] Chase, *Statutes*, I, 607.
[30] The Hamilton County Republican caucus nominated Kirker, but a secession group named Huntington. *Liberty Hall*, September 15 and 24, 1808. Benjamin Tappan wrote Worthington, September 15: "You have indeed made yourself extremely obnoxious to our judges by attempting to set bounds to their ambitions." He reported that a Federalist caucus in Trumbull County led by Judge Pease had named Huntington. Letter in WMOSL.

having supposedly agreed not to run if Worthington did. Worthington claimed that he would not have allowed his name to be submitted if he had known that Kirker was going to be a candidate.[31] Worthington's friends sought to aid him by circulating a report that Huntington was going to run for John Smith's seat in the United States Senate and was therefore not a candidate for governor, but this scheme seems to have failed miserably. Worthington, who naturally had no objections to electing Huntington to the Senate, took the report seriously. He wrote Huntington on July 29 that he understood he was not a candidate for the governorship but would run for the Senate, and asked him to announce his intentions publicly. He offered to support Huntington's senatorial candidacy, but added, ". . . If you prefer being a candidate for the office of governor be assured it shall in no wise interrupt our friendly relations. . . . I never have felt a desire to serve as the governor of the state, yet I am well aware this assertion with very many will not be credited. . . . I never would have suffered my name to be mentioned if I could have avoided it consistently with the duty I believe I owe my country."[32]

Huntington, who suspected a trap, refused to declare himself but let matters take their course; after all, the new legislature would not elect a senator until weeks after the governor's race was over. Who could foretell what Worthington and his friends would do then? Bezaleel Wells of Steubenville wrote Huntington that he had inside information that Worthington and Tiffin had conspired to get him out of the race by securing a federal judgeship for him or by inducing him to agree to run for the Senate rather than for the governorship. "You were to have been snugly laid up in drydock in order to prevent you from disturbing other family arrangements."[33]

It was a common trick in those days to get the papers supporting a candidate "to report," and all his friends to write, "Isn't it unfortunate that Jones [the opponent] has withdrawn?" or "Jones has refused at the last moment to run," with the result that many of his supporters voted for someone else rather than waste their ballots. Consequently, Huntington was understandably reluctant to trust a proffer of aid from any member of the Chillicothe junto, and he and his friends could at best only deny the rumor of his withdrawal.[34] Nevertheless, Worthington's efforts to clarify Huntington's candidacy were probably sincere, and

[31] T. Gibson to Worthington, September 1 (a memorandum of the agreement); Tiffin to Worthington, December 2, 1808, in WMOSL.
[32] Letter in the Huntington Papers, WRHS.
[33] Letter, July 20, 1808, in the Rice Collection.
[34] Huntington to J. Burnet, October 30, 1808, *ibid.*

Huntington's publication of Worthington's letters, especially those in which he deferred to his northern rival, was an unfair reply to a magnanimous gesture.

Worthington ran best in eastern Ohio, Huntington got the Federalist vote, and the three candidates split the Republican vote in the south.[35] Huntington received a plurality rather than a majority; thus Kirker's candidacy probably gave him the election. The vote was Huntington 7,293, Worthington 5,601, and Kirker 3,397.[36]

It appears that vituperation, deceit, and intrigue played a major part in the success of this campaign, as in most campaigns before 1815. Each candidate was picked by a partisan caucus, and his organization was so loose-knit that he scarcely knew who his loyal supporters were. Communications were poor, and candidates had to depend on local organizations and a personal following. The judicial contest had concentrated the conservative strength back of Judge Huntington and given warning to the radicals that the average citizen could not be driven too far. It was to take another campaign, however, to drive this lesson home. Worthington had tried unsuccessfully to steer a course between the extreme radical wing of his party and the regulars. His own hesitation, equivocation, and failure to electioneer and the shrewd manipulating and able electioneering done by Huntington's supporters had defeated him.

When the legislature met in December, Worthington did not show much interest in, or seriously oppose, the appointment of Meigs to the United States Senate to fill out the term of John Smith, who had resigned as the result of his implication in Burr's conspiracy. Nor did he try to prevent Meigs's election for the full six-year term. His pride had been hurt, and that subtle streak of arrogance which he always tried so hard to conceal had been aroused by his rejection at the hands of the electorate. He always espoused the principle—not that he always acted on it—that the office should seek the man. Alternately ambitious and indifferent, too often indecisive and noncommittal, this thirty-five-year-old Ohioan—now sometimes called "Old Sorrell"—was not quite capable of developing the egoistic confidence and the electioneering techniques which were becoming more and more necessary for popular success. Furthermore, he was inclined to be a little smug and supercilious at times and was too often disdainful of his critics. Sensitive to a fault, he never developed the callousness to criticism

[35] Tiffin to Worthington, December 2, 1808; J. Sloane to Worthington, April 11, August 6 and 20, October 3, November 13, December 11, 1808; Ephraim Quimby to Worthington, December 24, 1808, in WMOSL.
[36] Taylor, *Ohio Statesmen*, 56.

with which every real politician must insulate himself while he works for the public good. Moreover, he was too prosperous to avoid the jealousy of the rabble, too radical to please the conservatives, and too conservative to please the radicals. Yet his ability and influence could not be disregarded in any campaign.

5

Worthington spent the next two years in assiduous application to his business. The 1808 election had been such a disappointment that he refused to run again, even for the legislature. Home and business soon restored his spirits, however, and he kept in close touch with state affairs. His attitude toward the attempt to impeach Huntington, Tod, and Pease in 1809 was sympathetic, and it was no surprise that Huntington failed to appoint him to the Senate to succeed Tiffin, who had resigned. Tiffin had written Huntington requesting Worthington's appointment: "I believe no person in this state would be better received in the Senate of the U. States, or from the acquaintance & respectability of character which he acquired when there before, be more serviceable to the state."[37] Instead, Huntington selected for the interim appointment an able young lawyer from his own part of the state, Stanley Griswold of Cuyahoga County.[38]

It is interesting that Tiffin, too, had soon sickened of inactivity and party bickering in Washington and yearned for home. He proposed to resign in order to get back to what he called "the post of honor—private life." He chose to ascend, as he put it, from "servant to sovereign."[39] Moreover, his wife, Worthington's sister Mary, had died on July 1, 1808, and he was extremely lonesome in Washington.

Worthington took a six weeks' business trip East in the fall of 1809, during which he called on Gallatin, President Madison, and friends in Virginia. While in Washington, he took occasion to record this comment in his diary on September 30: "Many alterations in the President's house. Mr. Jefferson's stile was neat, economical and simple. Mr. Madison's more costly in furniture, etc. but I augur no good from it." Perhaps he was overcritical of the new President's ménage, since he and Nathaniel Macon had favored Albert Gallatin for the Presidency; if the ticket had to be Madison and Clinton, then Clinton should have been President and Madison Vice-President.

Home again by October 14, Worthington confined his activities to

[37] Letter, March 27, 1809, in the Huntington Papers, OSL.
[38] Taylor, *Ohio Statesmen*, 59.
[39] Tiffin to Worthington, December 2, 1808, in WMOSL.

business. On December 11, he wrote as follows in his diary: "Rode to town with Mrs. Worthington, declined being a candidate for the Senate of the U. States for a variety of causes but two principally, one on acc't of the intrigues practicing & the other on acc't of my domestic concerns. A[lexander] Campbell elected."

The battle over the judiciary was reopened in the legislative session of 1809-10 by the passage of the "sweeping resolution," which vacated all the judgeships in the state. The originator of this strange measure was a Chillicothe intriguer who proposed the plan in the *Supporter* under the signature "A Lawyer." He maintained that the seven-year term of judges was a block system and that a full change should occur, no matter when appointments had been made, at the end of each seven-year period.[40] This idea so caught the fancy of the radicals that it was adopted during the session, and a completely new set of judges was appointed. Tiffin, who was already back in the legislature and had been elected to succeed Alexander Campbell as speaker, was given credit for the passage of this dubious measure; at least Duncan McArthur called it "Tiffin's Resolution." Perhaps Tiffin supported it because he was a good party man; moreover, he was a doctor and a Methodist preacher, not a lawyer or a Calvinistic legalist, as were many supporters of the judiciary. His glee in helping pass the measure may also have been due in part to the ebullient delight he experienced when in January—at the age of forty-four—he became a father for the first time. His wife was Mary Porter Tiffin, whom he had married in April of the preceding year.

At this same session of the legislature it was decided to move the seat of government to Zanesville. McArthur claimed this loss was the price paid for the passage of the "sweeping resolution."[41] At least partly to blame, however, was the failure of Chillicothe citizens to provide adequate public facilities or subscribe generously enough to a new statehouse, as Worthington could testify, since he had spent several days in January trying to raise sufficient pledges to have his home town kept the capital. Boarding facilities were entirely inadequate; McArthur alleged there was not a "tolerable tavern in town."

Worthington greatly enjoyed the winter of 1809-10. He was not actually a legislator, yet he sat in on the sessions at times, dined with the legislators often, and attended their informal gatherings. Two or three evenings each week he would take from one to a dozen members of the assembly home with him for the night. Governor Huntington

---

[40] *Supporter* (Chillicothe), December 30, 1809.
[41] *Fredonian* (Chillicothe), October 9, 1811.

was not infrequently entertained, and the leaders of all political factions found the master of Adena a charming host. Guests about the roaring fireplaces of the mansion on the blustery nights of January and February, 1810, heard much political conversation of both a light and a serious nature. Worthington was present at the meeting of the legislature when the judges were appointed pursuant to the "sweeping resolution," and doubtless laughed up his sleeve at the discomfiture of his aristocratic opponents. He attended the sessions of the Tammany Society after its organization in February. Thus he and Tiffin in one way or another maintained a large measure of that domination in politics which they had secured when St. Clair was dethroned.

To Worthington these were years of progress in his agricultural pursuits, of domestic felicity, and of freedom from the cares of public office. He had time at least once each summer to visit his two daughters Mary and Sarah Anne, who had been at school in Kentucky since 1808, first at Mrs. Beck's academy in Lexington, and then at Mrs. Louise Keets's academy, Harmony Hall, near Frankfort. General Sam Finley's daughter and several other Chillicothe girls were also in attendance there, as well as Mary Anne Breckinridge and Worthington's nieces, Maria and Scota, daughters of William and Eliza Worthington. Mrs. Henry Clay was a close friend of the Worthington girls, and her hospitality was always available to them. Mary was awarded a medal of merit for excellence in scholarship at Mrs. Keets's school in October, 1809, which greatly pleased her father.

The Lexington firm of Mears, Trotter, and Tilford was the financial guardian of the Worthington children while they were in Kentucky. On his visits to Kentucky, Worthington usually stopped with the family of his old "respected, and lamented friend" John Breckinridge and never failed to visit the cemetery at Cabell's Dale to pay his respects. On these trips he also visited in the home of his brother William's widow, Eliza Worthington, who lived near Washington.

6

Tammany Society No. 1, which was organized at Chillicothe in March, 1810, with eighteen charter members, was sponsored by Senator Michael Leib of Wigwam No. 1 in Philadelphia. Thomas Scott was the first Grand Sachem for Ohio. Edward Tiffin joined on April 18, and Worthington was elected to membership on May 4. The Society soon became the political forum of the Ross County radicals, and Tiffin and Worthington were two of its leading lights. It was seized upon by the Republicans as a made-to-order vehicle for organizing their forces and maintaining their strength against the "Quid-Fed" forces of the "High Court Party." Wigwams were erected in Cincinnati, Zanesville, Hamilton, Xenia, Lancaster, Warren, and New Lisbon, where the Republican forces were strong.[42] Ross and Hamilton counties even had township organizations. Thus a new instrument of politics was substituted for the correspondence societies of an earlier day. The setting for its use was almost perfect in 1810. The conflict between the forces of conservatism and radicalism was at white heat. The "High Court Party" had pushed Huntington to victory in 1808, but the Republicans had achieved double satisfaction by the "sweeping resolution" in 1810, the passage of which had aroused much excitement in the state. It had caused a furore in the judiciary, for the holdover judges could not decide whether to fight the action and continue to function according to their commissions under the old order or meekly sacrifice salary, position, and prestige with a ready acquiescence which would keep them eligible for the party's future patronage.[43]

The gubernatorial election of 1810 was the first great test of the strength of the Tammany organization, which sought to unite the anticourt, liberal Republicans behind Worthington. The conservative-Federalist union supported Senator Return J. Meigs of Marietta. Meigs was an ideal candidate, for he was a Republican of the Huntington type and a Yankee by heredity and location, and he had been robbed of the governorship in 1807. It was something of a surprise that he should be willing to resign his seat in the United States Senate if successful in his campaign for governor, but when he found that Huntington did not care to run to succeed himself, he consented to be a candidate.[44] The legislative caucus endorsed Worthington.

The campaign was marked by a virulence seldom equaled in an Ohio election. The three Chillicothe newspapers vied with each other in attacking the character of the candidates. The *Scioto Gazette* backed Worthington; the *Supporter* and the *Independent Republican* supported Meigs. Scribes named "Timoleon," "Aimwell," "Democrat," "Old Seventy Six," and "House Joiner" took up the cudgels and belabored their respective opponents unmercifully. Practically the same epithets were applied to both candidates. They actually differed little in their democratic principles, as everybody knew, but the scribblers

[42] Tammany Society Collection, folder 4, and Minute Book, Tammany Society, Chillicothe, OHS.
[43] Sprigg to Huntington, February 28, 1810, and Sprigg to Tod, February 28, June 12, and July 11, 1810, in the Rice Collection.
[44] Meigs to Huntington, August 1, 1810, in the Rice Collection.

magnified what differences there were. Worthington was attacked because of his Tammany connections, his wealth, his attempted dictation of the state's politics, his attack on the judges, and his opportunistic brand of Republicanism.[45] Several critics of Worthington took great pains to prove that any comparison of the two candidates redounded to Meigs's credit. One contributor concluded, "The Tammanies are exhibiting in strong and striking colors their true characters and the hideous deformity of genuine democracy."[46]

In this inter-Republican fight Meigs had little if any advantage over his opponent at first, but the charges and countercharges so disgusted conservatives that he gained popularity steadily as the campaign progressed. Meigs was accused of favoring "judicial usurpation," but the charge had slight effect. The argument that he had already had his share of offices meant little in view of Worthington's record as an officeholder.

It would appear that the newspaper war did Worthington much more harm than good. Although it functioned well in Ross County, his splendid Tammany organization—and his press agents—damaged him irreparably elsewhere. "Tom Tickler" wrote on September 27 that

> an intended good has turned out the greatest curse;—Had Gen. Worthington silenced the Tammany Gazette six weeks ago, he would certainly have been elected . . . the old foul mouthed mortarpiece [Scioto Gazette] has bursted by the heavy charges of the Great Timoleon—the artillery is silent on the side of the General, and the firing commenced on the opposite side. I think now there is no doubt Meigs will be elected, owing to the improper conduct of the Tammany Gazette commencing too soon.[47]

The editor of the *Independent Republican* arrived at the same conclusion on October 25:

> From the accounts which have been received from the different counties in this state, we entertain no doubt of the election of Return J. Meigs. . . .
> Mr. Worthington may thank his good, kind and persevering friends, in a great measure, for the election of the above gentleman. The rude, indecent and unprovoked attack upon the character of Judge Meigs by "Timoleon," and other writers for the Gazette has done more to defeat the election of Mr. Worthington, than the whole host of writers who were opposed to him.

Undoubtedly, the old Federalists held the balance of power and were still unashamed of the label. Even in Chillicothe, a hotbed of Tammanyism, "Timothy Trowell" could exhort them, "Federalists

[45] *Independent Republican* (Chillicothe), September 13, October 25, 1810.
[46] *Ibid.*, September 13, 1810.
[47] *Ibid.*, September 27, 1810. The same sentiment is expressed in the *Supporter,* September 15, 1810.

come forward, take hold of our political ark. Unite with moderate republicans. Unite with all honest men in the election of Judge Meigs."[48]

Meigs won the election by a small but safe margin, carrying every county where the New England element was strongest. Worthington ran best in Ross, Adams, Fairfield, Highland, Butler, and Warren counties. The total vote was Meigs 9,924, Worthington 7,731.[49]

Worthington was not greatly disappointed by his defeat. Early in August he had threatened to withdraw because Meigs had decided to run against him, but his friends persuaded him to stay in the race.[50] Yet his business was so pressing that it was a relief to be freed from the obligation of serving.

When the legislature met at Zanesville, Worthington's defeat was turned into something of a victory by the determination of his friends. Carlos A. Norton wrote him, "Your name has somehow been brought forward";[51] and James Caldwell informed him, "Your friends has taken on themselves a considerable responsibility . . . without consulting you on the occasion. They had no alternative but bringing you forward . . . or have the state disgraced by the election of Huntington."[52] On December 12, despite his wishes and expectations,[53] Worthington had been nominated to the United States Senate by a party caucus. On the thirteenth, the *Independent Republican* reported, "We may not be imprudent to anticipate the election of that modest lover of the loaves and fishes, Thomas Worthington." On the fifteenth, he was elected on the sixth ballot to fill out his recent adversary's unexpired term. The vote was Worthington 35, Huntington 31, Pritchard 2.

One of Worthington's friends explained Huntington's strength as the result of an effort to secure a senator for that part of the state east of the Scioto River, a reasonable assumption since Alexander Campbell, the incumbent senator, was from Adams County. That the legislators from eastern and northern Ohio were unable to swing the election is surprising. James Caldwell wrote Worthington that the

---

[48] *Supporter*, September 22, 1810.
[49] Taylor, *Ohio Statesmen*, 66. See the *Independent Republican*, November 1, 1810, for results by county.
[50] Morrow to Worthington, August 21, 1810, in the Rice Collection.
[51] Letter, December 14, in the Meigs Papers.
[52] Letter, December 15, 1810, in the Meigs Papers.
[53] "Much perplexed in mind to know how I can leave home with propriety. The appt unexpected and unwished for, tho I feel gratified that friends have taken [me] up, not that I am elected." Worthington's diary, December 26.

Huntington supporters were "confident of success [and] their disappointment is very perceivable."[54]

7

Despite Worthington's subsequent absence from the center of political events in Ohio, he kept in touch with the situation there through numerous correspondents and watched developments with great interest. Moreover, he was at home each summer between Senate sessions, and took an active part not only in state politics but in Ohio's share in the war that broke out during his term.

Under Speaker Tiffin's leadership, the radical Republicans kept the whip hand in the Ohio legislature during the winter of 1811. William Creighton, Jr., and Henry Brush, Chillicothe lawyers who had opposed Worthington strenuously in the campaign for governor in the fall of 1810, were the leaders of the fight to break Tammany's power and repeal the "sweeping resolution," but they labored in vain.[55] Worthington wrote from Washington encouraging the Republicans to maintain their position against the doctrine of judicial supremacy and to keep the lawyer clique in subserviency, but his personal influence was missed.

In Worthington's absence the lawyers in the legislature continued their efforts to break the power of that "infernal institution," the Tammany Society, and concentrated their attacks on Tiffin. Indignation meetings were held in Chillicothe and elsewhere. After the assembly dissolved, a general campaign of propaganda was inaugurated over the state against the "political cabal," which in its opponents' eyes was perverting democracy. Such virulent attacks were launched against Tiffin that he was actually expelled from the local Methodist Church in which he had been lay preacher. Charles Hammond, a brilliant young Federalist lawyer from St. Clairsville, attacked him in a series of articles signed "Calpurnius" in the Chillicothe Supporter.[56] He particularly criticized him for being the Grand Sachem of the Chillicothe Wigwam of Tammany and for the speech he delivered on May 13 at the first anniversary of its establishment. Hammond accused him of having been with Burgoyne at Saratoga although he boasted of having fought for liberty at Bunker Hill; he charged that having in-

---

[54] Letter, December 15, 1810, in WMOSL.
[55] William T. Utter, "Saint Tammany in Ohio: A Study in Frontier Politics," *Mississippi Valley Historical Review*, XV (1928-29), 321-40.
[56] June 8, 1811.

effectually sought to destroy the infant republic, Tiffin had later sought a haven within her mature bosom.

Tiffin's cogent and sincere reply refuted all of Hammond's charges and largely nullified their effect.[57] The annual conference of the Methodist Church at Cincinnati reviewed his expulsion from the local church at the hands of the Reverend Ralph Lotspeich, who was supported by the anti-Tammany Methodist faction led by Creighton, and ordered his reinstatement. The conference ruled that membership in the Wigwam did not constitute idolatry or immorality. In this hearing Tiffin was ably supported by the Reverend Joseph S. Collins, a local preacher and the publisher of the *Scioto Gazette*.[58]

Meanwhile, the newspaper war continued, and partisanship reached a new high in the 1811 election of the members of the legislature. Both the supporters and the attackers of Tammany felt that the agitation had been carried too far;[59] Tiffin himself believed it would be best to dissolve the Society since it had been used by its critics to divide the party. This sentiment was widespread, and in Chillicothe a group of the citizenry, characterized by Jesse Spencer as "upwards of one hundred of the rabble," even went to the trouble of holding a mock burial of the great Tammany Chief's body in Winn Winship's mound. When the legislature met in December, the opposing parties found they were almost equal in power. The Tammanyites drew first blood when Huntington was defeated for speaker of the house, but a change of political atmosphere was evident when an attempt to disregard the "sweeping resolution" failed by only one vote. A direct attempt at repeal a little later was barely lost by a tie vote. Moreover, the impeachment of Judge John Thompson failed by a large majority, which seemed to show that the radical Republicans were gradually losing ground or that they were tired of the issue. In the end, partly because the Federalists tried to district the state so that Madison would lose some votes, the Republicans combined before the session closed to repeal that part of the Commissioning Act which embodied the "sweeping resolution."[60] There was a definite feeling

---

[57] *Supporter*, June 15, 1811.
[58] Samuel W. Williams, *Pictures of Early Methodism in Ohio* (Cincinnati, 1909), 195 *et seq*. Material on the two trials of Tiffin by the officers of the Methodist Church is to be found in RCHS.
[59] Tiffin to Worthington, October 31, 1811, in WM; *Muskingum Messenger* (Zanesville), August 2, 1811; *Independent Republican*, August 15, 1811.
[60] Van Horne to Worthington, January 4 and 8, 1812; McArthur to Worthington, January 26 and February 20, in WMOSL; Norton to Worthington, January 8, in the Meigs Papers.

that the conservative-Federalist faction was getting stronger, and that in order to reunite the Republicans radicalism must be moderated. General Isaac Van Horne informed Worthington, "It is a matter of consolation to us that we got our three judges & collector."[61]

The threat of war, with its concomitant recrudescence of patriotism, and the need for unity in the national election in the fall seem to have done much to clarify the vision of Ohio's legislators. Wyllys Silliman wrote Worthington as early as January 22, 1812, that he "had feared the consequence of this repeal, but the healing disposition manifested" in the legislature led him to hope that all would be well.[62] Duncan McArthur expressed much the same sentiment on March 3, when he wrote his neighbor: "Party quarrels are I hope about to subside in this quarter. I trust the Chillicothians will endeavor to behave themselves better for five years to come than they did the last five years the seat of government was with them."[63]

Carlos Norton, a Tammanyite, acknowledged the wisdom of pacification, conciliation, and compromise when he wrote Senator Worthington, March 4, both seriously and facetiously that

> with respect to the Tammany Society it "hath done us much evil"; And it is certain, that no good will come out of it. The minds of the people are prejudiced against it—and, for my part I see no use, in attempting to struggle against a stream, which must inevitably bear us down. I know you will acknowledge the truth of these remarks—& that you will say with me, in scriptural language "it is folly to kick against the pricks."[64]

James Foster of Circleville wrote Worthington that with one exception his public conduct had been "conformable to the strictest principles of Republicanism." The one error was his connection with Tammany, "a very impolitic step . . . it has given the Federalists room to hope that they will soon have in Ohio the Politics of Connecticut."[65]

The gubernatorial election of 1812 in Ohio has no particular significance for this account. Since there was much discontent with Governor Meigs, Worthington was urged to enter the contest, but he refused. The Federalist "High Court Party" nominated Supreme Court Judge Thomas Scott of Chillicothe. The Republicans swung to Meigs as the best vote-getter. Although there were some who hoped that

[61] Letter, March 11, 1812, in WMOSL.
[62] Letter in WMOSL.
[63] Letter in WMOSL.
[64] Letter in the Meigs Papers.
[65] Letter in WM.

Worthington might have a chance as a dark horse, their hopes were destroyed on June 17 when he voted in Congress against the declaration of war with Great Britain.

Worthington was at home from July to December, but he refused to be drawn into politics despite goading from the state's papers, which still claimed he was the power behind the radicals of the Tammany societies—a charge that was well founded. Meigs was reëlected with ease, polling 11,859 votes to Scott's 7,903. There were some scattered votes for Worthington, although he was not a candidate.[66] He had other irons in the fire.

The state went strongly for Madison in the presidential election. Tammany, anti-Tammany, and Clinton tickets were entered in the field, but the Tammany ticket polled more votes than the other two combined. "Dictator General W[orthington]," reported "An Elector" in the *Fredonian*, busied himself in seeing that the prospective presidential electors voted for Madison. It is significant that McArthur, Kirker, and David Kinkaid were on the committee headed by Worthington which made Madison's reëlection its business, for the union of these four marked the solidification of the Republicans.[67]

The Congressional election, in which Ohio chose six congressmen for the first time, was also a Republican victory; not a single Federalist was elected. It is significant that James Caldwell was the only Tammany man elected. On February 16, 1813, Jeremiah Morrow—Ohio's sole congressman since statehood—won an overwhelming victory in the race for the Senate. His election signalized the almost complete unification of the Republicans and the passing of the Tammany threat. Morrow defeated the Federalist candidate, Judge Calvin Pease, for the vacancy created by the retirement of Senator Alexander Campbell. The vote was 63 to 18.[68]

The course of the War of 1812 discredited the Federalists and sobered the Republicans. Sentiment changed greatly during the first two years of the conflict; the growing consciousness that unity of effort was necessary to make the war, so sanguinely entered, even

[66] *Trump of Fame* (Warren), September 16, 23, 30, October 21, 1812.
[67] *Fredonian*, September 23, 1812. See the "Circular" addressed to candidates for presidential electors signed by the four: one dated October 7, to J. S. Edwards, in the Rice Collection; the other of the same date to Massie, in Massie, *Massie*, 266.
[68] John Hamm to Worthington, December 13, 1812, January 15, and February 7, 1813, in WMOSL.

respectable solidified the state's support of the Administration. The change of feeling restored Worthington's slight loss of popularity. By June, 1813, it is reasonable to believe that he could have been elected governor; by 1814 he was the popular choice.

Anti-war Senator

WORTHINGTON left Chillicothe on December 29, 1810, and after traveling nine days on horseback through the rain, sleet, snow, and mud of winter, arrived in Washington on January 7. The next day he took his seat in the Senate. His second term, which extended until December, 1814, was to be overshadowed by the threat of war with England and by the conflict itself.

During this term, however, an important part of his work was concerned with internal affairs. He served almost continuously, most of the time as chairman, on the Committee on Public Lands. He had not been present a week before he made a motion for the appointment of a committee to investigate the measures necessary to provide for the sale of the public domain. As chairman of the Senate committee he helped secure the adoption of an act which provided for the sale of certain reserved sections of land. His committee pushed through another act which permitted a three-year extension of time for payment in default on lands purchased before 1808.[1] The need for the bill illustrates the fact that the situation of the land buyer in the Old Northwest was still very bad; usually he was able to make only the first payment, depending on the sale of his produce to meet future ones. Since buyers were continually in trouble, the area's representatives were constantly petitioned for aid. The Ohio legislature and the Indiana territorial legislature often petitioned Congress for relief.[2] Worthington was most attentive to these appeals, and did his best to get legislation for his constituents.[3] At each session, new enactments were needed, and either he or Jeremiah Morrow, chairman of the House Committee on Public Lands, introduced bills to ease the land

---

[1] *Annals*, 12th Cong., 1st Sess., 169, 170, 182, 193, 198, 199, 2275. See also *Annals*, 11th Cong., 3rd Sess., 96, 107, 294, 329, 981, 1009.

[2] See the *Annals, ibid.*, 104, for the petition from the Ohio legislature presented by Worthington, January 28, 1811. For the Indiana Territory, see the *Annals*, 100, 672, and 12th Cong., 1st Sess., 332, 1493, 1513.

[3] An example is the petition of Jacob Smith of Greene County, dated September 20, 1811, for inhabitants "between the great and little Mimmiae . . . to have a law passed to give them a little longer to pay for their land. Many of them have paid three payments and some two . . . it must be considered greavous when the land with all the improvements may be sold for one fourth of the original purchase money." In WM.

buyers' difficulties. In July of 1812, Worthington and Morrow succeeded in having a bill enacted which amended the earlier act so
that the original purchaser of lands might reënter them even though
they had reverted to the government through default. This bill
was applicable not only to purchasers northwest of the Ohio but to
the entire country.[4] Senator Worthington had maintained for some
time that land should be sold in smaller pieces by the government,
and had realized, at least since 1806, that a discontinuance of credit
would be beneficial. Long before the Land Law of 1820, Worthington
advocated the sale of eighty-acre tracts at one dollar an acre and
a discontinuance of credit but supported extension of credit to those
already obligated. These changes, rejected at the time (February,
1812), were later adopted with slight modifications as necessary and
wise.[5]

Perhaps Worthington's most important contribution to the management of the public domain was his introduction of a bill in 1812 which
resulted in the establishment of the General Land Office. The bill as
adopted provided for a commissioner and a chief clerk to take charge
of all records concerning the public lands of the United States, to
make a plat of all surveys, to record all warrants and patents issued,
and to furnish the Secretary of the Treasury with an annual fiscal
report.[6] Through the influence of Worthington, Edward Tiffin was
appointed the first commissioner by President Madison.[7]

After Worthington's break with the Republican party over the
declaration of war, he resigned the chairmanship of the Senate Committee on Public Lands and was succeeded by Allen B. Magruder of
the new state of Louisiana, and in 1813 by Jeremiah Morrow, his
new colleague from Ohio. He was second on the committee under
Morrow. His support of the Administration restored him to any esteem
he had forfeited; by the end of his term he was more active than ever,
serving on many more committees than did the very able Morrow.

During the period of the war, little was done in the way of internal
improvements. However, Worthington was able to push through two
appropriation bills for the completion of the first section of the Cum-

[4] *Annals,* 12th Cong., 1st Sess., 89-92, 95, 98, 311, 313, 315, 317, 523, 548, 585,
1489, 1513, 1567, 2358.
[5] Adams, *Memoirs,* I, 423 (March 25-26, 1806); *American State Papers, Lands,*
II, 439; Payson J. Treat, *National Land System, 1785-1820* (New York, 1910),
135; *Annals,* 12th Cong., 1st Sess., 19, 20, 93, 125, 127, 130, 147, 162, 163, 2252;
2nd Sess., 95, 100, 101, 117, 119, 1343.
[6] *Ibid.,* 12th Cong., 1st Sess., 107, 116, 128, 130, 2279 (January-April, 1812).
[7] See some twenty documents relating thereto in the McKell Collection, RCHS.

berland Road.[8] With Senator Alexander Campbell, he also sponsored a bill which authorized a sixty-foot road from the mouth of the Maumee River to Cleveland and another from Sandusky south to the Greene Ville Treaty line. He was chairman of a committee which secured legislation to establish many post roads in the Northwest for military communications. He also reported a bill for the extension of the Georgetown and Alexandria toll road and served on the Potomac Canal committee.

He was chairman of the Committee on Indian Affairs for a time. On March 11, 1814, he submitted to President Madison a plan signed by the Congressional delegations from Ohio and the Indiana Territory for moving the Ohio Indians to an area west of the Wabash River. He reasoned that all the Ohio Indians except the Wyandots, the Shawnees, and the Delawares had forfeited whatever rights they had hitherto had to the lands they occupied by joining the British. The three tribes excepted numbered no more than 3,000, owned little land, and could be suitably compensated for both their land and their loyalty.[9] Although Congress did not accede to the committee's proposals at the time, the plan helped lay the groundwork for later removal of the Indians to lands beyond the Mississippi River.

Worthington's stand on several other measures of a nonmilitary nature which came before the Senate during his second term should be noted. He supported the Louisiana Enabling Act, which was so violently attacked by Josiah Quincy, spokesman for the Federalists, in his famous "Secession Speech" of January 14, 1811. He voted against Senator Dana's proposal for the admission of trans-Mississippi states by amendment only. He voted in favor of an annuity for Arthur St. Clair, in favor of the districting of states for Presidential electors, and against the recharter of the United States Bank. His vote against the bank had surprising and far-reaching consequences because the measure tied in the Senate, 17 to 17; Vice-President Clinton then cast the deciding vote against it.

Worthington's vote against one of the pet fiscal projects of his excellent friend Gallatin can be explained only by his desire to stick with his party and by the influence of the provincial "wildcat" philosophy in Ohio which held, with some cause, that the monopolistic character of the United States Bank made it a menace to the American people.

[8] *Annals,* 11th Cong., 3rd Sess., 115, 174, 347, 349, 367, 992, 994, 1107-1108, 1352; 12th Cong., 1st Sess. 112, 199, 204, 206, 210, 2293; *Independent Republican,* April 4, 1811.
[9] The draft of the plan is in the McKell Collection.

His action is all the more surprising in view of the fact that throughout his life he was a bank official and a heavy investor in bank stocks —especially those of the United States Bank—and was usually regarded as a sound-money man. It is interesting that three years later (1814) Worthington worked with Gallatin and John Jacob Astor for the reëstablishment of the Bank.[10] Stephen Girard, David Parish, and Astor, who like Gallatin were all foreign-born, had taken five-eighths of the $16,000,000 federal bond issue of 1813 at $88 for each $100 share, and were anxious to establish a sound bank. The financial condition of the country was wretched, and it was believed that a national bank would have a stabilizing effect. Moreover, the average interest paid by the first bank during its twenty years of life was 8¼ per cent, an excellent return on such a secure investment. Gallatin's wisdom was amply borne out by the fiscal debacle in which the country became involved before the war was over, but Congress arrived at the tardy decision to recharter the bank only after a long and bitter fight.

2

When Worthington returned to Washington in the fall of 1811, he drove his own carriage and team of bays as far as Shepherdstown, Virginia. He was accompanied by Mrs. Worthington and the children—Mary, aged fourteen, Sally Anne (Sarah) eleven, Thomas four, Eleanor two and a half, and the three-month-old baby, Margaret (James, nine, and Albert, seven, were left in school at Chillicothe). Mary and Sally Anne were to enter Mrs. Hayward's school in Baltimore in November, but meantime they were to have a good visit at Shepherdstown with their maternal great-aunts, Eleanor Shepherd and Rachel Bedinger. The Senator took various members of the family for rides on the rather good roads of the Great Valley and told them stories of his early life in the vicinity. He found his birthplace strangely shrunken and changed but still occupied by his brother Ephraim's widow, Mrs. Thomas Breckinridge. He noted with sadness that his old property at Prospect Hill, and St. George's Chapel, where he had worshiped, had deteriorated badly.[11]

Mrs. Worthington and the children joined him in Washington on November 23, but Eleanor (Ellen) was not well all winter, and they returned to Shepherdstown in March. However, despairing of an early

---

[10] Astor to Worthington, April 26, May 16, September 18 and 20, November 23, 1814, in WM. See also the letters of Astor to Worthington, March 11 and February 26, 1814, in the King Manuscripts, II, 93, HPSO.
[11] Worthington's diary, October, 1811.

adjournment of Congress, the mother and children set out for Chillicothe on April 19.

In Washington, the Senator found himself in a Congress that was impregnated with a new spirit. The rest of his term was to prove a period of storm and stress in the life of the young republic, and he was to witness the most critical situation in which the United States had been involved since the adoption of the Constitution. The cautious Jefferson had met the threat of war by compromise. His embargo was intended to be the crowning event of his administration; instead, it had divided the country. Although Jefferson signed the bill for its repeal in 1809, his action appeared to be one of deathbed repentance, and he retired from office under a cloud. When his Secretary of State, James Madison, became President, the situation seemed to improve. Although the embargo was replaced by a nonintercourse act, it appeared for a time that amicable relations were to be reëstablished with Great Britain and perhaps with France. The repudiation of the Erskine agreement, the recalcitrance of the Canning ministry, and the unfortunate embassy of Francis James Jackson, however, left Madison as far from a settlement as ever. The Macon Bill No. 2, which removed all restrictions on trade, pleased the shipping interests, but Napoleon tricked the Administration into restoring nonintercourse with Great Britain and made a bad situation worse. Madison, who realized the significance of the election in 1810 of a group of congressmen who were soon to be called War Hawks, stiffened his attitude toward England. Lord Wellesley, Canning's successor, recognized this change. A new minister was sent to the United States, reparation was made for the Chesapeake affair, and Pinckney was requested to remain in England, but the revocation of the Orders in Council was flatly refused. As a result, Congress began to anticipate war.

Such was the situation when the Congress convened on November 3, 1811. The election of Henry Clay as Speaker made the new course immediately apparent. Randolph and the "old republicans" were to be curbed; party leadership had fallen to "the Boys" from the West. Madison's message practically recognized the inevitability of war, and the attitude of the whole Administration was one of paralysis and passive acquiescence. Worthington made this notation in his diary on November 5: "Received the message of the President which is strong and leaves little doubt but war must ultimately [be] adopted against England." War had been contemplated so often that it seemed to have no terrors, and no serious effort was made to avoid it. The seventy new members of Congress under the leadership of the young radicals swept all before them. They had never undergone a war, but they had experienced an inglorious peace. So, disregarding the Federalists, the commercial wing of their own party, and public opinion, they began the drive for war. Worthington noted on December 16 that "both branches of the Legislature [are] discussing propositions to raise a large army preparatory to war with England. No reflection of my life has given me so much concern; blessed with peace, liberty and plenty, beyond the controll of any earthly power yet [we are] insensible of the blessings we enjoy and do not consider the things which belong to our peace." The press took up the war cry and sought to popularize issues which for ten years had been deemed insufficient cause for war; almost everywhere except in New England the favorite topic of newspaper discussion was the conquest of Canada. The Virginia General Assembly pledged the support of its state to whatever policy Congress and the President should approve, holding that precious as was peace, war for honor was preferable.[12]

Despite the comparatively favorable trend which negotiations with England were taking, by April Madison and his counselors had decided that her refusal to repeal the Orders in Council left no alternative but an immediate embargo and preparations for war. Disregarding the enormous peacetime gains in Louisiana and Florida, the lack of preparation for hostilities, and the disapproval of a majority of the people, the Administration drifted toward war at the command of a group of young legislators who "cried out against the cowardice of further submission." The threat of Clay's coterie to disrupt the party and alienate all support from Madison in the coming Presidential election helped the President reach a decision to recommend war; thus a needless conflict was made inevitable.

The Federalists in Congress were solidly for peace, but, since they were impotent politically, many of them decided to support the Republican preparedness measures even at the cost of a short disastrous war.[13] They reasoned that a brief, abortive, and expensive war would discredit the War Hawks, pave the way for a political victory in November, and lead to an immediate peace and the restoration of commercial relations with Britain. They proposed a coalition of all the peace advocates of both parties to back the moderate Republican, DeWitt Clinton, for the presidency. Peace and prosperity could be secured if Madison were defeated and Clinton installed as chief executive.

---

[12] *Annals*, 12th Cong., 1st Sess., 112-14.
[13] Bayard to William H. Wells, January 12, 1812. Elizabeth Donnan, ed., "The Papers of James A. Bayard," in American Historical Association, *Annual Report*, 1913, II (Washington, 1915), 188.

Gallatin wrote Jefferson that he blamed the Administration's inability to maintain the peace on "domestic faction . . . ambitious intriguers, and internal enemies" who aimed at disunity.[14] John Randolph, Republican gadfly, saw the direction our foreign policy was taking and denounced as spurious the radical Republicans' arguments for a war of conquest, without money, leaders, army, or navy:

> We had by our own wise measures, so increased the trade and wealth of Montreal and Quebec that at last we began to cast a wistful eye at Canada. . . . Suppose it ours, are we any nearer to our point? . . . Go! march on Canada! leave the broad bosom of the Chesapeake and her hundred tributary rivers—the line of seacoast from Machias to St. Mary's unprotected! You have taken Quebec—have you conquered England? Will you seek for the deep foundations of her power in the frozen deserts of Labrador? . . .
> Will you call upon her to leave your ports and harbors untouched only just till you can return from Canada, to defend them? The coast is to be left defenseless, whilst men of the interior are revelling in conquest and spoil. But grant for a moment . . . that in Canada you touched the sinews of her strength. . . . In what situation would you then place some of the best men of the nation? As Chatham and Burke and the whole band of her patriots prayed for her defeat in 1776, so must some of the truest friends to their country deprecate the success of our arms against the only Power that holds in check the arch-enemy of mankind.[15]

Worthington mirrored the confused sentiments of the patriotic enthusiasts of Ohio who resented the insults of England but feared an Indian uprising against a practically defenseless frontier. Moreover, the western country was prosperous, and, although its citizens coveted the Indian and Canadian lands, war meant destruction and bloodshed. Since over half of our foreign trade was with England, war "would be a very unprofitable business." Worthington had consistently supported the neutrality of Jefferson and Madison but resented bitterly the New England shippers' policy of appeasement. He also deplored the growth of war sentiment in the West[16] and knew that so far as Ohio was concerned, the chief motivation toward war was the wish, born of fear, to destroy the Indians,[17] who were showing increased unrest under the urging of Tecumseh, of the Prophet, and, perhaps, of the British in Canada. Many Ohioans believed that once war was

---

[14] March 10, 1812, quoted in Adams, *Life of Gallatin*, 455.

[15] *Congressional Reporter*, 78, 80-85 (House of Representatives, December 10, 1811).

[16] See Julius W. Pratt, "Western Aims in the War of 1812," in the *Mississippi Valley Historical Review*, XII (1925-26), 35-50, for the best discussion of the situation in the West, especially on this subject. See also Pratt's *Expansionists of 1812* (New York, 1925).

[17] Adjutant General Van Horne wrote Worthington, December 12, 1811, that Ohio regarded war as inevitable. Letter in WMOSL. See also Tiffin to Worthington, April 16, 1812, in WMOSL.

declared, prompt and effective action by the regulars and the militia would make it possible to wipe out the Indians before British aid could arrive.

Worthington heard with alarm of Harrison's ill-advised march and the battle at Tippecanoe in October, 1811. "I am convinced," he wrote, "that this might have been prevented & all matters settled without loss of blood."[18] He foresaw the reign of terror which war would cause on every frontier and threw his whole energy into preparation for a conflict which he nevertheless did his utmost to delay.

In Congress there was a very serious division of sentiment among Worthington's Republican friends. Gallatin, Giles, Madison, and Clay were all leaders whom he sought to support, but there was little agreement among them. At one extreme, Gallatin was unreservedly opposed to resorting to war; at the other extreme, was Clay, the War Hawk; Giles considered war talk a Madisonian political stratagem, while Madison himself followed the dictates of the party majority. Worthington had many friends among the Federalists also. As a businessman he was interested in exports, sound banking, internal improvements, and the maintenance of peace. Hence he had a better appreciation of their point of view than most Republicans. However, he regarded himself as a true patriot and resented the long-accumulated insults suffered at the hands of the British. He was proud of his country, and approved of expansion, but expansion by peaceful means only. Purchase was preferable to war. Certainly, he had no sympathy with the constant attacks Quincy, Morris, and their Federalist colleagues made in Congress on slave representation and the need for New England secession if expansion and the admission of new states did not cease. His only wish was to support the Administration and to help legislate wisely, but how could he decide rightly when the Chief Executive had no policy but to please the dominant faction of his party? One thing he did know, that he would exert his influence against war to the very end unless there was at least a possibility of ensuring the safety of the frontiers and of winning ultimate success.

In the spring of 1811, Worthington voted to empower the President to seize and occupy the Floridas, partly because he believed the country needed the territory and could probably get it without a war, but more particularly because he understood the threat to the frontier from the Indians and from any power which might land forces there. Yet his concern for the safety of the Florida frontier was much less than that which he felt at that time for the northwest frontier. His first

[18] Worthington's diary, November 28, 1811.

and immediate responsibility was to Ohio. As the belief in the inevitability of war grew stronger, his apprehension for the safety of Ohio's people increased. Frequent letters came to him imploring provisions for defense and denouncing the warmongers, who did not have to live under the threat of Indians passing daily by their doors.[19] The reports from the governor of the Indiana Territory during the years 1810-11 left no doubt that Harrison was sure the Indians were ready to take up the hatchet.[20]

To meet this danger, Worthington introduced a bill, December 16, 1811, for the organization of six companies of rangers to protect the frontier, and secured its passage. Although in defense of the United States frontiers the 432 men and officers were only a corporal's guard, they constituted at least a beginning. Tiffin later said that without them "a great part of the frontiers would have been depopulated."[21] While the bill was being debated in Congress, Worthington secured a promise from Madison and Secretary of War Eustis that they would authorize Governor Meigs by letter to prepare for the use of rangers on the Ohio frontier. He was disheartened three weeks later to discover that they had taken no action, but he saw them again and secured a renewal of their promise. On January 8, 1812, he wrote as follows to Governor Meigs:

> Mr. Eustis has just told me the officers of our company would be immediately appointed and that the Gen'l direction of it would be given to you. . . .
> Knowing as I do Tecumse personally . . . unless measures are taken to prevent it . . . in the spring we may expect an Indian War, and especially in event of war with England which is now almost certain. . . . I have not ceased to press upon the President the necessity of availing himself of the favorable opportunity . . . to quiet the Indians.[22]

More warlike was a bill introduced by Giles which provided for ten regiments of infantry, two of artillery, and one of light dragoons —a total of 25,000 regulars added to the authorized establishment of 10,000—for a five-year tour of duty; Madison signed the bill on January 11, 1812. Martial, too, were bills Madison signed on February 6 enrolling 50,000 militia for one year, and on April 10 authorizing a militia of 100,000 to be raised by the states and held in readiness

---

[19] An eight-page letter from Sol Sibley (Detroit), dated February 26, 1812, is an excellent example. It portrays the terribly exposed condition of the Michigan frontier. In WMOSL.

[20] Moses Dawson, A Historical Narrative of the Civil and Military Services of Major General William H. Harrison (Cincinnati, 1824), 151, 153, 177; American State Papers, Indian Affairs, I, 800-805.

[21] Tiffin to Worthington, March 15, 1812, in WM.

[22] Worthington to Meigs, January 8, 1812, RCHS.

for instant service. Most discouraging, however, was the word from Governor Meigs on March 1 that he had been unable to get the legislature to authorize preparedness measures and that there were insufficient arms for the militia. Ohio seemed scarcely willing even to defend herself.

Worthington was distressed by the report of the Inspector General's office, which placed the strength of the regular army as of May 1 at 6,744 men scattered among twenty-two posts throughout the United States. Of these men, 1,125 had been recruited between January 1 and May 1; the Inspector General estimated that another thousand had volunteered during May. Worthington calculated that 5,000 volunteers would be secured as soon as war was declared, but he regarded an army of 13,000 as pitifully inadequate to meet the commencement of hostilities, especially since almost 8,000 of them would be garrisoning important posts. These posts needed to be reinforced rather than to have their troops put in the field. New Orleans was garrisoned with only 143 men; Charleston Harbor had 175; New York Harbor, 901; Newport, 193; Boston, 131; Detroit, 119, with 430 more ordered there; Michilimackinac, 88; Fort Wayne, 85; and Fort Dearborn, 53.[23]

The state of affairs was not improved when Secretary Eustis reported to Worthington on June 6 that the scattered returns from the forty-eight recruiting districts of the nation did not permit the Secretary of War or the Inspector General to make an estimate of the number of volunteers secured since March or to evaluate the state of their discipline. He reported that 3,500 militia and volunteers had been ordered to the most exposed posts of the nation but did not indicate where they were to come from.[24] Meanwhile, Worthington voted for every preparedness measure, since as early as March he had considered war to be inevitable. "The frightful exhibition by Gallatin of War taxes" necessary for the contemplated conflict added to his trepidation, but he favored the greatest possible preparation. He even approved the Giles bill authorizing twice as many regulars as Madison had asked for, could use, or could arm. He favored Madison's appeal for a temporary embargo and helped to extend it to ninety days. He then fought for an adjournment. Congress was doing nothing except wait for England's next move, and he believed an adjournment would be a good thing—the evil day might be postponed. Barely a quorum

---

[23] Report to Worthington, dated June 6, 1812, RCHS.
[24] Eustis to Joseph Anderson, June 6, enclosing report of Acting Inspector General Alexander Smyth, dated June 5, RCHS.

was present in each house, and all members needed a rest. The motion for adjournment passed the Senate on April 29, but the House refused to concur. Thus his attempt to alleviate the situation failed.

It is noteworthy that by May 8 Worthington was in favor of lifting the embargo which he had helped establish in April. Madison had meant it as a war measure, and the House had adopted it as such. The Senate, by extending it from sixty to ninety days, had changed its purpose to that of a negotiating measure. The embargo, together with the operation of Macon's bill pursuant to Madison's proclamation of November 2, 1810, and the act of Congress of March 2, 1811, was strangling the resources of the country and widening the schism with the shipping interests. The nation needed to marshal every resource of money, goods, and shipping before it could embark on war, but the attempt at repeal failed in both houses. Worthington and Pope of Kentucky were the only Republicans who voted with the six Federalist Senators in support of it.[25]

3

Despite Castlereagh's attitude of conciliation, during April and May the Administration moved steadily toward war. Madison had been badgered on both sides of the Atlantic until he was desperate. Nevertheless, a rump caucus of eighty-two members of the party had unanimously endorsed him for a second term. The country was little better prepared than in 1811 and much worse prepared than in 1807, but it was hoped that war would consolidate it by concentrating its animosities on the ancient foe. Worthington felt the ominous and irresistible drift of opinion and on May 12 confided to his diary:

> I have heretofore made no memo of my opinions of publick proceedings. I have been—and every day confirms me—in the opinion convinced that the govt are pursuing an improper course as to the powers of europe. It will be folly & madness to get into the war for abstract principles when we have not the power to enforce them. To withdraw would be wisdom but I fear she has fled our councils.

Madison seized upon Castlereagh's definition of retaliation in his note of April 10 as sufficient cause for defining the issue. On June 1, he sent his war message to both houses of Congress. Friday, June 5, by a vote of 79 to 49, the House of Representatives passed and sent to the Senate a declaration of war. Worthington joined with the Federalists and anti-Administration senators in attempting to change the House

---

[25] *Annals,* 12th Cong., 1st Sess., 237, 239, 1533, 1535-46.

bill from a war to a reprisal measure which would be applicable to France as well as Great Britain. On June 14, he called on Madison to protest the trend of affairs:

> Conversed near an hour and a half with the president on indian affairs and the subject of war. My objections candidly stated to him to wit, that we are unprepared—that 3 months must elapse before any invasion can be undertaken. that in the meantime the administration will be exposed to the attacks of its enemies the people disheartened . . . That although I may differ with my friends on this question or with him I will be the very last to agree to a disgraceful peace. will rise or sink with my political associates. That I believe the war is unavoidable but as we have it compleatly in our power to choose our own time to make it I cannot take the responsibility on me of entering into it in an unprepared [state].[26]

Attempts at delay and adjournment failed, and on June 15 the original bill was passed to the third reading. The next three days were spent by the opposition in debating amendments and urging delay. On June 17, Giles made a last effort, which Worthington supported, to make the declaration one of reprisal rather than of general war; but again the attempt failed. On the question, Shall the bill pass?, the vote was aye 19, nay 13, Worthington voting nay.[27] The President signed the bill the next day. Worthington wrote this comment to his wife:

> I have done my duty and satisfied my conscience. Thousands of the innocent will suffer, but I have borne my testimony against it, and, thank God, my mind is tranquil. . . . Now that the step is taken, I am bound to submit to the will of the majority, and use my best exertions to save my country from ruin.[28]

4

After the declaration of war, which came just five days before the Liverpool ministry repealed the odious Orders in Council, Worthington directed his efforts toward making the best of a bad situation and uniformly supported the Administration in all of its many financial and military measures.

He continued to act as chairman of the Committee on Military Appointments for the Indiana Territory and as a member of other military committees. It is important to note that he voted against the appointment of Generals Hull and Wilkinson, both of whom he regarded as incompetent. Although Worthington lost favor with his colleagues for a time as the result of his opposition to the war, his

---

[26] Worthington's diary, June 14, 1812.

[27] *Annals*, 12th Cong., 1st Sess., 297.

[28] *Private Memoir*, 60-61. Worthington confided to his diary, June 17, 1812: "The peace of the country is gone but who can tell when it will return. Alas poor man, how little dost thou know what is for thy peace. Oh my country if you but knew the horrors of war and the slavery it entails too often, pride would be repressed."

unswerving devotion to duty was rewarded when he was made chairman of the Committee on Military Affairs in December, 1813, and chairman of the Committee on Militia in 1814. In the latter capacity he sponsored unsuccessfully a conscription bill for a uniform system of militia throughout the United States, proposing that every able-bodied white male from sixteen to fifty years of age be enrolled in a local militia unit and armed and equipped for service. He was particularly solicitous for the welfare of the Ohio troops, and did his best to ensure their pay and to secure compensation for property and equipment destroyed by the enemy.

In 1813, Worthington introduced a bill to appropriate $75,000 for establishing a second military academy at Pittsburgh. He won the approval of Secretary of War Armstrong, but the chief engineer, Colonel J. G. Swift, estimated that both time and money could be saved by enlarging West Point, and so the plan was shelved by Congress.[29] The object of another bill which Worthington introduced and unsuccessfully supported was "to produce exact uniformity in the Army, viz., in the calibre, bayonets, locks & parts thereof so as to make any separate part of the gun fit any other, thereby saving a great expense to the public."[30]

Worthington upheld the Administration in its proposal to occupy the Floridas and Canada and opposed any limitation of the authority given the President, for he claimed that with the country at war it was unwise to restrict the Executive. He supported a resolution authorizing the President to issue an address to the Canadas promising them peace, security, and liberty if they came under the control of the United States. He voted for a bill to establish a government in any conquered territory and endorsed the many measures which were introduced to provide for the occupation and government of the Floridas. In 1813, he used his influence in favor of a bill calling for the forcible occupation of east as well as west Florida, which, after lengthy debate, was defeated. To General Jackson's extreme anger, Congress, on February 12, authorized occupation eastward only as far as the Perdido.[31]

Worthington's last two years in the Senate, then, were a period of arduous experience. A man of peace, he had had to study seriously the

---

[29] Armstrong to Worthington, December 30, 1813, enclosing estimates from Colonel Swift, dated December 28; two drafts of the bill and notes of Worthington's speech in support of it are in the McKell Collection, RCHS.
[30] McKell Collection.
[31] *Annals*, 12th Cong., 1st Sess., 324-25; 2nd Sess., 124-33; 3 *Statutes at Large*, 472.

cost of war in men, money, and property. He was certain that war was evil, but he was also firmly convinced that since periodic wars were seemingly inescapable, the country needed a better militia system and service of supply. He never ceased to maintain that a well-outfitted and well-disciplined militia was an indispensable part of the nation's peacetime equipment.

5

In concluding this sketch of Worthington's second term in the Senate, it should be observed that the Senator continued to spend a large portion of his time and energy in transacting business for his constituents. Ten to fifty letters came to him by every post from Ohio. Samuel Finley expressed fear for his health, and Worthington himself wrote, "The business I have to go through is more than anyone ought to bear." Everything from purchasing "5 doz. buttons & 4 stars" for General Cass's uniform to securing deposits of United States money in Ohio banks to pay war expenses fell to his charge. He found relaxation in attending church every week and visiting the stock farms of his acquaintances near Washington.

Worthington missed the company of his boys; in 1813, James was eleven, Albert nine, and Thomas six. James and Albert attended the private school of a young premedical student, Samuel C. Lewis, at Chillicothe during the years 1813-15. A letter Worthington wrote Lewis in January, 1814, reflects his solicitude for their welfare and some of his ideas concerning education:

> I wish him [Albert] first to be a perfect master of the Geography of his native state . . . knowing every river, creek, Bay, county, their relative distances &c. Next the adjoining states & Terr'ys & so on & then such a Knowledge of the great geographical divisions of the different countries of the world as will fit him . . . to understand something of history as he reads . . . give him some gen[era]l understanding of Chronology.
> [As to] the morals & manners of my poor boys . . . I am convinced that nothing of the frippery of this world will satisfy the soul. Religion alone, pure religion can only do so and the youth who believes and acts on this belief will never fail in after life to feel the greatest consolation from it.[32]

The presence of Worthington's daughters, Mary and Sally Anne, who were in school in Georgetown during the winter of 1812-13, was a great comfort to him. After school was dismissed, Sally Anne spent the summer with her father and participated in the gay social life of the capital. She was one of the many beautiful young ladies who flocked about the dashing young Elbridge Gerry, Jr., son of the Vice-President. This young man, a cousin of the President's wife, had a

---

[32] Worthington to Samuel C. Lewis, January 12, 1814, RCHS.

delightful time with the girls in Washington that summer. The nearness of the British seems to have disturbed him little or not at all. Observations in his diary do not indicate that anyone else was particularly worried.[33] Worthington took Sally Anne home with him when he departed from the city on August 1.

In reality, the capital was greatly disturbed by the depredations of Admiral Warren's sailors and soldiers in Chesapeake Bay and by the ineffectiveness of the American gunboats and batteries at Norfolk in defending that area against them. When the British entered the Potomac in early July, Washington and all the towns within fifty miles of the river were panic-stricken. Every able-bodied male was called to the colors, but John Armstrong, who had succeeded William Eustis as Secretary of War in January, had no organizing ability. In view of this, it was fortunate that Warren's action was only a feint and that for the next year he was content to maintain the blockade by cruising in the lower bay.

Worthington had little respect for Eustis' ability as Secretary of War, and he regarded his successors, Armstrong and Monroe, as almost equally incompetent. His fears for the outcome of the war stemmed primarily from his intimate knowledge of the men in Washington who were responsible for its conduct.

When in November, 1813, he returned to Washington for the next session of Congress, he took Mrs. Worthington and Sally Anne with him in the family carriage. They were accompanied by Nathaniel Massie Kerr, son of General Joseph Kerr, and General Duncan McArthur's daughter, Margaret, who was in school at Georgetown with Sally Anne. In the mountains east of Washington, Pennsylvania, their carriage was overturned and damaged, but after the loss of a day they managed to get on to Shepherdstown, where they stayed with Mrs. Worthington's aunt, Mrs. Abraham Shepherd. Worthington pushed on by stage the next day with Sally Anne, Margaret McArthur, Mrs. Shepherd's daughter, and young Kerr. On the second day of their journey, the stage suffered the same fate as the carriage, but no one was hurt, and they reached Georgetown that evening.

The next fall Worthington made the trip east by horseback. Since the public buildings at Washington had just been burned by the British and the enemy was still operating in Chesapeake Bay and all along the Atlantic coast, he did not venture to take any of the family with him.

He was mortified—though scarcely surprised—to discover how in-

---

[33] Townsend and Bowers, eds., *The Diary of Elbridge Gerry, Jr.*, 151-206.

competently the defense of the nation's capital had been handled. President Madison, well intentioned though he was, had been unable to discover military or executive leadership adequate to the occasion, and Congress—now sitting at the old Blodgett Hotel, recently the Patent Office—seemed to be unable to lift itself out of the lethargy into which the whole Administration had sunk. The treasury was empty, and banks everywhere were suspending specie payments; Gallatin was in Europe, and it was weeks before his successor, George W. Campbell, presented a tax plan. Before it could be debated, Campbell had resigned and had been succeeded by Alexander J. Dallas, who in due time proposed another tax schedule.

The military situation was equally desperate. The Maine coast was occupied by the enemy; 20,000 British were poised at Kingston to invade New York; a military and naval expedition was on its way to the Floridas. Even the timid Monroe saw the necessity for an immediate conscription of all available manpower, and the Giles and Worthington bills were introduced into Congress. Fought every inch of the way by the Federalists, the bills failed of adoption, and the Executive was left to fight in a seemingly hopeless cause with a regular army of 32,000 men supplemented by the state militias and whatever volunteers could be found.

Senator Worthington, Ohio's governor-elect, left Washington in late November, 1814, with his country on the brink of financial, military, and diplomatic ruin.

Wartime Service in Ohio

THE DRIFT toward war, which Worthington so strenuously opposed, had been watched by the people of Ohio with mixed emotions. Four attitudes apparently predominated in the winter of 1811-12: there was a minority group which shared the chauvinistic spirit of the War Hawks; another which was torn between the very real dangers and the glorious possibilities involved in the conquest of Canada; a third which shared Worthington's conviction that a declaration of war would be premature; and a fourth which opposed the conflict at any cost. A plebiscite would probably have shown that a decided majority of the people were against hostilities.[1]

Of course, the proponents of war did most of the talking. The officers of the militia and the genuine War Hawks, who looked for glory and honor in a conflict to defend the "independence achieved in the Revolution," constantly encouraged Madison to declare war. There was a feeling that an Indian uprising was the greatest danger to be apprehended—the British could do nothing to the interior of the country. The exaggerated reports of Harrison's "victory" at Tippecanoe in November, 1811, occasioned many demonstrations of pride and patriotism, and were cited as proof that nothing except the wilderness prevented the acquisition of Canada. The militia in coöperation with a small body of regulars could sweep to certain victory. James Caldwell wrote Worthington, December 14, 1811,

> In the event of a war with England, I think with you that the Indians would be troublesome, considering the defenseless situation of our frontiers, but I trust that with the assistance of arms from the Genl. Government and the aid of volunteers from Kentucky we shall have nothing to fear—and in the event of an army of the United States being sent to affect [sic] the conquest of Cannady we wont have no invation to apprehend from the British on that quarter, indeed from every view I can take of the subject I have been unable to discover on what quarter the British could do the U. S. any material injury and we would attack & conquer Cannady & humble their overbearing pride.[2]

Adjutant General Isaac Van Horne wrote Worthington the same month that war was already considered unavoidable: "Tod and

---

[1] John F. Cady, "Western Opinion and the War of 1812," *Ohio State Archaeological and Historical Quarterly*, XXXIII (1924), 427-505.
[2] In WMOSL.

McArthur seem now to vie with each other which shall dispense the most patriotism."[3] By the following spring, militia officers, newspaper editors, and the community braggarts agreed that it was time to strike for their "beloved country."[4] "In Ohio the public mind (not being cankered with mercantile cupidity) is prepared for war," wrote Levi Barbour, a staunch Marietta Republican.[5]

When the publication of the Henry Papers in March, 1812, discredited the Federalists nationally, some of the party in Ohio, perhaps in self-defense, denounced their New England leaders and asserted their loyalty. Being a cautious man, Madison had not hesitated to pay $50,000 to John Henry for the letters which exposed the major details of his effort to separate New England from the Union in 1809. The majority of the Federalists were very critical of Madison for wasting public funds for a batch of letters, maintaining that the Federalists as a group were as patriotic as the Republicans. John Kerr wrote Worthington, May 12, "The spirit of Patriotism and love of Country is high with us," but he warned that in his opinion war would ruin business.[6]

In spite of the high tide of patriotism, there were those who realized Ohio's vulnerability to attack from the north. Fear for the state's safety was undoubtedly increased by distrust of William Hull, governor of the Michigan Territory, who was regarded by many as a politician rather than a soldier. Some claimed that he did not have the confidence of his officers or men at Detroit; others believed that neither his officers nor his men were to be depended on. Lewis Bond of Detroit had counseled Hull's removal as early as January; he accused him of putting men in civil office who were un-American and pro-British—"not to be depended on in War." These appointments had been made, Bond realized, to make a favorable impression on the Canadians, but he was confident that very few of the men could be brought to fight either the British or the Indians. He further charged that some of Hull's officers and privates had actually changed sides in recent skirmishes. He was sure that if war were declared Detroit would be in great danger; with that frontier outpost captured, practically nothing would stand between Ohio and an invader.[7]

Newspaper editors were not consistent: one week they admitted

---

[3] December 19, 1811, in WMOSL.
[4] R. D. Richardson, Circleville editor, to Worthington, March 18, 1812, in WMOSL.
[5] Barbour to Worthington, May 17, 1812, in WMOSL.
[6] In WM.
[7] Bond to Worthington, January 15, 1812, in WMOSL.

a dangerous unpreparedness and the next week asked for war.[8] Contributed articles showed no great preponderance of sentiment for the precipitation of hostilities. Even General Van Horne admitted the "deficiency of arms and accoutrements" and stated that the militia would "present an indifferent barrier to an invading army."[9]

The declaration of war was hailed with general joy at Zanesville and "was signalized by 18 discharges from a Six pounder." At Worthington, on the Fourth of July, the proclamation was celebrated by toasts and resolutions, and Congressman Morrow was commended for his vote in favor of war, having "done honor to his own character and his state . . . meriting the highest confidence of his constituents."[10] The Circleville *Fredonian*, August 25, 1812, trumpeted a warning: "This western section of our country stands ready at the *signal of her Government to retrieve her dignity or CRIMSON the surface with a sluice of blood, rather than submit to the indignities offered her flag by the Tory advocates of England, that sink of perdition.*"

The celebrations which took place were more than spontaneous exhibitions of patriotic enthusiasm; they were, at least in part, displays of shameless political incitement. John Hamm, Grand Sachem of the Tammanies at Zanesville, was convinced that a declaration of war was the only thing that could save the Republican ticket: without a bold and vigorous foreign policy, Madison's reëlection would be impossible.[11]

On the other hand, the great silent majority of the Ohio people were opposed to the war. They realized that a conflict with Great Britain meant a war with the Indians. It was safe enough for the Kentucky papers and the politicians to urge war, for they were behind the frontier—Ohio was a part of it.[12] Both of Ohio's senators had opposed the declaration of war. Worthington believed that the "butchery" of war should be resorted to only as the "last means of redress." Senator Alexander Campbell was not present to vote against the declaration because of illness in his family, but he believed, and his constituents believed, that Congress had forced the Administration into the conflict. He would have preferred retaliatory measures.[13]

---

[8] Cf. editorials of March 16 and 27 in the *Fredonian*. See two columns against war by "Leonidas" in the March 11 issue.

[9] Van Horne to Worthington, February 24, 1813, in WMOSL.

[10] *Western Intelligencer* (Worthington), July 10, 1812.

[11] Hamm to Worthington, June 18 and 31, 1812, in WMOSL.

[12] Pratt, *Expansionists of 1812*, Preface and Chap. 1. Pratt indicates that there was a real popular sentiment for war in Ohio, but his proof is not convincing. Cf. Cady, "Western Opinion and the War of 1812," 27.

[13] Campbell to Worthington, May 24, June 17, 1812, and June 13, 1813, in WMOSL.

When Worthington returned from Congress in July, 1812, he was much concerned about the reaction of the Ohio people to the declaration of war, especially since Abraham Shepherd had just written him that nine-tenths of the people in western Virginia were opposed to it.[14] From contacts made as he traveled from Wheeling to Chillicothe he deduced that the people were divided in their sentiments, "those advocating it making much noise—those opp[ose]d more quiet."[15]

Certainly, much of the afflatus of patriotism subsided with the news of Hull's abject surrender at Detroit on August 16. The *Fredonian*, which had been so flamboyantly sanguine on August 25, characterized the capitulation in its next issue as "an act of treachery which has no parallel in the annals of human iniquity." Worthington's nephew William wrote him a few weeks later from Lexington that "the violent politicians of Kentuckey" are "pretty cule after being fanned for a month by the bleak winds of the north. . . . Most of the Democratic party have been disappointed, for instead of a frollicsome campain, they find themselves engaged in a tardy war."[16]

2

It might be supposed that Worthington's vote against the war would have made him too unpopular among the pro-war groups to be eligible for service in Ohio on his return from Congress. This was far from the case. His previous experience with the militia and in negotiations with the Indians was too well known. He had served as adjutant general under Governors Kirker and Huntington between 1807 and 1809. In 1807, besides his regular duties, he had organized the state's detachment of militia, authorized by an act of Congress, April 18, 1806, which called for 2,443 men in Ohio. In 1809, he organized another detachment, authorized by the law of March 30, 1808, which set Ohio's share at 2,384 men.

Worthington was criticized by some of his associates for his tardiness in providing for the safety of the Ohio frontier. Judge William Creighton, Jr., a fellow Chillicothean, wrote Judge Samuel Huntington that "love of office and influence consequent thereon" were Worthington's chief interests.[17] In anticipation of the need for armed forces in Ohio, Worthington had actually laid his plans to organize them immediately

---

[14] Shepherd to Worthington, July 2, 1812, in WM.
[15] Worthington's diary, July 13, 1812.
[16] William Worthington to Worthington, December 6, 1812, in WM.
[17] In the Huntington Papers, WRHS.

after the passage of the law of 1808. He knew, however, that militia could not be kept long in the field, and so he thought it unwise to call them out until they were needed. He believed that that time was approaching when he wrote General Gano early in 1809:

> *Whether war will be the result or not is yet uncertain. It is however believed it will. . . . The General government seem to be taking with earnestness the steps preparatory to such an event, under these circumstances the important relations in which you stand to your fellow citizens & soldiers cannot escape your notice. On you will greatly nay almost entirely depend the diffusion of orders & Military spirit throughout every inferior department of your division, your example will in a great measure give tone to every inferior officer.*[18]

Worthington's ability to deal with the Indians had been demonstrated in 1807. In September of that year, a thousand Indians had assembled on the frontiers of Ohio, and rumors of an extensive Indian war had caused great uneasiness throughout most of the state. On Governor Kirker's orders that they act as Indian agents, Worthington and McArthur had conferred at Greenville with over five hundred Indians under Tecumseh and the Prophet, and had secured their pledge of neutrality in case of war with Great Britain. After the negotiations, Tecumseh, Blue Jacket, Roundhead, and Panther had returned to Chillicothe with them and had stayed a week at Worthington's home as guests of Governor Kirker and his ambassadors.[19] Although he had fought against Wayne at Fallen Timbers in 1794, Blue Jacket was a trusted friend of the whites, and of Worthington in particular. Governor Hull regarded Blue Jacket as "the friend and principal adviser of the Prophet" and an unswerving advocate of peace.[20] Through Blue Jacket, who often stopped at Adena with other friendly chiefs, Worthington exercised no little influence over the Indians.

3

By 1811, then, Worthington was recognized as a leader in matters dealing with the Ohio militia and with Indian negotiations. He was fully aware of the inefficiency of the troops and the justifiable wrath of the Indians over the alienation of their lands by the treaties negoti-

[18] February 16, 1809, in "Selections from the Gano Papers," HPSO, *Quarterly Publication*, XV (1920), 35-37. See similar orders to General Wadsworth, February 16, 1809, in the Whittlesey Papers, WRHS. Worthington dismissed these troops May 15. See letter to Gano, May 15, in "Gano Papers," 40.
[19] Benjamin Drake, *Life of Tecumseh and His Brother the Prophet* (Cincinnati, 1852), 94-97; *Liberty Hall and Cincinnati Mercury*, October 13, 1807.
[20] Hull to Eustis, September 9, 1807, and July 14, 1812, in *Documents Relating to Detroit and Vicinity, 1805-1815* (Michigan Historical Collections, XL, 1929), 198.

ated by Indiana Territory's Governor Harrison. With impatience and misgivings, he watched Harrison's foolhardy expedition of November, 1811, and expressed profound regret at the news of Tippecanoe, for he believed the grievances resulting from encroachments on the Indian boundary could be settled permanently only by negotiation and the maintenance of amicable relations. He made this clear in a letter to Governor Meigs written from Washington:

> *The situation of our common country is becoming daily more serious and requires of those to whom the people have confided trust the exercise of their united exertions to manage the public affairs to the best advantage. . . . The late unfortunate occurence on the Wabash I fear will be the means of exciting the greatest alarm on the frontiers of Ohio and if it ends in alarm only I shall feel thankful. So soon as an account of this affair reached this place the delegation from Ohio called on the president, stated the exposed situation of our frontier and recommended in the strongest terms, 1st that you should be immediately authorized to call out as many companies of militia volunteers as should be considered necessary to be armed equiped & paid by the states who should act as rangers along our frontiers and protect the settlements. 2nd That a loan of arms should be immediately made by the U states to the state of Ohio. 3rd That the president should immediately appoint 3 commissioners who should go into the Indian country learn the causes of discontent of the Indians and if practicable, settle the differences without further bloodshed—whether this course will be adopted or not I cannot tell. I have thought it proper that you should be acquainted with what has been considered best under existing circumstances. You will in the event of an Indian war have the most arduous task to perform and I trust will not fail to attribute to me the proper motives in addressing you thus frankly for be assured sir whilst I do not mean to say anything which may have a tendency to offend, I can with great sincerity say that I have nothing to ask, hope or fear. At the same time it would give me the most sincere pleasure to live in peace and friendship with the whole circle of my acquaintances.*[21]

There was, indeed, sound reason for taking steps to prepare the militia and pacify the Indians of the Northwest. It was very fortunate that Tecumseh, at least for the time being, favored peace—unless the Americans got into a war with Great Britain—and did not plan immediate retaliation for the Tippecanoe insult. The Ohio-Indiana people who lived far from the frontier rejoiced at the blow Harrison had dealt the Indians; but the inhabitants on or near it shuddered for months in the expectation of a general attack. John Johnston, Indian agent at Piqua, wrote Meigs that "if war with the British is inevitable, the Government cannot take their measures with regard to the Indians too soon. It ought *never* to be forgotten that *fear alone* keeps the Indians quiet."[22]

---

[21] November 30, 1811, in WMOSL.
[22] Meigs to Worthington, February 5, 1812, quoting Johnston's letter of January 23, in WMOSL. Johnston set the number of Indians in Ohio at two thousand.

Meigs wrote Worthington on January 23, 1812, that the people on the frontier were uneasy, and suggested that a general treaty be made with the Indians before the British approached them.[23] As a result, President Madison appointed Senator Worthington, Congressman Morrow, and Governor Meigs to negotiate with the tribes at Piqua, August 1.[24]

Meanwhile, Congress had ordered the organization of twelve hundred militiamen and appointed Governor Hull to command them. They were to reinforce Detroit and be prepared for an invasion of Canada. They assembled at Dayton and started northward on the first of June. At Urbana they were joined by Lieutenant Colonel James Miller's regiment of regulars, the 4th Infantry from Vincennes. This motley, half-armed, ill-provisioned army took over a month to reach Detroit through the wilderness. The declaration of war alerted the British at Malden in time for them to capture the baggage of Hull's army (July 3), which he had foolishly sent by boat down the Maumee. This loss inaugurated a series of disasters for the American forces.

In the course of his Fabian maneuvers about Detroit, Hull managed to hold a council with the Indians at Brownstown during the second week of July. After explaining the situation, he felt he had convinced them that they should remain neutral or join the American forces. He wrote Eustis on July 21 that only Tecumseh and Marpot had joined the British and that he had sent the rest to the council at Piqua.[25]

On July 25, Worthington started for Piqua to meet the Indians, but when he learned from the papers that the council had been postponed until August 15, he returned home, where he participated in several conferences of Ohio leaders called by Governor Meigs to consider raising more troops and to plan for negotiations with the Indians. The news of the fall of Fort Michilimackinac came on August 5, reinforcing the Ohioans' fears concerning the fate of Detroit and impressing upon them the necessity for securing at least two thousand more troops and conducting a successful mission at Piqua.

On August 13, Worthington and Morrow reached Piqua, but no Indians had yet arrived. There they learned that Hull had invaded Canada, July 12, but that he had not yet struck the British. The Indians came in slowly and in nothing like the number expected. It became evident that Hull's sluggishness and the intrigues of the British had led

[23] In WMOSL.
[24] *Fredonian,* July 21, 1812; Robert B. McAfee, *History of the Late War in the Western Country* (Lexington, Ky., 1816), 111-12.
[25] Hull to Eustis, July 21, 1812, in *Documents Relating to Detroit,* 419-21.

many of the Indians to believe that the United States had no chance of winning the war and that if they placed themselves in the power of the Americans they would probably be massacred. Some groups which had halted near Fort Wayne joined in the siege of that post when they heard of the fall of Michilimackinac on July 17.[26] In spite of delays, however, by August 16 there were over seven hundred Indians present at Piqua to hear Worthington read the President's message. Their chiefs made appropriate replies.[27]

The Indians were sold large quantities of liquor by local dealers and were uncontrollable. Worthington spent most of his time riding about the camp quieting them and exhorting their chiefs to control them. When news arrived on the nineteenth that Hull had retreated from Malden, August 7-8, and had taken refuge in the fort at Detroit, it was decided to hold the Indians as long as possible while Governor Meigs left to raise more troops. Worthington and Morrow wrote Eustis, August 20,

> You will have learned before this reaches you that the commencement of the Indian council was postponed from the 1st to the 15th inst. when all the commissioners attended On the 15th and 16th insts near 800 Indians (men women and children) arrived composed of Shawanoes Delawares Wyandots Taw-ways & Kickapoes. It appears pretty evident that British agents have used every exertion to prevent the attendance of the Indians & not without success to a certain extent. This together with the unfavourable state of our affairs to the North has we apprehend had a considerable effect on the movements of the Indians and will on our part require additional exertion and caution. We deem it all important in the present critical situation of affairs to use every means in our power to keep the Indians quiet either at their homes or at the council untill the re-enforcements get to Detroit and a favourable change takes place. We have with a view to effect this sent confidential persons out among them to watch them to hasten such as are on the way in and to counteract the operations of the Brittish.
> You will perceive with this view of the subject that it will be necessary to prolong the council to a period beyond what might otherwise have been necessary. All is quiet at present on the frontier and we hope will continue so tho' we acknowledge we shall not be entirely without fear at least untill this army gets on the frontier We have only to add that we shall do all in our power to aid in the operations and effect the objects of the Government—
> P.S. Govr Miegs left on the 18th and is now at Urbanna using every exertion to start re-enforcements and supplies for this Army and [?] his return to the council is uncertain.[28]

The same day Worthington sent Eustis a second letter:

> I wrote you to day jointly with Mr Morrow on the subject of our duties here and now address you on several other subjects You will no doubt before this reaches you have learned through many channels the reverse our affairs

[26] McAfee, *Late War*, 111.
[27] In general, the account of the Piqua council is taken from Worthington's diary.
[28] In *Documents Relating to Detroit*, 457.

to the north have taken. Be assured things are bad enough and I shall not be surprised to hear of the loss of Hulls army before he is re-enforced. The great difficulty at present in carrying on our operations to the north is how to supply the army with provisions. you may remember that I pointed out this as the best route that is from this to fort defiance and then by water down the Maimia to the rapids & so on. I find on further examination—I was right and am satisfied Govr Hull was wrong in taking another rout. I should therefore advise that in future this should be taken as safest and best. I have heard since my arrival at this place that troops are about to be marched from Kentuckey to carry on an expedition against the Thousands of Indians which Govr Edwards has been collecting in Illinois between Michigan & Missi for two years past. How his great collection of Indians at piora [sic] have been supported so long I cannot conceive This man has excited more useless alarm in the west than any other I know and I most heartily wish him some berth where he will have less to fear.

If it be true this expedition is to be carried on if the Indians are about to be attacked soon the assertions of the Brittish to the Indians will be verified to wit, That the Americans whilst they [the Indians] were attending the council intend to distroy [sic] those of the Indians left at home about 30 Keckapoes from near piora [sic] are here and wait for the rest of there chiefs one principal chief is here. If the Govt intend to carry on war against the Indians I trust it will be general at all events let us not be treating and fighting at the same time If the force about to be called out be to protect the settlements it is all well but from the manner Govr Harrison writes us I understand hostile operations are to be carried on I have only to add and it is with reluctance & regret that Genl Hull I am satisfied has lost the confidence of the troops under his command[29]

The next day a friendly Indian brought bad news from Captain James Rhea at Fort Wayne: Fort Dearborn had fallen on August 15, and the garrison had all been massacred by the Indians. Rhea sent the following entreaty:

> Do all you can to give us some assistance—from the best information I can get they are determined on this place. . . . Everything appears to be going against us—for God Sake call on Gov. Meigs for to assist us in sending more men. . . . We shall start all our families from this [place] tomorrow. . . . We are very scant of provisions here—for God Sake try in Some way to get some forwarded to us.[30]

At 11:00 P.M., August 21, 1812, news came of the capture of Detroit on August 16. The Indians at Piqua were alarmed but friendly, and actually seemed concerned for the safety of the whites. Worthington moved among them and quieted their fears. He sat up until midnight writing letters and dispatches urging the militia officers and civil officers of the state to hasten troops to Fort Wayne. He enclosed Rhea's message in a letter to General Payne, who commanded one of Ohio's

---

[29] Ibid., 459.
[30] Rhea to John Johnston for Governor Meigs, August 19, 1812, in the Ohio State Archives, Executive Documents, 1810-12, OHS.

four regiments of militia, and importuned him to send as many volunteers as possible to Piqua.[31]

Worthington spent the next three days enrolling volunteers and collecting provisions at Piqua. He wrote Meigs and Harrison to hurry troops to Fort Wayne. He feared the whole frontier was "breaking up." His plan was to reinforce Fort Wayne immediately with four or five companies from Urbana; to recondition and garrison Forts Loramie, Murrys, St. Marys, and Adams; and to construct one other post between Fort Adams and Fort Wayne, thus establishing a cordon of outposts to guard the state's northwest frontier against the British and Indians if Fort Wayne fell and a general invasion of Ohio occurred.[32] Governor Meigs coöperated by ordering Colonel Bay to occupy these forts with his brigade and to protect the surrounding inhabitants. Worthington recorded in his diary, August 25, that "many troops arrive in consequence of a report that the indians have murdered Mr. Morrow and myself and seized the public property. My trials great, the people distracted and confidence lost in a great measure—never had so many difficulties to encounter."

On August 25, Worthington took the liberty of ordering Colonel Samuel Wells, in command of the 17th United States Regiment and a detachment of Kentucky troops at Cincinnati (actually at Newport), to march at once to the relief of Fort Wayne;[33] and both he and Governor Meigs urged Harrison, who awaited the arrival of four regiments from Georgetown, Kentucky, to hasten his departure from Cincinnati to the aid of that outpost. A majority of Harrison's troops departed on the nineteenth, and he joined them on the thirty-first near Dayton. They reached Piqua on the first of September, with the relief of Fort Wayne their immediate objective.

Meanwhile, so great was the fright at Chillicothe that a mass meeting was held on August 26 at which a committee was selected to see Governor Meigs and insist that he exert greater effort in recruiting troops. The committee was authorized to suggest to the Governor that he offer two hundred acres of land to each recruit who would serve twelve months and that he call to active duty every civil and military officer of the state.[34]

At the earnest suggestion of John Johnston, on August 26 and 27

---

[31] Worthington to Payne, August 21, 1812, in Benson Lossing, ed., *The American Historical Record* (3 vols., Philadelphia, 1871-73), I, 26. Lossing misdates the letter August 27.
[32] Ohio State Archives, Executive Documents, 1810-12, August 24.
[33] *Trump of Fame* (Warren), September 16, 1812.
[34] A copy of the mass meeting's resolutions, dated August 26, 1812, is in RCHS.

WARTIME SERVICE IN OHIO

Worthington organized seven mounted companies of forty men each and laid out a camp for them on the road to Fort Wayne, which was now reported besieged by six hundred Indians. The mounted companies were ordered to elect a commander, to hold themselves ready to march, and not to forage. Governor Meigs arrived in Piqua on the twenty-eighth with more troops and stores; the little army proceeded six miles to Fort Loramie the next day, and the following day marched to St. Marys. At this time it totaled some seven hundred mounted troops, temporarily commanded by "General Worthington, General Lytle, Col. Dunlap and Col. Adams." On the night of the twenty-eighth, Colonel Adams was elected commander by the troops, most of which refused to go any farther, much to Worthington's disgust, until General Harrison arrived.[35]

On the first of September, Worthington, with eight other whites dressed as Indians, set out with seven Indian guides to explore the country adjacent to Fort Wayne. They had covered thirty miles in two days without finding any sign of hostile Indians when a spy from Fort Wayne got through to them and reported that there were none farther east from the Fort than five miles. Nevertheless, the Indian guides refused to go farther and secretly returned to the army at St. Marys, much to Worthington's chagrin. The guides reported that they had been chased by hostile Indians—manifestly untrue—and consequently Colonel Adams did not move his troops forward as Worthington had planned but instead sent an express asking for information and advice. Worthington scratched this entry in his diary, September 3:

> The army do not march—the spies return to camp and we are 30 miles in advance in an enemy country. My plans completely defeated by the dastardly, cowardly conduct of a dozen cowardly scoundrels in camp, else we should have been able to have given the indians round the fort a good flogging.

After Worthington's scouts had pushed forward another four miles, a runner brought news from Jeremiah Morrow that Governor Meigs had left Piqua for Urbana and that the Indians were threatening to leave if Worthington did not return. He went back, on the fourth, to St. Marys, where he found nine hundred of Harrison's men, who had just arrived. On the fifth, he reached Piqua, where Harrison was encamped with 127 of his men. The next day Harrison pushed on toward St. Marys, picked up Colonel Adams' mounted volunteers at Shane's Crossing on the St. Marys River, and on the ninth, set out for Fort Wayne. One battalion of Colonel Adams' cavalry constituted the right flank of Harrison's army, and another rode a mile in advance of his

[35] Worthington's diary, August 31, 1812.

columns of infantry. Harrison's force now numbered about twenty-five hundred men. Fort Wayne was relieved on the twelfth, the Indians offering practically no opposition.

On the seventh, Worthington closed the Indian council and received from them "the most positive assurance of their determination to keep peace." The next day he arrived at Urbana, where Governor Meigs had assembled nine hundred volunteers. On the tenth, he reached Chillicothe and helped Samuel Finley prepare his men to march.

With their departure four days later, Worthington's military services for the summer were over, save as an adviser, and he returned to his farm and business interests for the short time remaining before he was to leave for his senatorial duties in Washington. During this interim of a month (he left for Washington on October 19), he served as acting president of the Bank of Chillicothe in General Finley's absence, milled three hundred barrels of flour for the army, had his corn harvested, surveyed a few tracts, closed several land deals, entertained Bishops Asbury and McKendree of the Methodist Church, and on October 17, dined "General Harrison, his aides & 20 others" who were on the way north.

It is interesting to note that the war, with its constant threat of British and Indian depredations, did not halt entertainment in Ohio's little capital. The *Fredonian* of September 30, 1812, announced the annual colt races for October 29; a circus played all week, September 28 to October 3, prices fifty and seventy-five cents; and a new dancing academy opened on September 29.

4

In Ohio the early enthusiasm for war was dispelled by the capture of Forts Michilimackinac, Dearborn, and Detroit. Mushroom patriotism and demagogic optimism wilted in the brilliant sun of criticism, pacifism, and recrudescent Federalist partisanship. Volunteering came to a standstill, and dissatisfaction and insubordination increased among the troops. Fear succeeded hopefulness: Harrison wrote Eustis, August 29, "The western country was never so agitated by alarm and mortification as at this time."[36] Adjutant General Van Horne complained because his men had lost the Spirit of '76: "Militia cannot march without a new blanket, a new gun & bayonet, shoes etc. and every company . . . must have a team of 4 horses to haul their baggage or they cannot

[36] In Logan Esarey, ed., *Messages and Letters of William Henry Harrison* (Indiana Historical Collections, IX, Indianapolis, 1922), II, 104.

march—if they are fifteen days out and no pay, damn the President."[37]

Ignorant of discipline, poorly officered, inadequately equipped, and provided with unsatisfactory commissary service, the troops lost most of their martial spirit before the year was out. Many of General Harrison's men by Christmas time had advanced only as far north as Fort Loramie, where hungry, sick, and unpaid, they deserted in droves.[38] The soldiers feared for their families and regretted their absence from home and business. Selfish politicians sowed dissension between commanders, encouraged desertion, and abused recruiting officers; some judges released recruits on writs of habeas corpus. The Ohio legislature and Congress were criticized for not safeguarding the frontier, and waves of panic swept the state from time to time. Tryal Tanner of Canfield wrote Worthington after the defeat of General Winchester's detachment at the River Raisin, January 22, 1813, "Have our War members & cabinet made no arrangements to defend the frontier . . . altho you are not considered a stickler for war we must look to our Senators for efficient War or Peace." The Northwestern Army dwindled to fifteen hundred men, and McArthur wrote Armstrong, March 30, 1813, that it would be five hundred in two weeks:

> *Some Persons have already been killed and scalped in the neighborhood of Piqua. . . .*
> *Great quantities of provisions and military stores are exposed at points far advanced in a wilderness . . . [those] at Sandusky are perhaps the most insecure. . . . The Indians . . . are almost daily visited by hostile Indians, who carry information to the British. . . . I understand . . . Genl Cass has returned to Zanesville. . . . Every day that the recruiting service is procrastinated will render it more difficult to obtain men. Very many . . . [once] sanguine of success, are now much discouraged; The constant inquiry is, "Why did not Genl Harrison make a requisition of men, in time to supply the places of those whose term of service had expired?" or, "Why is our frontier not guarded and the friendly Indians removed?"*[39]

A year later, things were no better. General Edward Tupper, commanding the Ohio militia, reported that when his men reached Zanesville in February, 1814, "there was not a single article of camp equipment to be found at that place." There and elsewhere, he related, the soldiers were urged not to march without tents and other equipment, and efforts were made to prejudice their minds and "introduce insubordination in their ranks." The legislature, he declared, "aided by

[37] Van Horne to Worthington, December 9, 1812, in WMOSL. Humphrey Fullerton wrote Worthington from Chillicothe, October 31, 1812, that two hundred Virginia troops had deserted and more were leaving daily. "Last night fifteen more . . . by the time they get to Detroit they will have few left." In WM.
[38] James Manary to Worthington, December 22, 1812, in WM.
[39] In *Documents Relating to Detroit*, 510-11.

two votes at one balloting from Charles Hammond," had displaced him from his command in favor of Robert McConnels. "I have therefore hung up my sword," he concluded, "till the enemy arrives at Chickamoga, that skirts the town of Gallipolis."[40]

The state of the war improved little the second year. Harrison was criticized for moving so slowly to avenge Hull's dishonor. After Winchester's defeat and while Fort Meigs, the chief center of resistance to the British, was being built, he even found time in March to visit his family in North Bend and to tour Chillicothe and other towns in the southwest quarter of the state in order to stimulate recruiting and counteract personal animosity toward him and the anti-war propaganda of the Federalists. Back at the defense of the fort in late April and early May, he gallantly held it against a British and Indian force twice the size of his own.

Between sessions of Congress, Worthington was useful in an advisory capacity, and often entertained Harrison, Governor Meigs, and the regimental commanders—Generals Cass, McArthur, and Findlay. Otherwise, he was constantly engaged in business. His mills ground steadily, and the contractors who had found it difficult to secure rations in some parts of the state drew heavily on him. Any surplus could be disposed of at a good price in New Orleans or in east-coast towns. Thus Worthington inadvertently benefited by the war he had opposed. In fact, the difficulty the sutlers had in securing grain for the army was partly due to the high price being paid at New Orleans. As early as July 8, 1812, D. C. Wallace of Cincinnati wrote Governor Meigs that the firm of Baum and Perry had bought up all the grain in that area for the New Orleans trade.[41] The same was true of woolgrowers; they sold where the price was best. Abraham Shepherd of Shepherdstown, Virginia, had opposed the war too, but he expressed the general economic sentiment of the farmers when he wrote Worthington, "I have a new hobby horse—that is to make Whiskey and raise Moreno sheep—Peace or war people will drink Whiskey and ware coats, I think my interest would be for the war to continue my life."[42]

Worthington was an ardent supporter of General Harrison even though he often criticized him for being slow and overcautious, and was inclined to agree with Charles Hammond that he was "little superior to every third man you would meet in a days journey through

[40] Tupper to Worthington, February 23, 1814, in WMOSL.
[41] See the Ohio State Archives, Executive Documents, 1810-12.
[42] December 10, 1813, in WM.

Ohio."[43] His confidence in Harrison was justified to a degree in 1813 by the General's first and second defenses of Fort Meigs and his victory at the Thames, October 5.

Worthington had confidence in McArthur's ability, too, and was happy to have him placed in command of the Northwestern Army when Andrew Jackson succeeded to Harrison's major generalship on the latter's resignation in May, 1814. Harrison was severely criticized after he decided to rest on his honors during the winter of 1813-14, and was in disfavor with Secretary of War Armstrong. Worthington had recommended to Armstrong that McArthur be appointed in Harrison's place. Instead, Armstrong appointed Jackson and gave McArthur a brigadier generalship and the command of the Northwestern Army.[44] McArthur was greatly displeased at not receiving the major generalship and the command of the district, and was very critical of Worthington for failing to secure him the desired appointment. His disgruntlement and lack of appreciation, perhaps added to the fact that he quartered a company of his troops on Worthington's estate without permission in January, 1815, led Worthington to note in his diary, January 28, that "McArthur [is] a most disagreeable neighbor." Worthington, who had never had much confidence in Lewis Cass as a military leader, welcomed his resignation to accept the governorship of Michigan Territory.[45]

He was himself urged to secure the command of the 8th Military District but was not seriously tempted despite his conviction that he could have done no worse than those whom Madison had appointed. In the Ohio area, military leadership, from Hull to McArthur, had not proved very efficient, and an increase in the willingness of a majority of men to fight and die either in defense of the region or for the conquest of Canada was no more discernible in 1814 than it had been in the two previous years.

Perry's victory on Lake Erie and Harrison's success on the Thames had caused rejoicing, but these victories were more than offset by defeats, the anti-war propaganda of the Federalists, petty politics, popular apathy, the greed and inefficiency of contractors, and the lack of coöperation between state and federal troops. By April, 1814,

---

[43] Hammond to Worthington, May 10, 1812, in the Hammond Collection, OHS.
[44] Worthington to McArthur, February 7, 1814, in the McArthur Papers; Dorothy Goebel, *William Henry Harrison* (Indiana Historical Collections, XIV, Indianapolis, 1926), 191-203, especially 198, n. 79; Clarence H. Cramer, "The Career of Duncan McArthur" (unpublished dissertation, Ohio State University, 1941), Chap. 3. McArthur was one of Governor Meigs's severest critics. See his letters to Meigs in the McKell Collection.
[45] Worthington's diary, March 9, 1814.

McArthur was willing to concede that a defense of the northwestern frontier was about all he could promise.[46] With the dispatch of Wellington's troops to Canada, affairs looked even darker.

In the East, the engagements at Chippewa, Lundy's Lane, and Lake Champlain raised the morale of the troops, but the burning of Washington in August, after a cowardly retreat at Bladensburg, took the heart out of the Administration. Worthington's years in the Senate ended in gloom. The prospect for Ohio was a little brighter, but for the nation the outlook was dark indeed.

5

Worthington's popularity with his colleagues in Washington and with certain groups in Ohio suffered for a time as the result of his vote against war. A month before the declaration, May 15, Joseph Collins had written him from Chillicothe: "I rejoice, my dear Sir that if uncontradicted reports may be credited you are very popular in Ohio—That you richly merit the love and confidence of the people, every candid man must acknowledge."[47] Two months later, July 14, sentiment had changed somewhat. Worthington's enemies seized the opportunity to attack him. William Creighton, a volatile patriot and Worthington's political adversary, wrote with considerable glee,

> Our old friend Worthington is opposed it seems to the effusion of human blood, a perfect Quaker in disposition opposed to fighting. He went on with the administration voting all the war measures untill he came to the pinch of the game and then turned tail to the government and his friends—his political days are numbered the people in every part of the State from which I have heard are pouring out their most precious curses on him for his vote—his vote is libel on the State—thank God friend we can wash our hands of the sin of sending him to the Senate.[48]

It is scarcely necessary to say that Creighton's sentiments did not express the opinion of the state, yet Worthington was attacked severely by the anti-Tammany newspapers. The *Fredonian* in July promised that the legislature would be petitioned to request his resignation (and Campbell's) "for deserting his post in the hour of danger." "Publico," in the *Liberty Hall and Cincinnati Mercury*, also asked for Worthington's resignation, claiming he no longer represented the people.[49] He was accused in the *Fredonian* of having been instru-

[46] McArthur to Worthington, April 15, 1814, in WMOSL.
[47] In WMOSL.
[48] Creighton to George Tod, July 14, 1812, in the Tod Manuscripts, WRHS.
[49] *Fredonian*, September 30. "Publico" was probably Jacob Burnet.

mental in the appointment of the "traitor" Hull; but that charge was easily refuted when Worthington showed the editor, Robert Richardson, a copy of the *Senate Executive Journal*. Richardson printed his documented denial "with sincere pleasure."[50] "A Friend of Merit" defended Worthington ably in the *Supporter* on August 1:

> *Before we condemn the opinion of those who opposed the immediate declaration of war, let us have a complete triumph, because we may, perhaps, need our united exertions before so desirable an event can be accomplished. . . .*
> *I am far from upholding Gen. Worthington as a perfect man; but where is the man who has encouraged population and manufactures more than he has done? Where is the man who has done more to encourage mechanics and to improve our country in general?*

In short, criticism of Worthington was largely the expression of political animosity and cannot be taken as representative of the attitude of the people at large or even of his home community. Governor Meigs was, if anything, more viciously and legitimately criticized. General McArthur found fault with the Governor for his "milk and water politicks" and alleged that the people "would support almost any other desent [*sic*] man in preference to him"; he particularly censured Meigs for campaigning for reëlection instead of raising troops, adding, "I suppose a company of rangers must be sent after him."[51] Edward Tiffin wrote Worthington, April 16, "The public will soon have a complete opportunity to observe we want a very different Man for Governor in [these] trying times—Volunteers I am informed cannot be obtained—no wonder."[52] After Hull's defeat, Meigs was accused of having received half the price of the General's treason, of having conspired to split the profits from provisioning the army, and of having withheld aid from Detroit.[53]

Worthington never had any occasion to regret his stand against the conflict. He wrote James Heaton of Hamilton, "I have often wished that there might be a state of things which would not justify my vote. I would willingly sacrifice selfishness to my love of country."[54] As time passed, the soundness of his position in regard to the war became more and more evident. The series of disasters and disappointments which had taken place rapidly restored him to general favor and

---

[50] *Ibid.*, September 16 and December 9; *Senate Executive Journal*, II, 243-45 (March 10, 1812).
[51] McArthur to Worthington, March 23 and April 7, 1812, in WMOSL.
[52] In WMOSL.
[53] Joseph Willen (Marietta) to Meigs, September 14, in the Ohio State Archives, Executive Documents, 1810-12. See also the *Trump of Fame*, September 16, 23, 30, and Carlos Norton to Worthington, April 17, in the Meigs Papers.
[54] January 22, 1813, in WMOSL.

justified the wisdom of his vote against the premature declaration of war. Even as early as November 23, 1812, John Kerr wrote him as follows:

> *I am much pleased to remark that the people are now not near so ready to burn your effigy . . . as they were in the summer. Consideration is always resumed by the multitude when it is of no great service to them. War is a pretty thing in theory, how it will terminate in practice is altogether a different consideration—If the people are heavily taxed for the support of the war, I wish it were a poll tax, the fever of war would be greatly reduced by such an application of the laws of Congress.*[55]

[55] In WMOSL. See the letters from Adjutant General Van Horne, December 9, in WMOSL, and from John Pollock (Milford, Clermont Co.), March 12, 1814, in the Meigs Papers, for an expression of the same sentiments.

Governor of Ohio

THE gubernatorial election of 1814 was a tame affair after the campaigns of 1808 and 1810. The war had so preoccupied the voters of Ohio that state politics had been relegated to the background. The agitation over judicial review, the "sweeping resolution," and the Tammany Society was largely forgotten.

Eight or more persons were pointed out by the newspapers as fit candidates for the position of governor, but the contest finally narrowed down to Worthington and Othniel Looker, who had been acting governor since March, when Meigs resigned to accept the postmaster generalship. Looker was from Hamilton County, and had a fair following in that part of the state.

Early in the campaign Worthington appeared to be the popular choice. His vote against war seems to have constituted no obstacle to his nomination for the governorship; rather, the course of the war had confirmed his judgment. A Muskingum County Federal-Republican caucus put him in nomination, recalling that he had "had the discernment to perceive the bad policy of going to war without being prepared and the firmness and independence to vote against it."[1] It is significant that the officers of an army regiment at Rossville (Piqua) nominated him in caucus,[2] and that General Reazin Beall of Canton scotched a north-state intrigue against him.[3] "Illius Ergo" of Butler County recommended him as "a man of unrivalled talents of unblemished reputation and unsullied honor."[4] "An Elector" in the *Scioto Gazette* wrote of him as follows:

> This gentleman possesses in an eminent degree, all the qualifications which the governor of the state of Ohio, ought to possess. He is inflexible in his political creed & strongly attached to the present administration—regular in his moral deportment; well acquainted with military discipline, and will no doubt perform the duties of governor with honor to himself & constituents.[5]

Worthington's neighbor McArthur had a following in the state, and particularly in Ross County. Early in the campaign, a group of

---

[1] *Zanesville Express and Republican Standard*, September 14, 1814.
[2] *Miami Intelligencer* (Hamilton), October 10, 1814.
[3] Beall to Worthington, October 24, 1814, in WMOSL.
[4] *Miami Intelligencer*, September 19, 1814.
[5] Copied in *Freeman's Chronicle* (Franklinton), August 5, 1814.

McArthur's supporters accused Worthington of using his influence to make Meigs Postmaster General in order to get him out of the way, but such a weak indictment had little weight, for Meigs had been none too popular as war governor. The resort to such an accusation indicates how little basis there was for any genuine opposition. McArthur would have run, however, since he was sick of the army, if he had been able to drum up sufficient support. He maintained that Worthington helped keep him in the army so that he could not be a candidate for the governorship.[6] Worthington had been instrumental in getting him appointed brigadier general in charge of the Northwestern Army; but McArthur felt that he should have had the major generalship vacated by Harrison and given to Jackson when the latter was placed in charge of the 7th Military District.[7] In a sense, McArthur had a legitimate complaint, for his army duty had prevented him from being a candidate to succeed Worthington as United States Senator, an office to which he aspired and for which he was considered a strong contestant.[8]

There was more truth than fiction in the sarcastic analysis made by "Calculator" in *Liberty Hall* for September 27, when he wrote that "everybody" was for Worthington:

> The federalists will vote for him because he was a violent federalist; the sweeping resolutionists because he is the father of that interesting measure; the Tammanies, because he is the head of that society; the opposers of the war, because he voted against the declaration of it; the supporters of the war, because he has regularly voted for war measures; the republicans, because he calls himself at present a republican; the military characters, because he has the title of general.

For the most part, the newspapers were unusually silent on political issues; at any rate, the result of the election was never in doubt. Concern over the course of the war filled the columns once devoted to personal abuse. Worthington and Tiffin were in Washington; the council fires of the Tammany wigwams were scattered; and the erstwhile combatants of the old junto were now largely in command of patronage.

The official count in the contest for the governorship was 15,879

[6] Joseph Kerr to Worthington, May 19, September 21, 1814, in WMOSL; Worthington to Kerr, September 30, 1814, in the McKell Collection. See the copy of a letter from Worthington to McArthur, October 30, in which he strongly rebukes him for being a party to such outrageous lies as had been started and cites many evidences of his continued loyalty to McArthur, both in peace and in war. In the McKell Collection.
[7] Worthington to McArthur, February 7, 1814, in the McArthur Papers.
[8] James Barnes, editor of the *Scioto Gazette*, to Samuel Williams, October 26, 1814, RCHS.

for Worthington to 6,171 for Looker.[9] Looker carried Clermont, Franklin, Greene, Scioto, and Hamilton counties; Worthington captured the rest, including the old Federalist strongholds of Jefferson, Washington, and Trumbull counties.[10]

2

Worthington's arrival in Ohio on December 2 to assume his new duties was greeted by the *Zanesville Express and Republican Standard,* December 7, 1814, as follows:

> At a time like this when war is raging upon our frontiers, and threatens the interior, to have so firm a patriot—so enlightened a politician possessing the confidence of all parties, placed at the helm of our State, is a subject of sincere gratification.

On December 8 Worthington rode into Chillicothe from Adena, appeared before a joint session of the legislature, and, having taken the oath of office, delivered his inaugural address. It was really a war message, a call to renewed devotion to a cause thus far made ignominious by party faction. The new governor praised the Administration for seeking to avoid war and engaging in it only after a long "series of injury and insult and in defense of its just rights," and for its willingness to negotiate at any time thereafter on reasonable and honorable terms. The negotiations at Ghent, he pointed out, had seemed to promise much, but they had disappointed reasonable expectations.

> England, intoxicated . . . in the plentitude of her power, has forgotten right and justice and has offered as a basis of a treaty, propositions as insulting as they are unjust . . . ; propositions which aim a deadly blow at the liberty and independence of the nation, and would, if accepted, lead to national degradation and ruin. That there should have existed a difference of opinion on the policy of declaring war . . . was to be expected. It was a question on which men of the best intentions might differ; but the measure once adopted, I believed every man owing allegiance to the government bound in good faith to take the side of his country . . . and that his best exertions should be used to support and defend it. . . . It is now in the strictest sense of the word, a war of defense. The enemy, by the manner he wages the war; by the means he uses in the employment of savages and slaves . . . gives a character to the war which cannot be misunderstood; and leaves strong ground to believe that a subversion of our happy form of government, and as a consequence the subjugation of the country, are among the objects he wishes to effect. We are therefore impelled by every motive and bound by every tie which can influence man, to defend the liberties of our country.[11]

Worthington warned the legislators of the dangers which threatened the country and reminded them that the power to provide adequate

[9] Taylor, *Ohio Statesmen,* 78.
[10] *Zanesville Express,* October 19, November 2, 1814; *Miami Intelligencer,* November 21, 1814.
[11] *Senate Journal, 13th General Assembly.*

defense for the state lay in their hands, not in the hands of the Chief Executive. He pointed out that although he recognized the value of the party system in a democracy, party animosity had so deeply affected the energies of the nation that three campaigns against the enemy had accomplished little. He appealed to them as representatives of the people to recognize the seriousness of their responsibility and to unite in a common defense of the state and the country.

3

Worthington made it clear in his inaugural address that his first concern was for the safety of the state. The pressing need was to provision the army at Detroit, which McArthur reported as living on the adjacent country.[12] In December, Worthington asked the legislature to authorize him to see that the soldiers were supplied. An investigating committee decided that McArthur's report was groundless, but gradually the contractors' service did improve. Had the situation not mended, Worthington would have supplied the posts with or without authorization.[13]

The state of discipline in the army was very bad, and morale was low. Deserters were legion; a fifty-dollar reward was outstanding for their apprehension. Five of the thirty court-martialed at Chillicothe in July were shot.[14] Worthington's vigorous activities soon brought about a change for the better. He firmly believed that the war was to be a long one and that preparations for an energetic defense were necessary. He had pointed out the frontier's lack of defenses to the Secretary of War just before leaving Washington,[15] and he now took in hand the effective organization of the militia. He ordered muster rolls completed and arms located, cleaned, and stored. A new spirit was manifested. In a special message to the legislature on December 21, he asked for a new set of militia regulations which would prevent evasion of military service and desertion and provide a creditable and efficient force from the forty thousand young men available. He urged that township trustees be empowered to arm all members of the militia not able to arm themselves and that stores of provisions be held in reserve. On the twenty-third, he recommended the construction

---

[12] McArthur to Looker, October 15, 1814, RCHS.
[13] Worthington's diary, December 9, 1814.
[14] *Miami Intelligencer,* July 20 and August 5, 1814.
[15] Worthington to Monroe, January 17, 1815, in Governor of Ohio, Executive Letter Book, 15, OHS.

of a line of blockhouses for the defense of the frontier. Constructed by rangers and guarded by militia contingents in shifts of two months each, they would cost little and provide a real defensive barrier. In the same message he asked that five new regiments be organized and mustered into service. (Incidentally, such a plan for strengthening the militia of the whole Northwest was being considered, at his suggestion, by Secretary of War James Monroe.)[16] When Adjutant General Van Horne demurred at carrying out his order to muster the new regiment of militia requested by McArthur, Worthington, determined on effective and speedy action, himself ordered them to Fort Meigs, and Van Horne resigned.

Joseph Kerr, who had been elected to serve out Worthington's unexpired term in the Senate, reported from Washington, January 30, that the fall of New Orleans was expected any minute and that Congress had authorized eighty thousand more militia. He advised Worthington to get the legislature to act for the safety of Ohio, for Monroe could not be depended on, and there was no prospect of peace.[17] Congressman James Caldwell informed Worthington, February 9, that eighty thousand British veterans had been dispatched to America.[18] John Johnston wrote from Piqua in February that the British were organizing an attack by Indians and regulars to take place in the early summer, and had arms and equipment for ten thousand Indians at Kingston. He reported frequent murders on the frontier: "23 persons were murdered in one day at the Pidgeon Roost I[ndiana] T[erritory]." In Johnston's opinion, no reliance could be placed now or ever on the Indians.[19]

Such reports stimulated the Governor to stronger measures, for the legislature had done little to improve the situation. On February 13, he urged the legislators in a strong message to take action on defense measures before they adjourned:

There is no evidence on which to rest even an opinion that peace will result from the present negotiations in Europe, . . . every arrival from thence strengthens the impression that the enemy are making the most vigorous preparation for prosecuting the war. The late desperate attempts at New Orleans, . . . affords full evidence . . . how much may be expected from a proper state of preparation. . . . Can it be necessary to remind you gentlemen of the extended and defenceless

[16] Copy of letter from Worthington to Monroe, November 21, 1814, in the Ohio State Archives, Executive Documents.
[17] Kerr to Worthington, January 30, 1815, in the Rice Collection.
[18] Caldwell to Worthington, February 9, 1815, in WMOSL.
[19] Johnston to Worthington, February 9 and 19, 1815, in the Ohio State Archives, Executive Documents.

frontier, which it becomes our duty to defend? . . . I feel bound from a most conscientious sense of duty . . . to recommend to your consideration the propriety of adopting such measures of defence, as the state of the country, in my opinion, imperiously requires before you adjourn.[20]

The same day, however, the legislature refused to ratify a hastily prepared bill which would have authorized the Governor to hold two regiments in readiness at all times for instant service.[21] To Worthington's chagrin, a weak substitute of volunteers was proposed but, after dallying for half a day with this measure, the legislators adjourned on February 16 without action. The Governor regarded this failure as most reprehensible, and explicable only on the grounds of ignorance, provincialism, and lack of vision. Luckily, and perhaps to some extent justifying the legislature's failure to act, a few days later there were rumors of peace—rumors which were fortunately confirmed on February 22. A most critical and anxious period in the history of Ohio was thus brought to a close, and thanksgiving assemblies succeeded prayer meetings. The Governor appointed March 31 as an official "day of Thanksgiving and prayer."

Throughout his term of office, Worthington never lost his interest in the militia. He continued to regard a strong and well-disciplined military organization as one of the most necessary and useful forces of the state, and his constant care was to make service in the militia popular. His annual inspection tours, in company with one or both of his aides, Colonel John Moore and Edward King, his son-in-law, were a pleasant duty. His motto was "In time of peace we must prepare for war." During the last year of his second term, he secured one hundred thousand dollars' worth of arms for the state's fourteen brigades, and by a personal trip to Washington settled the government's charge against Ohio for arms and accouterments for 1,200 soldiers issued during the war.[22] On this February trip he froze his nose and face, and was so sick with "bilious colic" on his return that he could not eat for seven days.[23]

4

On December 2, 1815, the Governor's second annual message was delivered. He requested that particular attention be given to pro-

---

[20] *Senate Journal, 13th General Assembly,* 420-23.
[21] *House Journal, 13th General Assembly,* 382, 391; *Senate Journal, 13th General Assembly,* 424.
[22] *Senate Journal, 17th General Assembly,* 11; *House Journal, 17th General Assembly,* 67.
[23] Worthington's diary, February 7 to 24, 1818.

visions for education, recommended an increase in judges' salaries, and urged a more responsible and effective expenditure of state funds for much-needed road improvement. Deprecating the custom of exploiting paupers by farming them out to contractors, he proposed the establishment of county poor farms under state regulation.[24]

On December 20, he sent a special message on land and banks to the legislature. He advocated that instead of selling land outright for taxes, only a portion of delinquent land sufficient on sale to pay the tax be forfeited in trust to the state with the privilege of redemption within two years: "Such a system . . . whilst it would afford ample indemnity to the state, would give a fair opportunity to the non-resident claimants to prevent the sacrifice of their property, and effectually put an end to the litigation and improper speculations produced by the former system."

He deplored the increase in the number of banks in Ohio and denounced their debasement through processes of speculation and overinflation. He proposed that the state regulate the banks by charter and coöperate with banks so chartered by investing state funds in their stock. Thus, if the state purchased one-fifth of the stock issues of banks about to be chartered or rechartered at an 8–per cent return, in a few years the tax burden on land might be reduced.

The legislatures of 1814 to 1816 did little in the way of legislation to meet the wishes of the Governor. They had denied him an emergency wartime militia, and now they failed to agree on a system of free education, on poor relief, and on an adequate road-building policy. Nevertheless, some modest and conservative measures were adopted. During the 1814-15 session, the militia regulations were revised; banks were restrained from issuing money without authorization, and a 4–per cent state tax was put on their dividends; the criminal code was amended; and the Governor was given authority to borrow funds to pay the direct tax.[25]

During the 1815-16 session, the legislature passed a law which went only so far as to make the erection of a poorhouse discretionary with each county and to provide that each township might erect its own poorhouse if the county failed to act. The compulsory pauper-care law was revised, but its provisions did not alter the arrangement by which the poor were cared for under contract and their children apprenticed.[26] Banks were again authorized to issue money, but the

[24] Senate Journal, 14th General Assembly, 10-18.
[25] Chase, Statutes, II, 856-901.
[26] Ibid., 928, 942-45.

stockholders were made responsible for it; however, the Governor's recommendations were carried out to the extent that each new bank was required to assign 4 per cent of its stock to the state, the dividends from which were to be applied to the purchase of more stock until one-sixth of its total was owned by the state.[27] The legislature also followed Worthington's wishes in refusing to endorse the resolutions of the Massachusetts and Connecticut assemblies providing for constitutional amendments excluding Indians not taxed and Negroes from the census for the purpose of representation, requiring a two-thirds vote of all states for the admission of new states, and denying Congress the right to lay embargoes of more than sixty days.[28]

5

The election of 1816 was dull, for Worthington had little opposition. He even found time during the months preceding it to lay out the town of Logan near his mill at the falls of the Hockhocking, a delightful country underlaid with large deposits of coal, which led him to hope that the town might soon become the Pittsburgh of Ohio. Judge Ethan Allen Brown of the Ohio Supreme Court, Colonel James Dunlap of Chillicothe, and Joseph Vance of Urbana were nominated to oppose him.[29] Worthington announced in August that he would serve again if elected, and he was nominated by numerous caucuses over the state. The election was held on October 8. The *Ohio Monitor* (Columbus) conceded on the tenth that Worthington was elected "by an almost unanimous vote" despite his "time serving policy" and his parsimony. An editorial in the *Western Spy* (Cincinnati) on the eighteenth expressed the hope that "his excellency . . . will not feel mortified . . . that he should condescend again to accept the office of Governor of this backwoods state. . . . It would manifest a spirit of condescension which ever gives additional lustre to true greatness." The vote was Worthington 22,931, Dunlap 6,295, Brown 1,607.[30] The "Grand Sachem of the [Tammany] Tribe of Ohio," as the *Liberty Hall and Cincinnati Gazette* called him, carried thirty-two counties, including the old Federalist strongholds of Trumbull, Hamilton, Warren, and Washington. Dunlap carried eight, including Ross County. Brown won four.

---

[27] *Ibid.*, 904-905, 913-24.
[28] Governor of Ohio, Executive Letter Book, 1814-18, 96.
[29] *Ohio Monitor*, October 3, 1816.
[30] *Senate Journal, 15th General Assembly*, 46-47.

6

The banking situation, which had engaged Worthington's interest during the summer of 1816, was to some degree a campaign issue. The failure to recharter the National Bank in 1811 had resulted in the establishment of a profusion of unauthorized "wildcat" banks, which flooded the country with depreciated money. The Ohio banks had not suspended specie payment until January, 1815, when the general inflation made it necessary to do so. Worthington had voted against the recharter of the United States Bank in 1811, but in 1816 he, like Clay, was in favor of it. There were now twenty-one authorized banks in Ohio and a very large number of wildcats; prices were inflated, and prosperity seemed to reign. It was "the jubilee of swindlers and Saturnalia of non-specie paying banks";[31] but a period of resumption and deflation had been forecast by the recharter of the United States Bank, which meant the day of judgment was near for the wildcats.

A contest arose as to whether a branch of the National Bank which had been authorized for Ohio should be opened in Chillicothe or in Cincinnati. At a meeting of Chillicothe stockholders, Worthington was selected to go to Philadelphia and Washington and use his influence to secure the bank for Chillicothe. Since Mrs. Worthington had been ill and the doctor had ordered travel, he took her and his youngest child with him. They visited in the homes of John Jacob Astor and Rufus King in New York, and traveled up the Hudson to West Point to visit the Governor's son James. While there, Worthington addressed the cadets.

Worthington was severely criticized by the papers of Cincinnati for having used his influence in behalf of Chillicothe. The *Western Spy,* November 15, reported that instead of being on the job as governor, he had "descended to the grade of a mere *pettifogging intriguer* for the pecuniary or commercial interests of *his own* particular section of the state . . . an *avowed* agent of sectional interests." In January, 1817, the directors of the National Bank awarded Cincinnati the branch, but Worthington, assisted by his son-in-law, Edward King, persisted in his efforts and made such a strong case for Chillicothe that in October that city also was given a branch.

The resumption of specie payment by the chartered banks was

---

[31] Richard Hildreth, *Banks, Banking, and Paper Currency,* 67, quoted by C. C. Huntington, "A History of Banking and Currency in Ohio before the Civil War," *Ohio State Archaeological and Historical Quarterly,* XXIV (1915), 280.

necessitated by the presence of the National Banks. As a result, their paper rose in value while that of the unauthorized banks sank still lower. The directors of the chartered banks, who wished the "wild-cats" destroyed, were naturally pleased. Unfortunately, however, not only the wildcat banks but also the chartered banks had overinflated their currency and accepted a good deal of doubtful paper, especially through the land offices. When the United States Bank restricted its issues and began to press the Ohio banks for redemption of the enormous amounts of paper money they held while refusing to accept any save their own paper and specie, a general collapse ensued. Thus an institution introduced as a great good lost its popularity because of an unavoidable but too precipitous operation. The history of the Panic lies outside the bounds of this account, but it may be said that Worthington's popularity declined because he seemed to be guilty of special pleading: he had not only supported the National Bank but was a director of both its Ohio branches. Moreover, he served on the committee of the federal bank which met in Philadelphia in November, 1819, and made a report on that bank's losses, gains, and general prospects—a report which, though none too encouraging at the time, was proved by later events to be overoptimistic.[32]

7

Ohio's seat of government was moved to Columbus during the summer of 1816. Worthington's friend, John Kerr of Columbus, had contracted in 1812 to erect the necessary buildings and, despite the war, had succeeded in getting the statehouse built on the corner of one of the two ten-acre lots donated by him for that purpose. These ten-acre donations were part of a 1,200-acre plot owned by Kerr and his associates, the remainder of which they laid off in in- and out-lots. Here, in the yet unfinished capitol building at the corner of Third and State streets, the Fifteenth General Assembly met on December 2. The capitol was not finished for another year. Worthington himself supervised the clearing of the grounds by the state's prisoners and had the area ploughed and enclosed by a five-rail mortised fence.

The Governor's annual message was read on December 3. Again he asked that a public school system, one of the most pressing needs of the rising generation, be established. He stressed the necessity for financing better roads and water routes in order to expedite the marketing of Ohio's abundant crops and products, and to that end

---

[32] *Niles Register*, November 18, 1819.

requested the legislators to abandon their plans to reduce taxes on land, a proposal which had been gathering strength for some time. He advised economy and industry as the proper means of recovery from the disorganized state of finances and urged a more liberal patronage of home industries.[33]

In his second inaugural address, delivered on December 9, he made a plea for penal recodification so that a vigorous program of reform might be made possible:

> The system with reference to the reform of offenders is defective. A criminal is imprisoned . . . and kept at hard labor, the proceeds of which, . . . goes into the state treasury; and at the expiration of his time he is turned out on the world, degraded, perhaps pennyless and with no other clothes than a penitentiary uniform, to be pointed at with the finger of scorn and contempt. . . . It is very true that crimes against society should always be held in abhorrence, and justice requires that they should be punished; but whilst we do justice let us not forget to love mercy. . . . It is our duty to give such a human being a fair opportunity of reform. Persuaded . . . that the good people of Ohio do not wish to profit by the miseries of the unfortunate, I recommend . . . the propriety of giving to persons confined . . . at the expiration of their terms, . . . the net proceeds of their labor. . . . Such an arrangement would unquestionably . . . encourage industry, sobriety and economy[;] the comforts and conveniences of this life may be obtained without resorting to means which violate the rights of others.[34]

Two days later, December 11, the Governor sent a message to the General Assembly asking its members to determine how the state could be of assistance in the Erie Canal project and urging that this important undertaking receive all possible encouragement. He enclosed a letter from DeWitt Clinton, president of the New York Board of Canal Commissioners, which urged Ohio to participate as fully as possible in the construction of the canal. Four weeks later, a committee made up of Robert Lucas, Almon Ruggles, and Aaron Wheeler reported enthusiastically in favor of Ohio's active participation in the project. A resolution was passed authorizing the Governor to continue correspondence with Clinton concerning what contribution Ohio could make.[35]

The legislature paid little heed to the Governor's other requests. Less legislation was passed than in any previous session. The land tax was reduced, the incorporation of turnpike companies was authorized, some changes were made in the criminal law, and several banks and towns were incorporated, but that was about all.[36]

---

[33] *Senate Journal, 15th General Assembly*, 8-12.
[34] *Ibid.*, 56-58.
[35] *Ibid.*, 67, 189-92.
[36] Chase, *Statutes*, II, 1000-1030; *Laws of Ohio*, XV (Columbus, 1817), 165-67.

In his annual message of December, 1817, the Governor discussed more vigorously than ever the matters on which he wished action. He deplored the inadequate number and inferior quality of the teachers available in the state. He made a strong plea for the establishment of a state system of education and a free state normal school at Columbus for indigent but able boys who, when qualified, could be employed as teachers. He lamented the folly of spreading the road-building funds so widely that none of the roads were good; he urged that the main roads be put in condition before expenditures were made elsewhere. He felt that supervisors of road-building and repair should be responsible for a particular section of each road, should not be permitted to dissipate their resources or shift their responsibilities by overlapping duties, and should be paid in accordance with the results obtained. Again, he urged the stimulation of home industry by buying at home:

> As far as circumstances will permit, every community should rely on its own resources. To depend on those of others, when by the exercise of economy and industry we have the means of supplying our own wants;—never fails to produce the worst effects. Since the late war the nation has been inundated with the manufactures of foreign countries. . . . What we do manufacture is better generally than that which we import. . . . [We should confine our buying in every instance where possible to the products of our own state and thus give] the proper encouragement to manufacturing in the state.[37]

Practically no legislation was passed during the 1817-18 session. Seven new banks were chartered and six counties established, but the greater part of the time was spent in "windy warfare" over the advisability of taxing the United States Bank.[38] Most of the matters recommended were considered in committee, and several bills were drawn, but none was passed.

During Worthington's second administration, an attempt was made to settle the dispute over the northern boundary of Ohio. The dividing line was rerun by William Harris under orders from Surveyor General Edward Tiffin, but Governor Cass of Michigan refused to accept it, and a controversy arose that was to result some years later in the so-called "Erie War."

8

President Monroe made a tour of Ohio in August, 1817. He visited the state capital in company with Governor Cass of Michigan, Gen-

[37] Senate Journal, 16th General Assembly, 11-14.
[38] Huntington, "Banking and Currency in Ohio"; House Journal, 16th General Assembly, 144 et seq.; Cramer, "Duncan McArthur," 112-17.

erals Jacob Brown and Alexander Macomb, and their aides. Governor Worthington took the whole party to Chillicothe and entertained them at Adena for dinner and the first night of their stay. They were given a reception by the citizens of Chillicothe, who were unanimous in their praise of the modest and affable manner of their new Chief Executive. He, in turn, appeared to be extremely grateful for the marks of affection and respect paid him, and was delighted with the splendid views afforded from the vantage points about town, particularly from "Mr. James' hill." Governor Worthington spent several days escorting him and his party about the central part of the state.[39]

9

If Worthington's own handiwork in the constitution of 1802 made him largely a figurehead as governor, it did not keep him from being very active whenever he could find constructive work to do. His most enduring monument, of course, is the state itself, which he helped to create. Of lesser importance but a substantial achievement, the Ohio State Library is his memorial. Dependent on politics and poorly financed as it has sometimes been since Worthington's day, at the time of its establishment it was a fine institution. Without authorization—something Worthington could scarcely get from a jealous legislature—but with the advice of Charles Hammond and a few other interested legislators, Worthington purchased from the contingent fund granted him 509 books as a nucleus for an Ohio State Library.[40] Moreover, he provided for its furnishings, appointed a librarian, and secured a set of rules for its government from the Library of Congress through his good friend William H. Crawford.[41]

In presenting the state with his purchase, he wrote as follows to the legislature, December 2, 1817:

[The contingent fund] has enabled me to purchase a small but valuable collection of books which are intended as the commencement of a library for the state. In the performance of this act, I was guided by what I conceived the best interest of the state, by placing within the reach of the representatives of the people, such information as will aid them in the performance of the important duties they are delegated to perform.[42]

[39] Worthington's diary, August 25-30.
[40] C. B. Galbreath, "Ohio State Library Centennial," Ohio State Archaeological and Historical Quarterly, XXVIII (1919), 112.
[41] Crawford to Worthington, July 9, 1817, in WMOSL. See also Daniel J. Ryan, "The State Library and Its Founder," Ohio State Archaeological and Historical Quarterly, XXVIII (1919), 98-109.
[42] Senate Journal, 16th General Assembly, 15.

The next summer, he inspected the penitentiaries of Pennsylvania and New York and secured plans and estimates for a new penitentiary for Ohio. In his first message of 1814, he had advocated reform of the penal code,[43] and now he was instrumental in making possible a more commodious and better-equipped institution for the housing and reformation of lawbreakers. Jeremy Bentham heard of his interest in prison reform and education and sent him, through Ambassador John Quincy Adams, a set of his works on those subjects, including both his *Christomathea* and *Panopticon*.

On January 20, 1818, while addressing the legislature regarding the Bentham gift, Worthington took the opportunity of announcing his retirement from the governorship:

> *I avail myself, gentlemen, of this opportunity, through you to inform my fellow citizens that I do not desire to be considered a candidate for the office of governor at the next general election. I have deemed this early notice proper, in order to give the good people of Ohio full time to select a successor.*

He suggested at the same time that the governor's salary be increased before a new incumbent was chosen and that provision be made for a governor's residence in Columbus.[44]

Ethan Allen Brown was the popular choice for governor in 1818, largely because he was in favor of taxing the United States Bank. James Dunlap of Chillicothe, the runner-up in 1816, was his opponent. McArthur was mentioned, but his opposition to taxation of the Bank made him unpopular. Worthington may have hoped that Jeremiah Morrow would be elected and that he would be chosen to replace him in the Senate; at least Brown and McArthur accused him of entertaining that idea, and many of McArthur's friends interpreted his trip to Washington in 1817 as part of the design. The argument lacked point, however, for Morrow refused to accept the nomination for governor or to run for reëlection to the Senate. McArthur also withdrew from the race for the governorship, and Brown overwhelmingly defeated Dunlap.

10

Governor Worthington's valedictory was read to the legislature, December 7, 1818, by his private secretary and son-in-law, Edward King. His first exhortation concerned education:

> *Among the measures which I have heretofore recommended to the Legislature, . . . and on which they have not acted, a good plan for the education of the rising generation, has been considered first in importance.*

[43] *House Journal, 13th General Assembly,* 101.
[44] *Senate Journal, 16th General Assembly,* 233-34.

Time, and further reflection have confirmed me in the opinions I have before communicated; and from a sense of duty to the state, I must again recommend the subject to your attention. Surely, nothing can be more important. . . . I feel convinced a perpetuation of that freedom, we now possess, greatly depends on the means, which may be used, under Providence, to produce that state of general information, which will enable the people to appreciate the liberty they enjoy. . . . I am fully convinced, it is the first duty of the Legislature to adopt, with as little delay as possible, a system for the establishment of elementary schools, throughout the state. . . . [If nothing is done] the poorer class . . . will be brought up in a state of comparative ignorance, unable to manage, with propriety, their private concerns, much less to take any part in the management of public affairs: and what is still more to be lamented, unacquainted with those religious and moral precepts and principles, without which they cannot be good citizens. . . . I avail myself of this the last opportunity, offered me, of recommending to your serious attention a subject of so much importance.[45]

Worthington urged the necessity of internal improvements as second only to educational planning. Roads needed to be improved and waterways made navigable so that commerce might flow easily and cheaply. He laid before the legislature a copy of a letter sent to William H. Crawford, Secretary of the Treasury,[46] urging completion of the National Road to St. Louis, as well as federal aid for certain post roads, notably those between Cincinnati and Toledo; Zanesville and Maysville, Kentucky; Portsmouth and Sandusky via Columbus; and Cleveland, Ohio, and Washington, Pennsylvania. He suggested that the Miami and Maumee rivers be joined by a canal and that other headwaters be similarly connected.

Worthington believed that the exportation of capital for goods of foreign manufacture was the principal cause of the depression; it had injured home industries and helped drain the nation of its specie. He maintained that with bountiful raw materials available for the manufacture of clothing and other necessary commodities at home, it was unpatriotic for citizens to "give a preference to foreign manufactured articles, generally inferior to those we can, and do make. . . . The result must be a state of dependence and embarrassment, producing the worst consequences to the country."[47]

He deplored the inhumane treatment of the poor and expressed regret that adequate care of them had not yet been made compulsory.

The act "to authorize the establishment of poor houses" leaves it discretionary with the commissioners to purchase land, on which to erect a poor house. The advantage, to every county from purchasing lands, before the price becomes

---

[45] *Ibid., 17th General Assembly,* 8-9.
[46] Worthington to Crawford, October 1, 1818, in *House Journal, 17th General Assembly,* 18-25.
[47] *Senate Journal, 17th General Assembly,* 12.

advanced, and by maintaining the poor in houses erected for that purpose, are so evident as in my opinion to make it the duty of the commissioners to purchase lands with the least delay. The present mode of maintaining the poor, besides the extraordinary expense it incurs, is not calculated to ensure them even humane treatment. Put off to the lowest bidder, their food, raiment, and treatment must be proportionably wretched. I . . . recommend to your consideration that the act be so amended as to effect the objects just stated.[48]

Worthington's concern about restoring banks and currency in Ohio to a sound and stable basis prompted him to recommend that the chartered banks be incorporated in a state bank and only their issues be received for taxes. Such a plan, he believed, in conjunction with the stabilizing effect of the National Bank would lessen the force of the depression. He did not denounce the projected plan to tax the Ohio branches of the National Bank, but since he was a director and stockholder, it was hardly necessary to announce his opinion on that subject.

It is most significant that he was the first governor to ask openly for a rigid regulation or suppression of saloons. He had seen many friends and neighbors die prematurely from the effects of drinking, and he was strongly opposed to the use of alcohol despite the fact that he himself had manufactured and shipped thousands of gallons of whiskey down the Mississippi. In his last address to the legislature, he voiced his concern:

The immoderate use of ardent spirits is productive of much evil in society. Need I attempt, gentlemen, to prove to you how often the unhappy mother, and her innocent children are brought to poverty and distress, and, often, to an untimely grave, by the intemperance of the more unhappy and wretched father? Need I remind you of the riots and litigation which have their origin in this vice, and is there not good ground to believe that many of the worst crimes against society have their origin in the same source. Nothing aids more in the practice of this vice, than what are usually called tippling houses, or dram shops. I have no doubt the putting down of such houses, would have the best effects as they are really nuisances in society.[49]

11

It appears that Worthington's popularity suffered little decline during his four years as governor. On December 12, 1818, the anti-Tammany *Western Spy*, which had attacked him for working for a branch of the National Bank at Chillicothe, hailed Ethan Allen Brown as an able successor to our "late worthy Governor." In the contest for United States Senator to succeed Jeremiah Morrow, who refused

[48] *Ibid.*, 13.
[49] *Ibid.*, 16.

to run again, Worthington made a good showing but was defeated on the fourth ballot after having led on the first three. Colonel William A. Trimble of Hillsboro, a wounded veteran and brother of Allen Trimble, was elected. Worthington's advocacy of the National Bank and the fact that he was a director of it probably were his chief handicaps, although he had not anticipated that the connection would be detrimental. He apparently expected to be elected, for William H. Crawford congratulated him on his contemplated return to "The Councils of the Nation," and his niece, Nancy Bedinger Swearingen, wrote her father that the Governor "is to be Senator."[50] It is noteworthy that the newspapers did not attack him and that there was considerable popular discontent with the choice of Trimble, who was relatively unknown and whose war services were his chief claim to preferment.

A review of the administrations of Governor Worthington shows that little of the legislation he suggested was enacted. There was a definite tendency on the part of the legislature to evade the inauguration of new or expensive projects. The state was young, and most of her people were just emerging from poverty. Comprehensive schemes involving tremendous expenditures were deliberately shelved, but more from necessity than from lack of interest. Even the canal project was adopted only after long delay and with much misgiving. Progress was dependent upon stabilization of the currency, disrupted by the war and the Panic of 1818-22. Worthington had argued that stabilization could be brought about through the influence of the National Bank, the regulation of state banks, and the stimulation of home manufactures.

It is worthy of note that during the administration of his immediate successor, the first important step toward curbing the liquor traffic in Ohio was taken; a law was passed regulating the establishment and licensing of taverns.[51] A free system of education, penal reform, and internal improvements were soon to follow. In no small degree, Worthington's labors were tardily bearing fruit.

In closing this chapter it seems appropriate to quote Worthington's own estimate of his four years as governor. On December 31, 1818, he wrote as follows in his diary:

Since the 22nd of last month I have been principally engaged in public duties and three weeks of the time at Columbus closing my duties as Gov-

---

[50] Nancy Swearingen to Henry Bedinger, December 20, 1818, RCHS.
[51] Chase, *Statutes*, II, 1046-47.

ernor & on a reviewing my conduct for the 4 years I have held this office I feel truly grateful to God to have nothing to charge myself with but regret it has not been in my power to do the good I wished to the state. I feel very conscious that I have left nothing undone in my power and I am content & grateful. I feel now a freeman & released from responsibility.

Business, Politics, and Internal Improvements

WORTHINGTON retired from active politics for three years at the end of his second term as governor. Having failed in the race for the United States Senate and having received no appointment from the Monroe administration, Worthington turned with energy and determination to advancing his business affairs. The times were bad, taxes were high, and labor was scarce; wheat sold slowly at twenty cents a bushel delivered, only a little corn could be disposed of at twelve and a half cents, and land transfers, except in bankruptcy cases, had stopped entirely.[1] Land sales at $1.25 an acre under the new Land Law of 1820 brought extremely few buyers, for even the formerly well-to-do citizens of the county and state could not raise the hundred dollars to buy the new minimum of eighty acres. More than half the citizens north of the Ohio were already deeply indebted for land purchased from the government, which in 1820 held paper against the people of the West in the sum of $22,000,000.[2] The Bank of Chillicothe was still solvent and paying dividends, but its stock was going begging at eighty dollars, and nobody who was lucky enough to have money in multiples of eighty was fool enough to put it in bank stock during the Panic.[3] Everyone's patience was short; Worthington had to admonish David B. Macomb, his son-in-law and the manager of his cloth mill, for overworking his help, displaying an ungovernable temper, and running up a bill of $2,000 with Kentucky cotton growers. His advice today seems as wise and humane as when he expressed it:

> *You should act with firmness tempered with calmness and kindness toward those under your controul. The man who has a good heart & genuine courage will never so far degrade himself as to wantonly insult and wound the feelings of his inferiors. Cowards only are capable of this. Let your conduct be kind, sincere and manly to all, and above all so govern & regulate your affairs by economy as to be able to spare some of your savings to the man who is needy.*

[1] Colonel James S. Swearingen to Major Henry Bedinger, November 12, 1820, RCHS.
[2] Burnet, *Notes*, 451.
[3] Colonel James S. Swearingen to Major Henry Bedinger, April 29, 1821, RCHS.

The pleasure such acts will give you is not to be compared with the little self denial you may use to enable you to do it. I write you as I would my own son. I can do no more.[4]

During the summer of 1819, Worthington himself turned to the breaking plow for the first time in his life. He could not obtain labor, he liked plowing, and he wished to set an example for his sons. He took up surveying again and resumed the buying of cattle and sheep. On July 16, 1819, Mrs. Worthington presented him with a son, the last of ten children, and he made this note in his diary:

This morning at 4 O'C[lock] my wife had a son being our 10th child born perfect. May it please my God to lead him through life in the Way of right-eousness. I would most humbly pray that he may be a sincere & able preacher of the Gospel under our Lord & Master—& may it please him to bestow a double portion of his spirit for that purpose.

The traveler Thomas Hulme visited Worthington in July, 1819, and was amazed at his 800-acre estate and his mansion. He reported him as chiefly interested in home manufactures, and added, "He is a true lover of his country." What seemed to impress Hulme more than anything else was the profligacy with which barnyard manure was wasted. Worthington had a pile growing out of and surrounding his barn that was larger than the barn itself, and he was threatening to move his barn to get away from it. Hulme estimated that not less than 300 loads of prime horse manure were dumped into the Scioto River annually by the one tavern at which he had stayed in Chilli-cothe.[5]

In October of the same year, the English farmer William Faux visited Worthington and was also much impressed by his prosperous estate, Adena, and by the thriving village of Chillicothe, the popula-tion of which was 3,000. Faux was surprised, however, at the large number of people who were pushing on westward and was moved to remark concerning this un-English phenomenon: "The American has always something better in his eye, further west; he therefore lives and dies on hope, a mere gypsey in this particular." Even more interesting than this comment is an impression he recorded of that eminent Chillicothe citizen, soldier, and congressman, Duncan McArthur, who three years later was again to serve in Congress and in 1830 was to be elevated by his fellow citizens to the governorship of the state. Faux related that, while walking with his friend "the squire" (Worthington),

[4] Worthington to Macomb, December 2, 1817, in WM.
[5] Thomas Hulme, *Hulme's Journal of a Tour in the Western Countries of America* . . . , in Reuben G. Thwaites, ed., *Early Western Travels, 1748-1846*, X (Cleve-land, 1904), 70-71.

they met General McArthur (he calls him McCarty), a "dirty and butcherlike [man] and very unlike a soldier in appearance, seeming half savage, and dressed as a backswoodsman." Worthington spoke to him, and after McArthur's surly nod remarked to Faux, "Like General Jackson . . . he is fit only for hard knocks and Indian warfare."[6]

In the summer of 1819, Worthington was instrumental in organizing the Scioto Agricultural Society, which was a great stimulus to the raising of better crops and livestock. He was the first president, and held that office for several years. An address he made before the Society in 1821 gives us a glimpse of his interest in home manufactures, which were as important to the members of the Society as agricultural pursuits:

> Nothing but industry, rightly directed, with economy, can relieve us from our present embarrassments. It should be remembered, that every article man-ufactured in the country is a saving of the price of that article to the country . . . . We must choose one of two alternatives, either to be in a state of dependence, clothed in foreign manufactures, or be independent, clothed in homespun, the products of our own labor. Indeed, necessity will compel us to choose the latter. . . . [Let us have] union of sentiment, and practice in the use of articles manufactured in this country, to enable us in a short time to lessen greatly, if not entirely remove the difficulties we are now feeling.[7]

Worthington was a breeder of Merino sheep. His stock in general rated second only to that of the Renick family, and was often bought by new settlers. His orchards were among the best in the community. In 1817, while on a trip to New York, he had induced several German redemptioners to go to Chillicothe and work out their indentures on his farms. These skilled horticulturists from the Rhineland replanted Worthington's vineyards and relandscaped his grounds; under their supervision Adena became a well-known beauty spot. Indentured for three years, the Palatines proved so industrious that Worthington shortened their terms and then employed them on his farms or in his mills.[8]

In August, 1819, he took a trip East on business and for his health, in the course of which he visited President Monroe, Rufus King, and William H. Crawford. Although Monroe had failed to appoint Worthington Secretary of the Navy the previous year, there seems to have been no ill will between them on that score. In this connection it may be noted that John Quincy Adams writes in his *Memoirs* that

---

[6] W[illiam] Faux, *Memorable Days in America, Being a Journal of a Tour to The United States* . . . , *ibid.*, XI (Cleveland, 1904), 179, 182.

[7] *Supporter and Scioto Gazette*, August 22, 1821.

[8] Worthington's diary, June 14, August 27, 1817, and April 7, 1818.

in October, 1818, he suggested Worthington as an available candidate for Secretary of the Navy: "The President said he was not personally acquainted with him, but he had been mentioned to him as a man of indirect ways upon whose steadiness no reliance was to be placed. He preferred men of a straightforward character." This characterization is a fabrication, at least in part. President Monroe and his staff had dined and stayed overnight with Worthington at Adena in August just a year earlier, and the Governor had spent several days in his company. Apparently it was difficult for Adams to write anything good about a western Republican.

In May, 1820, Worthington, accompanied by Mrs. Worthington's nieces, Elizabeth Bedinger and Ann Shepherd, went with a load of produce to New Orleans. There he spent a fortnight buying and selling, and showing his young companions the sights in the river metropolis. He was personally pained to see the citizenry making the Sabbath "a day of amusement and gambling." On the fourteenth, he hurried from his hotel at ten o'clock in the night to view a great fire at the navy yard which, "from total want of caution," resulted in a loss, he calculated, of between $300,000 and $400,000.

On May 24, they sailed for Philadelphia, arriving there on June 11. Having placed the girls on the stage for Fredericktown, Worthington went on to Washington. There he attended to a number of business transactions and met his niece, Sally Bedinger, whose school had just closed. On the fifteenth, they went by stage to Shepherdstown, and after a day's visit there he pushed on to Ohio.

That fall, Worthington and John Waddle spent six weeks in the East on business. Worthington attended to some banking affairs in Washington, visited Rufus King in New York, and then took a steamer to Boston, where he inspected the Waltham Cotton Mills, "said to be the best in the World," having a capital and surplus of $600,000 and paying annual dividends of 15 to 20 per cent. On October 19, he attended a cattle show at Brighton and visited John Adams, whom he found "very feeble." He arrived home November 4, after stops at New York, Philadelphia, Washington, and Shepherdstown.

Shipping meat and flour down the Mississippi continued to be one of Worthington's chief enterprises. In this business he had no local monopoly; to mention only two competitors, Sam Finley and Drayton Curtis established a steam flour mill early in 1818 with three pairs of stones which turned out fifty barrels a day. Joseph Kerr was one of his strongest competitors in the export of meat. In 1820, there were seventy-three steamboats coursing the western rivers, and others were being built. Innumerable arks and flatboats were used to float products to New Orleans, and 33,000 tons of goods were carried by steamboat up the river in 1820 alone.[9] Worthington built boats for the river trade at his own sawmills and loaded them with his own flour, beef, pork, and whiskey, as well as products which he purchased locally. His flatboats were usually fifty or fifty-six feet in length and had a sixteen-foot beam. The cost of building these flimsy boats was only one dollar a linear foot; thus, not counting the lumber, a fifty-foot boat cost Worthington a mere fifty dollars.

Too often, these homemade craft were defective, and failed to navigate the falls at Louisville or sank in the river before they reached New Orleans. Once on March 12, 1823, during the freshet which was always awaited to make the Scioto navigable, one of Worthington's heavily loaded boats broke loose, ran on a stump, and sank within sight of its wharf. Drayage around the Louisville rapids in times of low water was expensive, and each shipment was both a physical and a financial gamble. The canal movement in the West envisaged a Kentucky and an Indiana waterway around this obstruction in the Ohio, and Worthington heartily supported every scheme for expediting navigation toward the Gulf. Like the Ohio canals, however, this improvement was not secured until after his death. Sometimes he shipped from Portsmouth, Cincinnati, or Louisville by steamer (the charge was $1.50 a barrel from Portsmouth), but usually he sent his goods all the way from Chillicothe in his own flatboats. From 1819 until his death, the flow of exports from the Scioto country grew in volume continually.

In addition to his independent enterprises, Worthington was also a member of the firm of Worthington, [John] Waddle, and [Amaziah] Davisson of Chillicothe, Portsmouth, and Cincinnati, which during these years supplied provisions to the army posts of the Southwest and to military expeditions such as the one conducted by Colonel Henry Atkinson in 1819-20 to explore the upper reaches of the Missouri. Joseph Kerr was also an associate in this commercial venture. Worthington's diary for May, 1821, briefly itemizes the difficulties of supplying New Orleans, Fort Smith, and Natchitoches with provisions, and tells how storage, freight, and spoilage consumed expected profits. Low water in the rivers was a major obstruction to success. Sometimes Worthington's cargo was held up for weeks at the mouth of the Red River after its transfer to a steamer. Navigation up the Arkansas to Fort Smith was subject to the same hazards. Deliveries at ports on the

[9] Grant Foreman, "River Navigation," in the *Mississippi Valley Historical Review*, XV (1928-29), 39.

Gulf or the Atlantic coast (Worthington supplied the Washington and Norfolk navy yards) were much more predictable, although they necessitated a transfer of cargo to ocean-going vessels at New Orleans.

The brief diary account of the nine-week business trip Worthington made to New Orleans in the spring of 1823 illustrates the hazards and uncertainties of river traffic. With Mrs. Worthington and their four-year-old son Francis, he accompanied his two partially loaded flatboats from Chillicothe to Portsmouth, March 14-15. There the three attended church on Sunday, the sixteenth. From the seventeenth to the twentieth the boat loadings were completed, including the cargo of a third boat which had arrived from Chillicothe on Sunday. New crews having been secured for the flatboats, the Worthingtons proceeded to Cincinnati, where Worthington loaded the contents of one boat on the steamer "Magnet," a 120-foot vessel which could withstand the current of the Red River to Natchitoches. The consignment for this army post consisted of the following items:

240 *barrels of pork*	1 *box of bacon*
123 *barrels of flour*	10 *barrels of vinegar*
47 *barrels of whiskey*	3 *boxes, 1 barrel, of apples*
49 *barrels of beans*	2 *half-barrels of beer*
52 *boxes of soap*	1 *pot of apple butter*
11 *boxes of candles*	

At Cincinnati, Worthington sold the emptied flatboat for $37.00, filled out his shipments by the purchase of forty-four barrels of beans at $3.00 a barrel, and, setting out again on the twenty-fourth, reached Louisville that evening. Aboard the "Magnet" next day, Mrs. Worthington was exceedingly ill, probably as a result of exposure to the continuous wet weather. That day they reached the Mississippi; both it and the Ohio were very high. On the twenty-eighth, they passed the mouth of the Arkansas, and on the twenty-ninth, they arrived at Natchez, where freight was discharged. On the thirtieth, the "Magnet" entered the mouth of the Red River, which, owing to the high water in the Mississippi, had a fifty-mile backwater that had inundated much of the country. Though heavily laden, the "Magnet" steamed well, passing Alexandria on the thirty-first and reaching the straggling settlement at Natchitoches on the third of April. On transferring his consignment to the military authorities, Worthington noted with some disgust that his pork was two barrels short.

On April 6, they were back on the Mississippi, the river "higher than I ever seen it." At 7 A.M., on the seventh of the month, they reached

New Orleans, where they were met by their son Albert, who for several months had been acting as a business agent there.

Having safely lodged Mrs. Worthington and Francis, Worthington and Albert prepared another steamer load of produce for Natchitoches from the flatboats and by purchase, which was dispatched on the "Hornet" under Albert's care on the twelfth. It consisted of the following merchandise:

342 *barrels of flour*	38 *boxes of candles*
34 *barrels of whiskey*	18 *small and* 21 *large boxes*
4 *barrels of pork*	*of salt*
12 *barrels of vinegar*	

From the twelfth to the thirtieth of April, Worthington was busy selling the remainder of his produce and purchasing goods to take home—two bales of cotton, nine bags of coffee, twenty hogsheads of salt, one tun of rice, and one barrel of oil, among other items. He had hoped to show his wife and son the city and its historic places, but it rained almost continuously, and they were all ill with fever. They bade Albert farewell on April 30, had a wet and disagreeable return trip, ran aground once, and arrived home on May 23, where they all continued to be sick for the ensuing week.

Worthington and George Gibson, commissary general of subsistence, entered into a typical army contract November 18, 1819. It bound the firm of Worthington, Waddle, and Davisson to deliver at Natchitoches, Louisiana, the following shipment, one quarter on June 1, 1820; one quarter on September 1, 1820; one quarter on December 1, 1820; and the final quarter on March 1, 1821:

> 208 *barrels of pork, "one head to the barrel, the pieces not to exceed ten pounds in weight"* @ $16.30
> 420 *barrels "fine fresh" flour* @ $8.00
> 2,304 *gallons proof whiskey "in good white oak barrels"* @ 62½¢
> 2,920 *pounds "good" soap* @ 20½¢
> 1,100 *pounds "good" candles* @ 21¢
> 46 *bushels of salt* @ $1.00
> 730 *gallons "good" vinegar "in white oak barrels"* @ 26¢
> 164 *bushels peas or beans* @ $2.50
> 93 *barrels corn meal—"kiln dried"* @ $6.25

What the Panic and the hard times of the twenties did to prices is shown by a comparison of this bill of lading with an order received by Worthington in a contract signed with Gibson on November 23, 1825, for supplying the same post. It bound Worthington to deliver the following items at Natchitoches, one-half on June 1, 1826, and one-half on December 1, 1826:

180 *barrels pork @ $11.25*	1,240 *pounds tallow can-*
375 *barrels flour @ $5.50*	*dles @ 14¢*
2,400 *gallons whiskey @ 28¢*	42 *bushels salt @ $2.00*
165 *bushels beans @ $1.50*	675 *gallons vingear @*
7,640 *pounds soap @ 9¢*	*24¢*[10]

For several years after 1820, the effects of the Panic were still being felt, and credit was extremely difficult to arrange. In 1823, it was hard for Worthington to secure enough credit to buy pork at $6.50 per hundred which he had contracted to deliver to the army at New Orleans for $8.50. This meat had to be examined in New Orleans to see if it would stand the army's inspection on receipt. To wash and repack the meat and rehead the barrels was an expensive process. Moreover, government payment was exceedingly slow, and even if a small profit had been made on the shipment, too often it was eaten up by interest charges.

Worthington engaged in up-river trade also, purchasing goods in large quantities at New Orleans or at other points on the river. When not too busy, he accompanied his shipments down to the Louisiana metropolis and bought merchandise for himself, for his neighbors, and sometimes for the merchants of Chillicothe. The same was true when he went to the eastern seaboard. A typical bill of lading, dated April 4, 1822, of a Worthington shipment from New Orleans on the "Car of Commerce," Joseph Pierce, master, was made up of the following items:

3 *hogsheads sugar*	3 *kegs salt petre*
4 *kegs nails*	1 *cask empty bottles*
1 *barrel coffee*	½ *barrel lamp oil*
1 *barrel loaf sugar and coffee*	1 *chest earthenware*
1 *barrel loaf sugar and rice*	1 *barrel white Havana sugar*
1 *barrel rice*	1 *box spermaceti candles*
½ *and ¼ chests tea*	2 *boxes raisins*
1 *barrel brown sugar*	1 *box books*
1 *bale verdigris*	2 *bags corks*
1 *basket s[perm?] oil*	2 *half-barrels sugar and coffec*
1 *keg verdigris*	44 *bags "turkistand" salt*[11]

---

[10] Consignment lists and bills of lading, in WM.
[11] In WM.

Shipping to New York, Baltimore, or abroad by way of New Orleans was at best a circuitous and wasteful route, and agitation grew for more direct connections with the East. Measures for the completion of the Erie Canal were watched with great interest in Ohio. Worthington had always had a great interest in canal-building projects. While he was governor, he had been requested by Governor Clinton and other prominent New Yorkers to use his influence in getting the Ohio legislature to assist in the construction of the Erie Canal because Ohio would benefit so greatly by it. Worthington had brought the matter, together with the correspondence concerning it, before the legislature in his message of December 11, 1816, and the idea had been enthusiastically received,[12] but no actual financial aid was made available. Nevertheless, from that time on, the project of canals for Ohio took shape, and was the subject of lively debate each year in the assembly.

2

Worthington reëntered politics in 1821 by running for the state legislature. He was elected from Ross County, together with Archibald McLean and William Vance, from a field of ten candidates. Bills for free education, poor relief, a canal system, and other projects which he had recommended while governor or in which he was interested were pending, and his influence was needed to get them adopted. His return was not an occasion for great rejoicing among his colleagues, however. They resented his reassumption of leadership and tried to keep him in the background. He was suspected of desiring the speakership, with which the house might well have honored him, but he was denied it. The death that same month of United States Senator William A. Trimble gave him a chance to try his strength against the younger men in control. Governor Brown was the only candidate who was considered strong enough to defeat him in the senatorial contest, although General Harrison, Robert Lucas, and John McLean received some votes on the first few ballots. It took nine ballots to elect, on five of which Worthington led. He eventually lost to Brown by one vote, 50 to 51.

Thus Governor Brown succeeded Senator Trimble, and Speaker Allen Trimble, William's brother, succeeded Governor Brown for the remainder of his term. Worthington, greatly chagrined at his defeat, wrote his friend William H. Crawford, then Secretary of the Treasury, of

---

[12] *Senate Journal, 15th General Assembly*, 67-68, 189-92, 222. 321.

the circumstances concerning it. Crawford tried to cheer him up by praising his past achievements but had to break the further bad news to him that there seemed no likelihood that the postmaster generalship, for which Worthington had been angling, would be vacated soon by Meigs.[13] Rufus King declared that Meigs would never resign so long as he could contrive to hang on to the job.[14] Actually, when Meigs retired in 1823, Crawford and King recommended to Monroe that Worthington be appointed. Instead, his fellow statesman, John McLean of Cincinnati, who had succeeded Meigs in the general land office, secured the position.

During this session of the legislature, Worthington was successful in having the tax on land raised so that the deficit would be covered, in getting an extra session of the legislature called to redistrict the state, in having a resolution denouncing the Osborn bank decision rejected, and in getting an improved pauper bill passed. He failed in his attempt to have a constitutional convention called to reform the judiciary.

In 1822, Jeremiah Morrow was elected governor over Allen Trimble, and Worthington was reëlected to the house. The session of 1822-23 was noteworthy for little except canal legislation. Worthington's advocacy of a constitutional convention again failed, and so did his efforts, as chairman of the committee on finance, to get the land tax raised again.

In 1824, Worthington ran for the legislature again and polled the highest vote in the sixth district from a field of nine candidates. He was beaten for speaker by Micajah Williams on the third ballot. Morrow was reëlected governor, defeating Allen Trimble in a very close race. Worthington opposed Trimble "bitterly," but Ross County supported him nevertheless.

3

In Ohio, the Presidential campaign of 1824 was an exciting one. The number of eminent Presidential candidates gave every voter a wide latitude in his choice. Clinton was boomed in 1822, and, had New York come out in support of him, Ohio would probably have followed suit. A Columbus caucus for Clay, December 10, 1822, was stalemated by Clinton's supporters, who insisted on a postponement until New York acted. Clay was second choice, but the longer the campaign went

[13] Crawford to Worthington, November 3, 1821, and January 17 and June 14, 1822, in WMOSL.
[14] Rufus King to his son Edward, November 3 and December 25, 1822, in the King Manuscripts.

on, the stronger his support grew. His equivocal attitude toward slavery hurt him a good deal at first and gave Clinton the advantage, but, when the latter failed to get the backing of New York, his friends turned to Clay and the "American system."[15]

Worthington and Morrow were both mentioned as possible Vice-Presidential candidates on a Crawford or Clinton ticket, but the Clay forces suspected that this was a stratagem on the part of the Adams party and refused to be alienated from Clay. Worthington was personally in favor of Crawford for President, although his son-in-law Edward King rightly believed that most Ohioans favored Clay.[16] Worthington helped Senator Benjamin Ruggles engineer a caucus for Crawford and Gallatin at Washington in February, 1824. Ruggles made the following report: "I have followed your opinions on the subject of a caucus. We held one last evening under a general notice . . . about 70 attended, Mr. Crawford received 64 . . . Mr. Gallatin 57 votes for Vice president."[17]

Thus two of Worthington's best friends were put in nomination. So far as their views on internal improvements were concerned, there was little to choose between Clinton, Clay, and Crawford. New York eliminated the first, Crawford's sickness put him out of the running, and Ohio supported Clay, with Jackson in second place. There is little doubt that Worthington was prejudiced in favor of the Crawford-Gallatin ticket because both men on it were his close friends and because Crawford had attempted to get the postmaster generalship for him when Meigs resigned. In Ohio 19,255 votes were cast for Clay, 18,489 for Jackson, and 12,280 for Adams, a poor third. It is interesting to note that after the elimination of Clay, the vote of Ohio's delegates in the House of Representatives was 10 for Adams, 2 for Jackson, and 2 for Crawford.[18]

4

By 1824, Worthington's influence was not as strong as it had been. He had lost touch with the growing population of the state, and the legislators were looking to younger men for leadership. His advocacy

[15] Eugene H. Roseboom, "Ohio in the Presidential Election of 1824," *Ohio State Archaeological and Historical Quarterly*, XXVI (1917), 161 *et seq.*
[16] Edward King to his father, Rufus, November 24, 1822, and January 23, 1823, in King, *Rufus King*, VI, 487, 497.
[17] Ruggles to Worthington, February 15, 1824, in WMOSL. See the excellent letter from G. A. Worth to Worthington, February 14, 1824, for an account of the situation in New York. In the Ethan Allen Brown Manuscripts, OSL.
[18] *Supporter and Scioto Gazette*, November 11, 1824.

of the canal system was largely responsible for his election to the legislature, but his popularity was not sufficient to elect him to the United States Senate to succeed Ethan Allen Brown. In the legislative jockeying to secure this position, William Henry Harrison electioneered for ten days before and after the legislature met. His chances were injured, however, by the report that he had seduced the daughter of a prominent doctor.[19] Brown was thought to have done little in Congress for his constituents, and he suffered from Harrison's rivalry in the southwestern part of the state. Worthington did not offer himself as a candidate for the position until rather late, when he saw that he had a chance to win because of the scandal about Harrison and the prospect of a divided vote. He had been elected, however, to work for canals, not to go to the Senate. Wyllys Silliman also offered to run for the office, and each candidate had his party of supporters in the legislature. Harrison was the popular figure as events proved; a general "sympathy" in his "favor seemed to prevail," and he was easily elected on the fourth ballot, Silliman being his nearest rival, Worthington in third place, and Brown fourth.[20]

This appears to have been the last election in which consideration was given to Worthington as a representative of the state in Washington. He was widely popular, and his talents were respected, but his services were regarded as more valuable in local projects than in national politics. Moreover, the vigor of Jacksonian populism had little charm for him, and he viewed the growth of the General's popularity with a jaundiced eye. St. Clair, had he been alive, would have enjoyed his rival's discomfiture as the same turgid stream of American democracy which had overwhelmed him—now more turgid—changed its course and left Worthington in the shallows of Jeffersonian conservatism.

5

The legislative session of 1824-25 was a very important one. The tax system was reformed, an elementary school law was adopted, and canal construction was authorized. In this session Worthington helped bring to fruition some of his fondest hopes.

---

[19] A. Kelley, in a letter to Brown, January 28, 1825, reported that Harrison's chances were less bright as a result of the story that "has lately come out of his having seduced the daughter of Doct. Brower, though it is contradicted by his friends." In the Brown Manuscripts. See also William Doherty to Brown, January 29, in the Brown Manuscripts; *Cincinnati Advertiser*, February 9; and Trimble to McArthur, December 22, 1824, and January 24, 1825, in the McArthur Papers.
[20] *House Journal, 23d General Assembly*, 345.

Every governor after Worthington had advanced his arguments for the establishment of a public school system. Critics had argued the poverty of the state, but gradually that objection failed to be convincing as papers and public-spirited citizens pleaded for schools unceasingly. In 1819, Ephraim Cutler had introduced a public-school bill which failed in the senate. In 1822, a commission headed by Caleb Atwater had been appointed to study the situation, but its report to the legislature of 1823-24 met with no serious response. Governor Morrow's message in December, 1824, urged action, and by this time public opinion was strong enough to compel a more positive attitude. Under the chairmanship of Nathan Guilford of Cincinnati, a bill was introduced and adopted. Thus, the first important step was taken toward the realization of one of Worthington's greatest desires. He had sent his own children to the finest private schools, but education for all was his ideal.

While Guilford and Cutler exerted their efforts in behalf of the education bill, Worthington, as chairman of the finance committee, pushed for tax reform. Under his capable leadership a bill was introduced and passed which reallocated the three-class evaluation on land and inaugurated the extension of taxes to practically all forms of property. The law, mild as it was, met with much opposition; but it was maintained, and it blazed the way for our modern system of taxation. On the whole, the large property owners, including most of the legislators, were slow to advocate progressive measures when they meant increased taxes, but a few aggressive leaders made good headway in the session of 1824-25. On February 3, the following letter from Worthington was printed in the *Supporter and Scioto Gazette*:

> I have much pleasure in stating to you, for the information of my constituents, that the Canal bill was this day passed into a law, with only thirteen dissenting votes in the House of Representatives, and two in the Senate.
> The bill changing the Revenue System has likewise passed; and a bill for the encouragement of Schools, is before the House, and will most likely pass. These are, indeed, three most important subjects to the state of Ohio. With a well regulated system of Common Schools, which shall diffuse information to the rising generation throughout the state, and consequently produce the best effects on their morals, and the most lasting advantages; a good and well regulated system of internal improvements, executed with energy and integrity—and both based on a just and equitable system of taxation— Ohio, under these blessings, if duly appreciated, cannot fail to be prosperous and happy. Having spent the prime and strength of my younger days, with others, in endeavoring to promote the best interests of the state, every step having this tendency is most grateful to me. I am now getting to a time of life which reminds me that I must soon pass away; therefore feel the higher gratification, when I consider that I have given my aid at the present session, to effect objects which will benefit millions when I am no more. That there

should be a difference of opinion, on subjects so important in their nature and tendency, was to be expected; but that there should be so much harmony, is truly pleasing.

6

Worthington's activities in getting the Ohio canal system started may be regarded as his last achievement in behalf of the state for which he did so much. Although Ohio's canals were not fully completed until 1845, Worthington was instrumental in getting the state to authorize their construction, in selecting the routes they were to follow, and in stimulating popular approval of them.

The construction of the Erie Canal was watched with great interest, and the newspapers kept agitating for a similar project for Ohio. Governor Brown made it the chief object of his messages to the legislature. The first canal bill, introduced in 1819, provided for private construction, but it met with great opposition. It was generally thought that the state, not a private company, should finance and reap the benefits of such an enterprise. Uncertainty as to just how the project should be approached was removed in February, 1820, by the passage of a bill authorizing the appointment of three commissioners, who were to hire an engineer, survey projected routes, and petition Congress for a grant of land.

Not until Worthington came to the house in the session of 1821-22, did the canal movement really gain much momentum. He was a member of the canal committee of five headed by Micajah Williams of Hamilton County. The committee's report of January 3, 1822, was so clear and convincing that the bill for the necessary surveys was enthusiastically passed. Benjamin Tappan, Alfred Kelley, Thomas Worthington, Ethan A. Brown, Jeremiah Morrow, Isaac Minor, and Ebenezer Buckingham were appointed commissioners to manage the details. They were instructed to supervise the survey of the possible routes and make a report at the next session.

The canal committee represented all parts of the state. Its composition was meant to placate each political group, for then, as now, it was necessary to play politics. The routes over which the canals were to run were of no small importance to landowners. By September, 1824, when the surveys were not yet complete, "lands within a reasonable distance" from the canal routes had risen in price 50 to 125 per cent.[21] When Morrow refused to serve on the committee, Worthington successfully blocked an attempt to replace him with his old enemy Allen

---

[21] *Supporter and Scioto Gazette,* October 7, 1824.

Trimble; but Micajah Williams, a close friend of Trimble, was appointed. The Brown-Trimble-Williams political faction had little use for Worthington. It was difficult, they claimed, "to keep him within the traces." Even Alfred Kelley wrote Senator Brown that Worthington was "a bad selection but necessary."[22] He was a bad selection because he was a political rival of long standing and too rugged an individualist to coöperate readily with men at least some of whom he regarded as his inferiors. He had been defeated for speaker by the coalition, and Brown had defeated him for the Senate. The committee members knew he would dominate the committee if they gave him a chance. As already noted, three years later, in the 1824-25 session of the legislature, Williams himself was to defeat Worthington for speaker and was again to help humiliate him in the senatorial election when Harrison was chosen. Worthington was more popular with the rest of the board, however, and succeeded before the summer was over in getting them to elect him their chairman. Williams accused him of unduly influencing the engineer in favor of the Scioto route, but the canals were, after all, a local as well as a state project, and Worthington's preference for that route, other things being equal, was only natural. In fact, one of the interesting features of the intrigue was this recrudescence of the old rivalry between Cincinnati and Chillicothe: for the capital in 1802, for the bank in 1817, and now for the canals. As in 1817, the answer was to be a compromise, for both cities had secured banks and both were to get canals. Since Worthington's dogged perseverance had been tested before, it is not surprising to find that his opponents, especially those from Cincinnati, had little use for him. They hoped to run the first canal from the Maumee to Cincinnati, but other parts of the state had other designs. Worthington had ample support in braving his opponents.

7

During the summer of 1822, numerous surveys were made and routes charted to determine the best and cheapest locations for the proposed waterways. Judge James Geddes of New York was employed as consulting engineer, and the canal committeemen chose Alfred Kelley to work with him as their representative. Since his own son James was one of the surveyors employed by Geddes, Worthington had a reliable reporter on the scene of action who kept him fully informed of the progress being made. The four routes under consideration were the

---

[22] February 3, 1822, in the Brown Manuscripts.

Maumee-Miami, the Sandusky-Scioto, the Cuyahoga-Muskingum, and the Grand-Mahoning. The preliminary surveys proved that the first of these routes would probably be feasible. Because of the topography, the Sandusky-Scioto route had to be modified by eliminating the Sandusky River and connecting the Scioto River at Lockbourne (near Columbus) with the Cuyahoga-Muskingum route by a cross canal from the headwaters of the Licking. The results of the surveys (900 miles by the end of the year) and the recommendations of the committee were laid before the legislature by Chairman Worthington on January 3 and 23, 1823. The committee recommended that the survey work be continued and that steps be taken to secure finances for actual construction.

On January 27, the legislature authorized further surveys of the Hockhocking and Licking rivers and of the cross connection with the Scioto. The legislature instructed the committee to choose two of its members to serve as acting commissioners and authorized the two thus selected to open negotiations for loans, secure concessions for right of way, and employ competent engineers. The acting commissioners were granted a per diem by the legislature; the others received only their expenses. Alfred Kelley and Micajah Williams were selected as the acting commissioners.

While on a trip east in May, 1823, Worthington called on Governor Clinton, inspected the Erie Canal, then nearing completion, secured as much information as possible about construction methods and costs, and opened negotiations for the employment of Judge David S. Bates of Rochester as supervisory engineer. At the same time, Alfred Kelley canvassed New York for financial backing.

During the summer, the Maumee-Miami route was declared impracticable because of the summit height between the two rivers. The Sandusky-Scioto route was also found to be definitely undesirable because of the summit grade and the lack of feeders—a most "unexpected and unwelcome intelligence," said the *Ohio Monitor* (Columbus) —but the Scioto half was carefully surveyed with the object of using it in case a connection was made with the Muskingum. The most crucial decision necessary before progress could be made concerned the choice of the river to connect with Lake Erie. The engineers, therefore, concentrated on the Grand, the Black, and the Cuyahoga—the Maumee and Sandusky having been rejected temporarily.[23]

In March, 1824, the surveyors definitely laid out the canal line down the Scioto. The northern connection had not yet been selected, but the

---

[23] Williams to Worthington, September 8, 1823, in WMOSL.

Sandusky route seemed to be the best choice. Nevertheless, the plans now included a cross canal to the Muskingum from near Columbus and a Dayton-Cincinnati canal along the Great Miami which, it was promised, would be ultimately extended to the Maumee.

The same month, Worthington accompanied a boatload of produce to New Orleans and then went by sea to New York; his health was bad and he needed a vacation. On May 22, he reached New York and found on inquiry that Ohio could float canal loans there easily. The following notes appear in his diary on May 22 and May 31:

> Dined with George Clinton. . . . Considers Mr Wright best engineer in the state, Mr Geddes the best for exploring the canal route and Mr (Judge) Bates as of the secondary class N. York of engineers. . . .
> Monday Tuesday . . . engaged in endeavoring to make arrangements to obtain funds for the making the Ohio canal and find if the legislature will do their duty there will be no difficulty. . . . Treated with much politeness indeed kindness by Mr Clinton and others. . . .
>
> Find the canal [Erie] too narrow in places for the passage of 2 boats which are 15 feet wide . . . their boats are drawn by 3 horses & go 3 to 3½ miles per hour. Freight or transportation boats by 2 sometimes one horse who hauls with a boat over 8200 lbs at the rate of 2 miles per hour or 25 miles per day The passage of a boat through a lock when it is to be filled takes 8 to 10 minutes. When ready filled 5 & when an ascending & descending boat meet the 2 are passed the lock in about 10 minutes.

Worthington's exertions in behalf of the canal doubtless accounted in part for his easy election to the legislature after a year's absence. The education and tax bills, important as they were, did not create nearly so much interest as the canal project. Judge Bates made his report, January 8, 1825, and Worthington reported for the commission two days later. Bates recommended the route by way of the Cuyahoga, Muskingum, Licking, and Scioto rivers, connecting Cleveland and Portsmouth. Worthington's committee report approved the same route and urged immediate construction at state expense.[24] A bill incorporating the committee's recommendations was passed in the senate, January 21, and in the house, January 28. It provided for seven commissioners —three of them acting commissioners who were to supervise construction of the canal—and three canal-fund commissioners who were to raise and disburse the necessary monies.[25] Cincinnati was mollified by

---

[24] House Journal, 23d General Assembly, 186-229, 238-51; Senate Journal, 23d General Assembly, 254. The Supporter and Scioto Gazette carried Bates's report, February 3, 1825.

[25] Chase, Statutes, II, 1472-76. The new commission was made up of Kelley, Williams, Worthington, Tappan, John Johnston, Isaac Minor, and Nathaniel Beasley (House Journal, 23d General Assembly, 355). E. A. Brown, Allen Trimble, and Ebenezer Buckingham were the fund commissioners.

the authorization of a canal to Dayton which would eventually extend to Lake Erie. Although the citizens between the towns of Worthington and Sandusky were incensed at not getting a canal, they received no satisfaction.

Worthington was elected by the construction committee as one of the three acting commissioners and was assigned to supervise the Scioto route. Since he owned land on both sides of the Scioto, it made little difference to him on which side of the river the canal ran, but the merchants of Circleville and of Chillicothe wanted it to run through their towns. In as much as the terrain east of the Scioto required that a crossing be made either at Chillicothe or farther north, Worthington was instrumental in having the canal overpass the river at Circleville so that it went through both the towns.

Commissioner Williams let the first contracts and arranged the inaugural ground-breaking ceremonies for July 4, 1825, at the Licking Summit near Newark. Governor Clinton turned the first spadeful of dirt. Several thousand people, including "half the town" of Chillicothe, assembled for the gala event. A reception committee and a detachment of dragoons met Clinton's entourage six miles from Newark on the Granville road. On July 7, an ebullient reporter for the *Columbus Gazette* wrote an account of the great occasion:

> Immediately upon meeting, GOV. CLINTON alighted from his carriage, and was introduced by Governor WORTHINGTON to the suite of the Governor of Ohio—Canal Commissioners, with whom he was unacquainted, and accepted of an invitation to a seat in the carriage of Mr. BUCKINGHAM with Gov. WORTHINGTON and Mr. BUCKINGHAM, and was escorted to Newark, where he was received by Capt. STAUNTON of the Artillery, with twenty-four ample rounds.
>
> A little later the approach of Governor Morrow was announced and he was similarly met and given the salute of twenty-four rounds.
>
> At 11 o'clock the cavalry were paraded, and escorted Gov. Clinton, Gov. Morrow, Ex. Governors Worthington and Brown, the Canal Commissioners, Commissioners of the Canal Fund, and a number of distinguished strangers, and citizens to the Licking Summit, where the Throne of Grace was addressed by the Rev. Mr. Jenks, and an oration delivered by Thos. Ewing, Esq. . . .
>
> After the exercises were closed at the rostrum, a procession was formed to the ground where the first manual operation of the great work was to be performed. Upon arrival at the spot, Messrs. Kelly and Williams acting Canal Commissioners, each presented a spade to Judge Minor, President of the Board, with the request that he would present them to the two distinguished guests of the Canal Commissioners, with the proper request for them to commence the work. The two Executives, each at the same time proceeded to break the ground and place the earth in the barrows . . . and were immediately succeeded in the same operation by Governors Worthington and Brown, followed by the Canal Commissioners, Messrs. Lord and Rathbone, contractors for the loan, and Gen. Vanrensselear. . . . The barrows . . . were wheeled out by Colonels Bacon

and King, amidst the reiterated shouts of some thousand souls, the roar of
cannon and discharge of musquetry. Upon the whole it was a scene only to be
felt—it defies description.

The extraordinary optimism of the times is reflected in another
reporter's conclusion about the significance of the event: "They removed the first sod upon a work which will be admired when the
pyramids of Egypt are effaced. At this interesting moment the voices
of thousands rent the skies."[26] A similar celebration was held at
Middletown, July 21, when ground was broken for the sixty-seven-
mile canal between Dayton and Cincinnati.

Clinton and his entourage were feted from town to town during the
month. He arrived in Chillicothe on the twenty-fourth and spent the
night at Worthington's "hospitable mansion." The next day he was
escorted from Adena by the Chillicothe Blues, Colonel Edward King
commanding, to his quarters at the Madeira House, where he was
greeted by artillery and introduced to leading citizens. In the afternoon he was banqueted in Chillicothe's "best style" at Madeira's,
where Worthington, assisted by William Creighton and John Woodbridge, acted as toastmaster. At 6:00 P.M. he addressed the Masons
of Scioto Lodge, and after a cold collation accompanied by several
toasts was escorted back to the Madeira House by the lodge brothers
in procession. He left town the following day.

8

Canal construction in Ohio during the next two years moved slowly
because competent engineers were scarce, and money, despite early
advice to the contrary, was difficult to borrow. The legislature was
very conservative in its appropriations, even refusing by a two-to-one
vote to pay the expenses of the acting commissioners. Moreover, winter
freezes and spring floods were so disastrous to the wood and dirt
construction of the canals that expenses, as usual, greatly exceeded
estimates. Worthington kept in close touch with the progress being
made, and interested capitalists like John Jacob Astor in the Ohio
project. By this time, however, he was finding it necessary to devote
most of his energy to his own business and to his health. His illness
necessitated trips to Saratoga Springs in 1825, 1826, and 1827, and his
business affairs took him away from home often. Although his mills
ground steadily, his meat-packing went on apace, and his distillery
proved profitable, he was not able to give these and other personal

---

[26] Quoted in Morrow, "Jeremiah Morrow," 127.

enterprises the supervision they needed, with the result that some of them lost money. For instance, because of miserable management and the high price of hemp, his ropewalk became unprofitable. His son James was forced to assume more and more responsibility for his father's duties in connection with canal affairs and even for his business interests as the failure of Worthington's physical forces gradually incapacitated him and brought his career to a close.

Last Years

WORTHINGTON's last years were clouded by debts, business reverses, and illness. In 1816, he had given John Jacob Astor his note at 7 per cent for $10,000 to invest in stock in the newly established Bank of the United States. He was never able to pay any of the principal on this purchase, and during the Panic of 1820 he could not even keep up payment on the interest. To make matters worse, he had given surety to numerous friends and relatives who were caught in the bank crashes which took place at that time. One of these was his son-in-law Edward King, for whom he paid a debt of $6,010 in 1826. Another was his old and trusted friend Samuel Finley, president of the Bank of Chillicothe, whose former wealth had dwindled to the point where it would pay only half his debts at the time of his death —"all gone to the dogs like so many others" as a result of the Panic.[1] Finley had borrowed more than $20,000 from the Bank of the United States to pay the United States Treasury arrears of $40,000 on a debt incurred while he was receiver of public monies. Worthington, who was one of Finley's bondsmen, found himself liable for half of the amount in arrears,[2] and devoted his energies to meeting this obligation as well as lesser ones of a similar nature which he considered himself honor bound to satisfy.

He never lost touch with Albert Gallatin, his confidant for more than twenty years. Over a long period of time he had urged him to come and live on his Scioto lands, where they could be neighbors. Gallatin and his family, however, refused to settle permanently in the western wilderness. They tried living in New Geneva, Pennsylvania, for a while in 1824, but were not happy there. Like Worthington, Gallatin had suffered business reverses; his glassworks had collapsed, and he had lost heavily in the failure of the Bank of Columbia. The move to New Geneva had been made of necessity, but the sale of much of his western land subsequently enabled Gallatin to settle in New

[1] James Swearingen to Henry Bedinger, April 29, 1821, RCHS.
[2] Charles Hammond to Worthington, March 7, 1818, regarding Finley's debt to the United States, in the Hammond Collection. W. H. Crawford wrote Worthington, August 17, 1819, that the judgment was for $22,278.74. Worthington also owed $4,500 to his old friend Henry Bedinger of Shepherdstown, Virginia, and $2,000 to the Bank of Lancaster.

York City. In 1824, however, he was in such bad straits financially that he chided Worthington with some bitterness for charging him his agent's annual fee of thirty dollars.[3] Nevertheless, they remained friends to the end.

2

The last four years of Worthington's life were complicated by almost continuous illness; his financial worries militated against his recovery, for complete peace of mind was impossible as long as he owed any man.

In 1823, after an exceedingly rainy winter, the Scioto Valley was swept by an epidemic of fever, and all the members of the household at Adena were very ill. The family took a trip to New Orleans in late March, but Worthington and his wife were both constantly unwell, and he never completely recovered his strength. Nevertheless, he made a trip to New York in May on behalf of the canal commission and continued to be as active as ever in business affairs. In April, 1824, he took a boatload of meat to New Orleans, there secured a $10,000 order for a December delivery of pork, and went by steamship to New York on canal business for the state. He had hoped that the salt air would benefit his health, but during the first part of the voyage he was very ill and oppressed by the heat and "muschetoes." In sight of Cuba he was well enough, however, to record in his diary, May 11, that he had seen a Columbian privateer overhaul and take a Spanish schooner.

In the spring of 1825, he took another trip to New Orleans with a consignment of produce, accompanied by his son James T. and his daughter Sarah King. From New Orleans James sailed to Europe for a tour of the manufacturing towns of France and England with a view to improving the methods and processes used at Chillicothe. He was much impressed by the industry of the British workers, but even more by the smallness of the manufacturing establishments, the squalor in which the European laborers lived and worked, and the persistence of the domestic system.[4]

Meantime, at New Orleans on April 10, Worthington, Governor Henry Johnson, and other distinguished gentlemen of Louisiana met Lafayette when he disembarked at Chaumette and accompanied him

---

[3] Gallatin to Worthington, October 21, 1824, in WMOSL.
[4] James Worthington to Thomas Worthington, August 10, 1825, in WM; December 14, 1825, in RCHS.

over the historic ground of Pakenham's defeat. Worthington had an opportunity to converse with the state's distinguished guest on the ride back to the city, after which he attended the reception and banquet in Lafayette's honor. Lafayette, whom Worthington had previously met in New York, was extremely interested in news of the Ohio country —its growth and progress since statehood—and expressed a determination to visit it. He regarded its rapid increase in population and prosperity as a complete vindication of an opinion he had formed at the time of his first trip to America, namely, that a republic of free men under a good government would succeed better than a state where slavery was permitted to exist.[5] Worthington wrote out an itinerary for Lafayette's proposed trip up the Mississippi and Ohio rivers which the General agreed to follow.[6]

When Lafayette sailed up the Ohio River in the second week in May, he had a most unfortunate experience. His steamboat, the "Mechanic," struck a snag 120 miles below Louisville at midnight and sank in ten minutes. No lives were lost, and the General and his baggage were put ashore safely. Lafayette was provided with a cot on which to spend the rest of the night, but a few hours later the "Paragon," en route to New Orleans, was signaled, and the captain readily agreed to turn about and take Lafayette and his party back up the river to Louisville. The General sent regrets to Worthington that he could not go to Chillicothe to see him as he had hoped, since he had to hurry east for the Bunker Hill celebration.[7]

In August, 1825, accompanied by his daughters Margaret and Eleanor, Worthington took a trip to Saratoga Springs to try the waters for his health. He had now been suffering for some years from periodic attacks of "pain beyond description" which the doctors had been unable to relieve—probably gall bladder trouble or gastric ulcers, but called "bilious colic" in those days. His father and grandfather had succumbed to the same complaint. The Worthington party went by boat from Sandusky to Buffalo. On the trip, Worthington, who regarded card-playing as the stupidest and most foolish way of spending time, was mortified to have his daughters see the "disorderly gambling passengers." He and the girls visited Niagara Falls and then went to Troy, where Margaret and Eleanor were placed for the year in Mrs.

---

[5] Worthington's diary, April 10, 1825. Sarah King assisted the hostess at the reception. See also J. Bennett Nolan, *Lafayette in America Day by Day* (Baltimore, 1934).
[6] James T. Worthington to Thomas Worthington, April 11, 1825, in WM.
[7] A. G. Burnet to Worthington, May 14, 1825, in the Comly Collection.

Emma Willard's Academy. Worthington spent several days at Saratoga Springs, but the waters seemed to do him no good. His next stop was New York, where he stayed a few days visiting friends—among them John Jacob Astor and Rufus King—before going on to Washington. There he dined and had a good visit with President Adams, with whom he was well pleased. He told Adams frankly that he had not supported his election but that as President he might count on his undivided loyalty. President Adams urged him to communicate with him freely whenever he felt the Administration was in error.[8] Worthington reached home on September 19, feeling somewhat rested, but his bilious attacks were increasingly severe and no less frequent. A second trip to Saratoga Springs, in 1826, definitely convinced him that the waters there would do him no good; if anything, they seemed to add to his misery.

The year 1827, which was to prove his last, opened like any other. Butchering in January, boat-building in February, and canal work in March were his major activities, but he was not the indefatigable stalwart of former years. Nancy Bedinger Swearingen, a niece of Mrs. Worthington living at Adena, reported that it was now customary to refer to Worthington as "the old man."[9] He had been sick practically all winter, and grew steadily weaker during the spring. On March 6, he confided to his diary, "I seem to be sinking gradually & hope my suffering will soon be over." He drew his will on the fifteenth of the month, and a few days later despite the protests of his family, insisted on accompanying his boats to New Orleans. His stay there did him no good, nor did the thirty-five-day voyage to New York, which he reached on May 15 in a critical condition.

Judge McGeehee, a fellow traveler from New Orleans, saw him put up comfortably at the American Hotel. There the Reverend J. D. Disosway found him the next day reading his Bible and hymnbook, very weak but cheerful and in excellent spirits. Shortly thereafter, he was moved to quieter quarters, and his son Thomas, a cadet at West Point, was in constant attendance, spending several hours with him almost every day. The Reverend Julius Field of the Methodist Episcopal Church called regularly, as did two other clergymen—Burch and Ketchum. He had the best of medical care from Dr. David Hosack and his son, Dr. Alexander Eddy Hosack, who called in Dr. Wright Post and a Dr. King for frequent consultations. Their efforts were ineffectual. Worthington gradually weakened, and died peacefully

---

[8] Worthington's diary, September 11, 1826.
[9] Nancy B. Swearingen to Sarah Bedinger, February 19, 1827, copy, RCHS.

on June 20 at the age of fifty-three, conscious and cheerful to the end, full of thoughts of his family and, characteristically, consoled by the precepts of his religion. Mrs. Worthington and her son-in-law Edward King arrived in New York the next day and accompanied the body to Ohio.

3

The *National Intelligencer* for June 26, 1827, noting Worthington's death, called him

> *a conspicuous politician of the Jeffersonian school. . . . He was particularly useful from his familiarity with the interests of the West and is believed to have been the legitimate father of the beneficent measures which have reduced and almost annihilated the Public Land Debt of the Western country and by establishing a reduced cash price for the lands of the United States have prevented the possibility of its reaccumulation. Governor W[orthington] has been, in a word, a very useful citizen.*

News of the death of Worthington was the occasion for a mass meeting in Chillicothe at which preparations for his funeral were entrusted to a committee made up of William Creighton, Thomas Scott, Anthony Walke, and Samuel Williams. The pallbearers were William McDowell, William McFarland, Duncan McArthur, Thomas James, George and Felix Renick, James English, and John Woodbridge.

A troop of dragoons met Worthington's body at Hopetown, four miles north of Chillicothe, and a company of the Chillicothe Blues, together with a large concourse of people, joined them at the Scioto bridge near the edge of town for the march to Adena. The order of the procession was as follows: the dragoons, the hearse, the pallbearers, the committee of honor, the Masons, the judges and other Ross County officials, the members of the county bar association, the city officials, the teachers and pupils of the public and private schools, the citizens, and the Chillicothe Blues. At 2:00 P.M. the cortege reached the Worthington home, which had been crowded since 8:00 A.M. The services consisted of a prayer and a short but eloquent sermon delivered by old Bishop William McKendree.

The trip home and the fatigue of the day were almost too much for Mrs. Worthington, but she was able to be present at the interment in a lot dedicated to that purpose northwest of the house. At a later time, Worthington's remains were removed to beautiful Upland (now Grandview) Cemetery, just south of Chillicothe, where an appropriate memorial marks his resting place.

The resolutions of respect drafted by William Key Bond on behalf of the committee of honor admirably sum up Worthington's career. They describe him in part as

> the builder of his own fame and fortune . . . conspicuous in that small but enterprizing band of pioneers, who, in less than a quarter of a century, caused the wilderness "to blossom as a rose" . . . without disparagement to any, it may be truly said, that he was greatly instrumental in promoting us from the Territorial to the dignity of State Government. . . . In all his various stations he met and performed his duties with that ability, promptitude and indefatigable industry, which commanded the respect of his associates, and inspired his constituents with renewed confidence.[10]

On July 5, 1827, the editor of the *Scioto Gazette* wrote on the death of "our distinguished fellow-citizen":

> Endowed by nature with a vigorous and discriminating mind, and great firmness of purpose . . . he always maintained the reputation of a faithful, zealous and vigilant public officer, and a true friend to the interests of his country. As a man of business he was remarkable for untiring industry, uncommon penetration, and astonishing perseverance. . . . The ordinary difficulties which usually arrest the operations of other men, seemed only to increase his ardour; and neither the rigors of the season, the infirmities of nature, nor even bodily suffering, appeared for a moment to impair his mental and physical activity.

4

In his will Worthington listed his debts at $38,000. He estimated his estate conservatively at $146,000. At the time of his death he owned at least 15,000 acres of choice land and a great number of town lots, but much of this property had to be sold to satisfy his creditors. Adena and its 1,500 acres, however, were left unencumbered to Mrs. Worthington and the unmarried children. It took Worthington's executors twelve years to settle his very complicated business and personal affairs.[11]

5

The achievements of Thomas Worthington illustrate what could be accomplished in early Ohio by a man of vision, courage, and perseverance. Left an orphan early in life, he lifted himself from obscurity by the exercise of these qualities and by unrelenting devotion to the work at hand. Arriving at the age of maturity, he manu-

---

[10] *Scioto Gazette*, July 5, 1827.
[11] Report of Henry Massie, "Special Commissioner," filed July 4, 1839, in Ross County Probate Records.

mitted his slaves and moved to a virgin country which beckoned to his perspicacious mind. Others recognized the qualities of leadership which he divined within himself; whether on the bench or in the land office, working at home or surveying in the wilderness, conciliating Indians or commanding militia, directing a state or following a plow, he was never at a loss as to how to proceed. His record is one of outstanding accomplishment. Equally at home in the Ross County courthouse or the Senate chamber of the United States, in the company of his servants or among the élite of the nation's capital, his courteous and dignified conduct won the respect of his associates and the affection of most of his intimates.

No man did more than Worthington to make Ohio a state in the Union and a force in the councils of the nation. His services in the Senate were of extraordinary value. During wartime no one carried a heavier load of self-imposed responsibility for the safety of the people of Ohio. As governor, his recommendations to the legislature were simple, straightforward, and reasonable; conciliatory in tone and noble in sentiment, they stimulated the growth of a new philosophy among many of Ohio's lawmakers. Free education, state control of banking, pauper welfare, reformation of criminals, regulation of the liquor business, stimulation of home manufactures, construction of internal improvements—these were measures too advanced, it is true, for immediate realization in their entirety, but they were soon to be achieved.

Indefatigable in his numerous private concerns, Worthington attacked public problems with the same energy. Bold and decisive when convinced of the merit of a proposition, nevertheless he could be most cautious and discreet if necessary. Impatient of delay when a course of action was discernible, he rarely committed himself until he was sure of his ground. Slow to make up his mind, he was inflexible in his opinions; just in his judgments, he always believed that he was in the right. The force of his personality sometimes stimulated his political adherents to excesses for which he was blamed; he suffered from political vituperation of which he was aware but for which he did not feel personally responsible. Disdainful of counsel when his judgment was once formed, he often gave an impression of smug, supercilious conceit. When he had not yet reached a decision, his hesitation seemed to be equivocation, and his caution often appeared to be indifference. His prosperity caused jealousy, and in his advocacy of any project he was suspected of being motivated by self-interest; certainly no one was benefited more than he was by the constructive measures of his day. A radical Republican in theory, he was restrained from rashness by his economic interests, which gave balance to his opinions. Although he was too able and influential to be disregarded, his assumption of leadership often smacked of condescension; he failed to appreciate fully the honor bestowed upon him in his election and appointment to the many offices in which he served. His greatest personal handicap, observable when he was under restraint, was an unconscious egotism which was disconcerting and irritating. A suspicious eye and a disdainful air of shrewdness often gave an impression of cunning, subtlety, and lack of candor.

Worthington was fundamentally a rugged individualist. He followed no man but failed to understand when, upon occasion, few followed him. His closest friends were constant in their loyalty, but most of his political support came from those who respected him for his superior abilities. He appeared to be an authority on any subject— law, land, Indians, wheat, cattle, politics, war, or mechanics—not because he had superior knowledge or formal training but because by the very intensity of his interest he gave an impression of omniscience. When he had complete control of a project, he was an excellent administrator; but he was annoyed when limited by the necessity of securing authorization for each step taken. He could not brook delay in carrying out a course of action which, to him, was obviously right. His diary portrays the impatience with legislative delay or the inability of his associates to make decisions which is characteristic of a man of action. Consequently, his four years as governor of Ohio were somewhat unhappy, for he was too often merely a figurehead. The man of deeds had to find an outlet for his energy and leadership in creating a library, in clearing and fencing the statehouse grounds, in establishing a bank, in planning a penitentiary, and in directing activities at his farms and mills.

Although he attacked Plumer and persecuted St. Clair, Worthington was opposed to principles rather than to men. He forgave his enemies, conciliated his critics, and trusted his friends. His correspondence and diary are free from abuse and personal recrimination. As a true humanitarian, he opposed the useless sacrifice of lives, whether Indian, British, or American. As a senator, he disapproved of the death penalty for sabotage because he believed that capital punishment violated "the principles of humanity."[12] As governor, he favored solitary confinement rather than corporal punishment for prisoners, believing that contemplation would do them more good than

---

[12] Plumer, 105; Adams, *Memoirs*, I, 286. This was in reference to conspiracies to collect insurance by burning ships at sea (1804).

physical suffering. No man could abuse dumb beasts or servants in his presence. A well-digger's life was worth the risk of his own.[13] He despised card-playing and condemned drunkenness as inexcusable because of the suffering it brought to the innocent.

Worthington built the finest mansion of its time in Ohio and surrounded it with splendid lawns, beautiful gardens, and noble trees. A lover of the humanities, his unusual private library was a mark of his devotion to learning. He was the sponsor of the Chillicothe Academy and a trustee of Ohio University. A true philosopher, he read Seneca on horseback rides to farm and mill, pondered the significance of man's earthly existence, and sought by faith to apprehend the next.

His family life was a measure of his character. A devoted husband, he kept the love and respect of his spirited wife through the vicissitudes of a frontier life. An indulgent father, he sought to train his children by precept and example rather than by dictatorial command. An appreciation of the dignity of labor was an essential aspect of their discipline. Religious by nature, he instituted family prayers as a part of daily living. He was often misunderstood because of his concern with spiritual matters, and the elevated level of his thought was regarded as superciliousness by many, but the dedication of his youngest son to the ministry of the gospel bore witness to the seriousness of his convictions.

Worthington was comprehensive in his theology and had no sectarian prejudices. Buffeted by the selfish cares of business and politics, away from home he found his greatest relaxation in the calm atmosphere of a Quaker meeting. At home, he accompanied his family to the local Protestant churches, to all of which his means were distributed according to their need. His spiritual horizons broadened with the years, and his diary came to be given over more and more to expressions of gratitude and homage to his Maker. He bore physical pain with fortitude, but his suffering helped confirm his desire to escape the trials of this life. A sense of having realized the purpose of his creation gave him peace of mind. He died at a comparatively early age after an amazingly full and fruitful career.

6

Every man has a right to the last word concerning his own life and works, his success and failure, his hopes and desires for the future.

---

[13] Worthington's diary, August 17, 1811.

As Worthington approached the end of his second term as governor of Ohio, he evaluated the aims and aspirations of his career perhaps better than has the author of this volume. On March 24, 1817, in one of the longest entries in his diary, he penned the following statement:

> *At home & this day commence the setting my affairs in order. My mind has an overcharge of business including public and private. . . . As I have heretofore made great exertions in the fulfilment of all my duties and by honest industry acquired a competency I now only desire either by the sale of part of my estate or my income from the whole to pay my debts & support my family—additional wealth has no charms for me. Experience has proved to my satisfaction that to increase it will only add to my troubles, Excite envy and increase my responsibility. I am now 43 years old and in the vigor of life and to my God I return the most sincere thanks for these impressions, for they have been on my mind from my youth up. The rem'r of my life I desire to make useful if I can but not in acquiring property—What I have is more than enough for myself & children if rightly used & too much if abused. I have endeavored with all my soul from my youth to do justice. I have loved mercy and desired to walk humbly with my God & to give him a satisfactory acc't of my stewardship—I have passed through many trials and tribulations and now my worldly affairs are settled and my soul longs for the presence of its God—I have a large family of children. To bring these up "in the nurture & admonition of the Lord" will be the greatest happiness I can enjoy whilst I live. In a word to fulfil the object of my creation is the first desire of my soul and to my God & saviour I humbly look up for aid having no reliance but on him. With Pope I can most sincerely say*

> If I am right, thy grace impart
> Still in the right to stay:
> If I am wrong, oh teach my heart
> To find that better way.

Selected Bibliography
Index

SELECTED BIBLIOGRAPHY

Manuscripts

Papers of the Breckinridge Family, 1752-1904, 400 vols., Library of Congress. The first ten volumes are of some value for this study.

Ethan Allen Brown Manuscripts, Ohio State Library, Columbus. Several boxes of letters and papers concerning his governorship. They are sometimes called "Canal Letters." Valuable for politics and the early part of the canal era, 1818-28.

James N. Comly Collection, 30 vols., Ohio Historical Society, Columbus. Pertains chiefly to the period 1837-87.

Paul Fearing Papers, Marietta College Library, Marietta, Ohio.

Governor of Ohio, Executive Letter Book, 1814-18. Official correspondence of Governor Worthington. Ohio Historical Society, Columbus.

Charles Hammond Collection, Ohio Historical Society, Columbus.

Samuel Huntington Papers.
Ohio State Library, Columbus. Important for Huntington's governorship, 1808-1810, and for his service as paymaster in the War of 1812.
Western Reserve Historical Society, Cleveland. Several volumes of correspondence.

Thomas Jefferson Papers, Library of Congress. Some scattered correspondence of value for this study.

King Manuscripts, 3 vols., Historical and Philosophical Society of Ohio, Cincinnati. Chiefly letters of Rufus King and his son Edward King. The latter was the son-in-law of Worthington, and there are many letters of the Worthington family in the collection.

Duncan McArthur Papers, 54 vols., Library of Congress. Important source of material concerning the early history of Ohio, economic and political. Extensive Worthington correspondence.

Return Jonathan Meigs, Jr., Papers, Ohio State Library, Columbus. Some 300 important letters, written chiefly during his governorship, 1810-14.

Miscellaneous Collection, Historical and Philosophical Society of Ohio, Cincinnati. An important collection of some 600 letters and documents covering the period of Worthington's life. Especially valuable for Hamilton County. Includes letters of Worthington, Meigs, Creighton, Huntington, Bellamy Storer, and others, some of which have been printed.

Ohio State Archives: Executive Documents, Ohio Historical Society, Columbus. Several boxes of important documents. Catalogued for the period of Worthington's governorship.

Rice Collection, 18 vols., Ohio Historical Society, Columbus. A valuable miscellaneous collection made by C. E. Rice of Alliance, Ohio.

Ross County, Ohio, Probate Records, Courthouse, Chillicothe. Approximately 1,000 documents relating to the business and family affairs of Thomas Worthington.

"Memoir of the Hon. Thos. Scott, by Himself," dated July 19, 1852, 15 pages, Ross County Historical Society, Chillicothe, Ohio.

Nancy Bedinger Swearingen Letters, 100 typed copies in the Ross County

Historical Society, Chillicothe, Ohio. These copies were made from the originals in the hands of Robert Scott Franklin, Charleston, West Virginia. Franklin is now dead and the whereabouts of the original letters is unknown. The letters are chiefly to Nancy's husband, Lt. James Swearingen, the builder of Fort Dearborn. Nancy was the daughter of Major Henry Bedinger of Martinsburg, West Virginia.

Journal of Executive Proceedings of the Territory Northwest of the River Ohio, Including the First and Second Stages of Territorial Government, 1788-1803, Ohio Historical Society, Columbus. The executive record from 1788 to 1803, chiefly in the hand of Winthrop Sargent, secretary of the territory. Published in *Territorial Papers of United States, III, Northwest Territory,* edited by Clarence E. Carter.

George P. Torrence Papers, Historical and Philosophical Society of Ohio, Cincinnati. Fifty-seven boxes of about 3,000 letters and documents, collected by Aaron Torrence. Especially valuable as a source of information about early Ohio and Hamilton County history.

Elisha Whittlesey Papers, Western Reserve Historical Society, Cleveland. A large collection, which sheds valuable light on the history of northern Ohio, chiefly of a date later than 1827.

Thomas Worthington Manuscripts:

Library of Congress. Thirty invaluable notebooks cited as Worthington's diary. Letter book for 1801, a valuable collection of copies of letters (approximately 70) covering the periods 1801-1804. Letter book at Portsmouth [Ohio], some 50 letters written between 1822 and 1825, chiefly relating to business.

Ohio Historical Society, Columbus. Prior to 1949, the letters and documents in this collection, numbering about 5,000, were in the possession of James T. Worthington, Washington, D. C., the great-grandson of Governor Worthington. They are chiefly personal but very valuable. They include Thomas Worthington's twelve-page "Account of his Ancestors and of His Own Early Life," written in March, 1821; it is unreliable in some details and brings the account of his life only to May, 1791. It was annotated by his children. Here also are notebook 23, cited as Worthington's diary, and microfilms of all notebooks in the Library of Congress.

Ohio State Library, Columbus. The 1,000 letters in this collection appear to be a select group, and are invaluable for information concerning the economic and political history of Ohio. They include approximately 100 from Tiffin, 80 from McArthur, 40 from Creighton, 50 from Massie, 30 from Cass, and 20 from Gallatin.

Ross County Historical Society, Chillicothe, Ohio. Some 500 letters relating chiefly to Sarah Worthington and her husband Edward King. Two Thomas Worthington notebooks cited as Worthington's diary. Photostatic copies of Worthington's diaries and all other Worthington manuscripts in the Library of Congress and the Ohio State Library have recently been secured. McKell Collection of Worthington-Meigs papers relating to the War of 1812.

Public Documents and Miscellaneous Printed Sources

American State Papers. Washington, D.C. *Foreign Affairs,* II, 1832; *Indian Affairs,* I, 1832; *Military Affairs,* I, 1832; *Public Lands,* I, 1832; *Miscellaneous,* I, 1834.

Annals of the Congress of the United States. Washington, D.C., 1851.

Carter, Clarence E., ed. *Territorial Papers of the United States.* 22 vols., in progress, Washington, D. C., 1934— .

Chase, Salmon P., ed. *Statutes of Ohio and the Northwest Territory.* 3 vols., Cincinnati, 1833.

Congressional Reporter. Concord, 1811. Library of Congress, Rare Book Collection. Privately printed and meant to carry all messages, reports, and public documents. Only one volume printed.

Documents Relating to Detroit and Vicinity, 1805-1815 (Michigan Historical Collections, XL). Lansing, 1929.

Journal of the House of Representatives of the State of Ohio. Various places and dates.

Journal of the House of Representatives of the Territory of the United States North-West of the River Ohio . . . 1799 (Cincinnati, 1800); *ibid., 1800* (Chillicothe, 1800); *ibid., 1801* (Chillicothe, 1801).

Journal of the Legislative Council of the Territory of the United States, Northwest of the River Ohio . . . 1799 (Cincinnati, 1799[?]); *ibid., 1800* (Chillicothe, 1800); *ibid., 1801* (Chillicothe, 1801).

Journal of the Senate of the State of Ohio. Various places and dates.

Kilbourn, John, ed. *Public Documents Concerning the Ohio Canals, Which Are to Connect Lake Erie with the Ohio River*. Columbus, 1828.

Pease, Theodore Calvin, ed. *Laws of the Northwest Territory, 1788-1800* (Illinois State Historical Library, Collections, XVII). Springfield, 1925.

Ryan, Daniel J., ed. "From Charter to Constitution," *Ohio State Archaeological and Historical Quarterly*, V (1897), 1-164. A valuable collection of documents. The constitution of 1802 and the journal of the first constitutional convention are in this collection.

[Worthington, Thomas]. *Communication to Those Citizens of the Northwest Territory Opposed to an Alteration of the Boundaries of the States as Established by Congress and Who are Favorable to the Formation of a Constitution*. Chillicothe, 1802.

Worthington, Thomas. *Letter of Thomas Worthington, Inclosing an Ordinance Passed by the Convention . . . Together with the Constitution . . . and Sundry Propositions to the Congress*. Washington, D. C. 1802.

Newspapers

Chillicothe:
Chillicothe Advertiser
Chillicothe Times
The Fredonian (published at Circleville from October 9, 1811, to August 11, 1812)
Friend of Freedom
The Independent Republican
The Scioto Gazette
The Supporter
The Supporter and Scioto Gazette
Cincinnati:
Cincinnati Advertiser
Liberty Hall
Liberty Hall and Cincinnati Gazette
Liberty Hall and Cincinnati Mercury
National Republican and Ohio Political Register
The Western Spy
Western Spy and General Advertiser
Western Spy and Literary Cadet
Columbus:
Columbus Gazette
Ohio Monitor

Ohio Monitor and Patron of Husbandry
Ohio State Journal and Columbus Gazette
Western Intelligencer and Columbus Gazette
Franklinton:
Freeman's Chronicle
Hamilton:
Miami Herald
Miami Intelligencer
The Philanthropist
Lebanon:
Western Star
Marietta:
American Friend
New Lisbon:
The Ohio Patriot
Steubenville:
Western Herald and Steubenville Gazette
Warren:
Trump of Fame
Worthington:
Western Intelligencer
Zanesville:
Zanesville Express
Zanesville Express and Republican Standard
Muskingum Messenger
Muskingum Messenger and Ohio Intelligencer

Biographies, Memoirs, and Contemporary Writings

Adams, Charles Francis, ed. *Memoirs of John Quincy Adams, Comprising Portions of His Diary from 1795 to 1848.* 12 vols., Philadelphia, 1874-77.

Adams, Henry. *The Life of Albert Gallatin.* Philadelphia, 1880.

——, ed. *The Writings of Albert Gallatin.* 3 vols., Philadelphia, 1879.

Asbury, Francis. *The Journal of Francis Asbury.* 3 vols., New York, 1821.

Bates, James L. *Alfred Kelly, His Life and Work.* Columbus, 1888.

Bond, Beverley W., Jr., ed. "Memoirs of Benjamin Van Cleve," Historical and Philosophical Society of Ohio, *Quarterly Publications,* XVII (1922), 1-71.

Brown, Everett Somerville, ed. *William Plumer's Memorandum of Proceedings in the United States Senate, 1803-1807.* New York, 1923.

Burnet, Jacob. *Notes on the Early Settlement of the North-Western Territory.* New York, 1847.

Campbell, John W. *Biographical Sketches with other Literary Remains of John W. Campbell.* Columbus, 1838.

Cleaves, Freeman. *Old Tippecanoe: William Henry Harrison and His Time.* New York, 1939.

Cole, Frank T. *Thomas Worthington of Ohio, Founder, Senator, Governor and First Citizen.* Columbus, 1903.

Cramer, Clarence H. "The Career of Duncan McArthur." Unpublished Ph.D. dissertation, Ohio State University, 1931.

Cuming, Fortescue. *Sketches of a Tour to the Western Country.* Pittsburgh, 1810. Republished in Reuben G. Thwaites, ed., *Early Western Travels,* IV.

Cutler, Julia Perkins. *Life and Times of Ephraim Cutler, Prepared from His Journals and Correspondence.* Cincinnati, 1890.

Cutler, William P., and Cutler, Julia P. *Life, Journals and Correspondence of Manasseh Cutler.* 2 vols., Cincinnati, 1888.

Darnall, Elias. *Journal of Elias Darnall.* 3rd ed., Philadelphia, 1854.

Dawson, Moses. *A Historical Narrative of the Civil and Military Services of Major General William H. Harrison.* Cincinnati, 1824.

Dickoré, Marie. *General Joseph Kerr of Chillicothe: Ohio's Lost Senator.* Oxford, Ohio, 1941.

Donnan, Elizabeth, ed. *The Papers of James A. Bayard* (American Historical Association, *Annual Report*, 1913, II). Washington, D. C., 1915.

Drake, Benjamin. *Life of Tecumseh and His Brother the Prophet.* Cincinnati, 1852.

Esarey, Logan, ed. *The Messages and Letters of William Henry Harrison* (Indiana Historical Collections, VII and IX). 2 vols., Indianapolis, 1922.

Faux, W[illiam]. *Memorable Days in America, Being a Journal of a Tour to the United States.* London, 1823. Republished in Reuben G. Thwaites, ed., *Early Western Travels*, XI.

Finley, Isaac, Jr., and Putnam, Rufus. *Pioneer Record and Reminiscences of the Early Settlers and Settlement of Ross County, Ohio.* Cincinnati, 1871.

Finley, James B. *Autobiography of James B. Finley; or Pioneer Life in the West.* Cincinnati, 1853.

———. *Sketches of Western Methodism; Biographical, Historical and Miscellaneous.* Cincinnati, 1854.

Gilmore, William E. *Life of Edward Tiffin, First Governor of Ohio.* Chillicothe, 1897.

Goebel, Dorothy. *William Henry Harrison* (Indiana Historical Collections, XIV). Indianapolis, 1926.

Hulme, Thomas. *Journal of a Tour in the Western Countries of America.* Republished in Reuben G. Thwaites, ed., *Early Western Travels*, X.

King, Charles R., ed. *Life and Correspondence of Rufus King.* 6 vols., New York, 1894-1900.

King, Margaret R. *Memoirs of the Life of Mrs. Sarah Peter.* 2 vols., Cincinnati, 1889.

McAllister, Anna S. *In Winter We Flourish; Life and Letters of Sarah Worthington King Peter, 1800-1872.* New York, 1939.

Massie, David Meade. *Nathaniel Massie, A Pioneer of Ohio: A Sketch of His Life and Selections from His Correspondence.* Cincinnati, 1896.

Parish, John C., ed. *The Robert Lucas Journal of the War of 1812.* Iowa City, 1906.

Peter, Mrs. Sarah Anne (Worthington). *Private Memoir of Thomas Worthington.* Cincinnati, 1882.

Porter, Kenneth Wiggins. *John Jacob Astor, Business Man.* 2 vols., Harvard University Press, 1931.

Smith, William Henry. *The Life and Public Services of Arthur St. Clair.* 2 vols., Cincinnati, 1882.

Trimble, Allen. *Autobiography and Correspondence of Allen Trimble.* Columbus, 1909.

———. "Selections from the Papers of Governor Allen Trimble," *Old Northwest Genealogical Quarterly*, X, XI (Columbus, Ohio, 1907, 1908).

General Works, Local Histories, and Monographs

Adams, Henry. *History of the United States During the Administrations of Jefferson and Madison.* 9 vols., New York, 1921.

Alsbach, James R. *Annals of the West.* Pittsburgh, 1856.

Atwater, Caleb. *A History of the State of Ohio, Natural and Civil.* Cincinnati, 1838.

Bond, Beverley W., Jr. *The Civilization of the Old Northwest.* New York, 1934.

Downes, Randolph C. *Frontier Ohio, 1788-1803* (Ohio Historical Collections, III). Columbus, 1935.

Evans, Lyle S. *A Standard History of Ross County, Ohio.* 2 vols., New York, 1917.

Evans, Nelson W. *A History of Scioto County, Ohio, Together with a Pioneer Record of Southern Ohio.* Portsmouth, Ohio, 1903.

———, and Stivers, Emmons B. *A History of Adams County, Ohio.* West Union, Ohio, 1900.

Galloway, William A. *Old Chillicothe, Shawnee and Pioneer History.* Xenia, Ohio, 1934.

Gephart, William F. *Transportation and Industrial Development in the Middle West* (Columbia University, "Studies in History, Economics, and Public Law," XXXIV). New York, 1909.

Gilkey, Elliott H., ed. *Ohio Hundred Year Book.* Columbus, 1901.

Harlow, Alvin F. *Old Towpaths, the Story of the American Canal Era.* New York, 1920.

Hinsdale, B. A. *The Old Northwest.* New York, 1899.

Howe, Henry. *Historical Collections of Ohio.* 2 vols., Cincinnati, 1904.

Hulbert, Archer B. *The Cumberland Road* (*Historic Highways of America*, X). Cleveland, 1905.

Hutchinson, William T. "The Bounty Lands of the American Revolution in Ohio." Unpublished Ph.D. dissertation, University of Chicago, 1927.

King, Rufus. *Ohio, First Fruits of the Ordinance of 1787* ("American Commonwealth Series"). New York, 1903.

McAfee, Robert B. *History of the Late War in the Western Country.* Lexington, Kentucky, 1816.

McClelland, C. P., and Huntington, C. C. *History of the Ohio Canals, Their Construction, Cost, Use and Partial Abandonment.* Columbus, 1905.

McMaster, John B. *History of the People of the United States.* 8 vols., New York, 1914.

Pratt, Julius W. *Expansionists of 1812.* New York, 1925.

Randall, Emilius O., and Ryan, Daniel J. *History of Ohio.* 5 vols., New York, 1912.

Renick, L. W., Fullerton, M. D., and Nipgen, P. N., eds. *Che-le-co-the—Glimpses of Yesterday—A Souvenir of the Hundredth Anniversary of the Founding of Chillicothe, Ohio.* New York, 1896.

Slocum, Charles E. *The Ohio Country between the Years 1783 and 1815.* New York, 1910.

Taylor, William A. *Ohio in Congress from 1803 to 1901.* Columbus, 1900.

———. *Ohio Statesmen and Annals of Progress.* Columbus, 1899.

Thwaites, Reuben G., ed. *Early Western Travels, 1748-1846.* 32 vols., Cleveland, 1904-1907.

Treat, Payson J. *The National Land System, 1785-1820*. New York, 1910.

Utter, William T. *The Frontier State, 1803-1825* (Carl Wittke, ed., *The History of the State of Ohio*, II). Columbus, 1942.

———. "Ohio Politics and Politicians, 1802-1816." Unpublished Ph.D. dissertation, University of Chicago, 1929.

Weisenburger, Francis P. *The Passing of the Frontier, 1825-1850* (Carl Wittke, ed., *The History of the State of Ohio*, III). Columbus, 1941.

Williams Brothers. *History of Ross and Highland Counties, Ohio*. Cleveland, 1880.

Williams, Samuel W. *Pictures of Early Methodism in Ohio*. Cincinnati, 1909.

Wittke, Carl, ed. *The History of the State of Ohio*. 6 vols., Columbus, 1941-44.

Young, Jeremiah S. *A Political and Constitutional Study of the Cumberland Road*. Chicago, 1904.

Articles

Andrews, Israel Ward. "Kentucky, Tennessee, Ohio, Their Admission into the Union," *Magazine of American History*, XVIII (1887), 306-16.

Beals, Ellis. "Arthur St. Clair, Western Pennsylvania's Leading Citizen," *Western Pennsylvania Historical Magazine*, XII (1929), 75-96, 175-96.

Bogart, Ernest L. "Taxation of the Second Bank of the United States by Ohio," *American Historical Review*, XVII (1912), 312-31.

Mississippi Valley Historical Review:

Baldwin, Leland D. "Shipbuilding on the Western Waters, 1793-1817," XX (1933-34), 29-44.

Bond, Beverley W., Jr. "American Civilization Comes to the old Northwest," XIX (1932-33), 3-29.

———. "William Henry Harrison in the War of 1812," XIII (1926-27), 499-516.

Coleman, C. B. "The Ohio Valley in the Preliminaries of the War of 1812," VII (1920-21), 39-50.

Downes, Randolph C. "Trade in Frontier Ohio," XVI (1929-30), 467-94.

———. "The Statehood Contest in Ohio," XVIII (1931-32), 155-71.

Galpin, W. F. "The Grain Trade of New Orleans, 1804-1814," XIV (1927-28), 496-507.

Goodman, Warren H. "The Origins of the War of 1812: A Survey of Changing Interpretations," XXVIII (1941-42), 171-86.

Hacker, Louis M. "Western Land Hunger and the War of 1812: A Conjecture," X (1923-24), 365-95.

Nettels, Curtis P. "The Mississippi Valley and the Constitution," XI (1924-25), 332-57.

Pratt, Julius W. "Western Aims in the War of 1812," XII (1925-26), 36-50.

Utter, William T. "Judicial Review in Early Ohio," XIV (1927-28), 3-24.

———. "Saint Tammany in Ohio: A Study in Frontier Politics," XV (1928-29), 321-40.

———. "Ohio and the English Common Law," XVI (1929-30), 321-33.

Weisenburger, Francis P. "John McLean, Postmaster-General," XVIII (1931-32), 23-33.

Morrow, Josiah. "Jeremiah Morrow," *Old Northwest Genealogical Quarterly*, IX (Columbus, 1906), 1-27, 99-133, 227-59.

Ohio State Archaeological and Historical Quarterly:

Bartlett, Ruhl J. "The Struggle for Statehood in Ohio," XXXII (1923), 472-505.

Cady, John F. "Western Opinion and the War of 1812," XXXIII (1924), 427-76.

Dial, George W. "The Construction of the Ohio Canals," XIII (1904), 460-81.

Douglas, Albert. "Major-General Arthur St. Clair," XVI (1907), 455-76.

Downes, Randolph C. "Thomas Jefferson and the Removal of Governor St. Clair in 1802," XXXVI (1927), 62-77.

Dudley, Helen M. "The Origin of the Name of the Town of Worthington," LII (1943), 248-59.

Hulbert, Archer B. "The Old National Road—The Historic Highway of America," IX (1900-1901), 405-519.

Huntington, C. C. "A History of Banking and Currency in Ohio before the Civil War," XXIV (1915), 235-540.

M'Clintock, William T. "Ohio's Birth Struggle," XI (1903), 44-70.

"Ohio Day at the Jamestown Exposition," XVII (1908), 173-92.

Randall, Emilius O. "Ohio in the War of 1812," XXVIII (1919), 597-604.

Roseboom, Eugene H. "Ohio in the Presidential Election of 1824," XXVI (1917), 153-224.

Ryan, Daniel J. "Nullification in Ohio," II (1888-89), 393-401.

———. "The State Library and Its Founder," XXVIII (1919), 98-109.

Sears, Alfred B. "The Political Philosophy of Arthur St. Clair," XLIX (1940), 41-57.

———. "Thomas Worthington, Pioneer Business Man of the Old Northwest," LVIII (1949), 69-79.

Williams, Samuel W. "The Tammany Society in Ohio," XXII (1913), 349-70.

Williams, Elizabeth. "M[icajah] T[errell] Williams," *Old Northwest Genealogical Quarterly,* I (Columbus), 1898.

Index

Hastings, Seth, 82, 130
Heaton, James, 191
Henry, John, 176
Henry Papers, 176
Henry, Patrick, 8
Highland County, 153
Hockhocking River, 226
Hoffman, George, 112
Home industries, TW's encouragement of, 204, 207, 213
Hosack, Alexander Eddy, 234
Hosack, David, 234
Hull, William, 170, 179, 181, 182, 183, 189; criticism of, 176, 178
Hulme, Thomas, on TW, 212
Huntington, Samuel, 79, 107, 122, 143, 149-50, 151, 153, 154, 155, 178; attemped impeachment of, 145; as a candidate in the 1808 elections, 146-47; offices held by, 111, 147; relationship with TW, 110, 148

Illinois country, 54
Independent Republican (Chillicothe), 151
Indiana Territory, 83, 117, 131, 167; establishment of, 55
Indians of the Northwest Territory, 131, 133, 175; Ohio settlers' relations with, 9, 37, 46, 47, 161, 165, 166, 167; role of, in the War of 1812, 181, 197; TW's negotiations with, 179, 180, 181-86
Ingles, Mary Draper, 20-21
Internal improvements, 221; action in U.S. Congress on, 124-28, 160-61; TW's advocacy of, 207
Irwin, William, 143
Isle of Orleans, purchase of, 116

Jackson, Andrew, 171, 189, 213, 221, 222
Jackson, Francis James, 163
Jackson, John G., 125, 127, 131
James, Thomas, 235
Jay's Treaty, 123
Jefferson, Thomas, 26, 60, 79, 85, 103, 104, 107, 115, 120, 122, 127, 130, 138, 148, 163; action taken by, in the removal of St. Clair, 88, 97; Plumer on, 119, 135; role of, in the impeachment of Samuel Chase, 129; TW on, 75, 76
Jefferson County, 73, 109, 195
Johnston, John, 180, 184-85, 197
Judicial review in Ohio, 143-45, 193

Judiciary, powers of, under Ohio constitution, 98, 100-101, 149, 151
Judiciary Act of 1801, 75

Keets, Louise, 150
Kelley, Alfred, 224, 226, 228; on TW as canal commissioner, 225
Kerr, John, 176; donor of Columbus capitol site, 202; on War of 1812, 192
Kerr, Joseph, 173, 197, 214, 215
Kerr, Nathaniel Massie, 173
Kickapoo Indians, 182
Kilbourne, James, 28; town founded by, named for TW, 42-43
Kimberley, Zenos, 143
Kincaid, David, 157
King, Edward, 198, 201, 206, 221, 229, 231, 235
King, Rufus, 201, 213, 214, 220, 234
King, Sarah Worthington, 232; see also Worthington, Sarah Anne
Kirker, Thomas, 101, 142, 144, 145, 147, 157, 178, 179

Lafayette, and TW, 232-33
Lake Erie, 226, 228
Lancaster (Ohio), 151
Land laws: of 1800, 24, 39, 55; of 1820, 160, 211; TW's sponsorship of, 131-32, 159-60
Land sales (Ohio): percentage of, to be used for roads, 125, 126; TW's plan for, 199
Land speculation in the Ohio country, 8, 9, 10, 23-24, 25
Land taxes, 50, 220
Langham, Elias, 48, 49, 56, 111, 140; attacks of, on TW, 42, 86; opposition of, to territorial division law, 66
Latrobe, Benjamin, 30
Lewis, Samuel C., 172
Liberty Hall (Cincinnati), on TW, 194
Liberty Hall and Cincinnati Mercury, 141
Licking River, 226, 227
Licking Summit (Ohio), 228
Ligonier (Pennsylvania), 98
Lincoln, Levi, 41
Liquor traffic, control of, 209
Logan, George, 75, 85
Logan (Ohio), 200
Looker, Othniel, 193, 195
Lotspeich, Ralph, 155
Louisiana Territory: government of, 117-18; purchase of, 115-18